Catholicism on the Web

Catholicism on the Web

Thomas C. Fox

A Subsidiary of Henry Holt and Company
New York

MIS:Press
A Subsidiary of Henry Holt and Company, Inc.
115 West 18th Street
New York, New York 10011
http://www.mispress.com

Catholicism on the Web

Limits of Liability and Disclaimer of Warranty

The Author and Publisher of this book have used their best efforts in preparing the book and the programs contained in it. These efforts include the development, research, and testing of the theories and programs to determine their effectiveness. The Author and Publisher make no warranty of any kind, expressed or implied, with regard to these programs or the documentation contained in this book. The Author and Publisher shall not be liable in any event for incidental or consequential damages in connection with, or arising out of, the furnishing, performance, or use of these programs.

All products, names and services are trademarks or registered trademarks of their respective companies.

First Edition—1997

10 9 8 7 6 5 4 3 2 1

ISBN 1-55828-516-4

MIS:Press and M&T Books are available at special discounts for bulk purchases for sales promotions, premiums, and fundraising. Special editions or book excerpts can also be created to specification. For details contact the Special Sales Director of Henry Holt at the address listed above.

Editor and Publisher: Paul Farrell
Executive Editor: Cary Sullivan
Copy Edit Manager: Shari Chappell
Production Editors: Joe McPartland
Copy Editor: Suzanne Ingrao
Indexers: Edward J. Prucha, EdIndex

To My Sister

VIRGINIA

Who Has Taught Her Family Much About Love

The Prader-Willi Connection
http://www.visink.com/pwhome.htm

Prader-Willi Syndrome Association (USA)
http://www.athenet.net/%7Epwsa_usa/index.html

CONTENTS IN BRIEF

CONTENTS

Chapter 2: Religious Orders 31

Chapter 3: Organizations 83

Chapter 4: People 105

PART II: CATHOLIC IDEAS 131

Chapter 5: History 133

Chapter 6: Teachings 145

Chapter 7: Education

Chapter 8: Communications 197

Chapter 9: Information 219

PART III: CATHOLIC ACTIVISM 227

Chapter 10: Peace, Justice, and the Environment 229

Chapter 11: Renewal Groups.......................... 287

Chapter 17: Liturgy and Worship 387

Chapter 18: Art and Meditation 399

Appendix: On-Line Directories 413

Index 423

With the advent of computer telecommunications and what are known as computer participation systems, the Church is offered further means for fulfilling her mission. Methods of facilitating communication and dialogue among her own members can strengthen the bonds of unity between them. Immediate access to information makes it possible for her to deepen her dialogue with the contemporary world. In the new "computer culture" the Church can more readily inform the world of her beliefs and explain the reasons for her stance on any given issue or event. She can hear more clearly the voice of public opinion and enter into continuous discussion with the world around her, thus involving herself more immediately in the common search for solutions to humanity's many pressing problems. . . .

—Pope John Paul II
World Communications Day
May 27, 1989
http://listserv.american.edu/catholic/
church/papal/jp.ii/computer-culture.html

PREFACE

I am a Catholic by birth, twenty-six years married and the father of three grown children. By vocation, I'm a newspaperman, with sixteen years at the feisty lay-edited newsweekly *National Catholic Reporter*—*NCR* for short. The paper reports on, analyzes, and editorializes on the Catholic Church and the many complex moral issues that face U.S. Catholics and the wider society. In some circles, *NCR* is viewed as progressive, even radical. In others, recognizing our love and support for the Church, it is seen as intrinsically conservative. But labels don't fully explain *NCR*, and they don't fully explain me.

In my work as a journalist and as the Editor of *NCR*, hardly a week goes by in which I fail to receive some reader's grateful letter or telephone call saying something like, "Keep it up, your paper is my lifeline to the Church." Both as a newspaperman and a Catholic, I find such comments enormously satisfying. They tell me a lot about the need people have for connectedness, for finding other voices that speak to their hopes and fears, doubts and beliefs, joys and sorrows. What's gratifying to us at *NCR* is that sometimes—from our offices in Kansas City, Missouri—we can publish those voices that answer needs felt by Catholics spread out across the U.S. and around the globe.

In one sense *NCR* is no different from other newspapers in the U.S. Almost without knowing it, we have become participants in the electronic communications revolution. In one decade, we've moved from typewriters to desktop publishing, from waiting days for articles to arrive by mail, to fax reception and most recently email. And of course we are now thinking about, reporting on, and participating in the

World Wide Web, potentially the most revolutionary medium for communication to appear in our lifetime. On the Web, everyone can become a publisher, and that makes it an empowering medium.

By most any reckoning, the Web is unruly and represents untamed territory—a kind of Wild West in which visitors can easily feel threatened and become lost. At the same time, it is the most fascinating, colorful, exciting, and potentially useful, not to mention fastest growing, domain of cyberspace. This book seizes and attempts to tame momentarily just one section of that domain—what might be called "the Catholic Web." After months of plowing through thousands of Catholic Web pages, I chose and organized into categories the 500 or so that I found most interesting, or useful, or typical, or otherwise significant. Not every page I selected was authored by a Catholic, but all involve Catholic ministries and concerns. Some, particularly in Chapter 10 ("Peace, Justice, and the Environment"), are sites I believe, perhaps giving in too much to my own biases, will be especially helpful or relevant. And without a doubt, I have missed some good Catholic sites, as well as included those to which some Catholics will take exception. But this book, like any other, is a reflection its author's own best judgments about what matters, and there's no doubt that my personal feelings about the importance of inclusiveness and openness are revealed on almost every page.

The Catholic Web, like the wider World Wide Web, is a moving target. New Catholic sites are coming on-line every day. Thus, I have come to see this book as not just a directory, but as a starting-point for conversation, for dialog, and I cannot think of any institution more likely to be served by increased dialog than the global Catholic Church. United in basic faith, but spread throughout five continents, Roman Catholics are using the Web to learn more about each other and their varied interests as never before. What is new about this new medium is that it is based on no hierarchy and is peculiarly democratic—even chaotic—in its operation. In Catholic terms, it is a new medium through which the People of God can share—one-to-one—in their common journey of faith. A Brazilian pastoral director can set up a site that will appear, in a Web search, alongside the Vatican's official home page. The Web—with its magnificent, tangled, oddly linked, and infinitely diverse global reach—is curiously suited to bringing untold numbers of like- and unlike-minded Catholics and Catholic communities together in unexpected ways.

And I'm not myself immune to the Web's unexpected effects. Perhaps it was being raised in the heady idealism of the 1960s, or having experienced Vatican II at a formative stage of my spiritual and intellectual development, but I have always been attracted to Catholicism's pastoral call to serve the poor and disenfranchised of the world by working to build more compassionate, just, and peaceful communities. Writing this book reinforced my love for this vision. However, it has also helped me better understand the many other ways—the "thousand paths"—Catholics take to enter and embrace the Church. This recognition has nudged me to be more generous in judgment and wider in embrace, and I suspect others who read this book and browse the Catholic Web may be similarly moved—and changed.

> —Thomas C. Fox
> Kansas City, Missouri
> www.natcath.com

Acknowledgments

I want to acknowledge Paul Farrell, the editor of this volume and Publisher of MIS:Press, for having encouraged me to write this book, and write it quickly. Also at MIS:Press, editors Ann C. Lush and Andy Neusner deserve thanks for their efforts in facilitating this project. Thanks as well to Suzanne Ingrao for her copy editing. My assistant, Jean Blake, in the *National Catholic Reporter*'s Kansas City, Missouri, newsroom, was helpful as always. And my wife, Hoa, made the greatest sacrifices while her husband sat long evenings at the home computer reviewing Web sites; for this and for the cups of tea she would often bring me and for countless other blessings, I am grateful.

Publisher's Note

Live links to all the sites listed in this book can be accessed at the following page:

http://www/mispress.com/catholicism

At the site, the author and publisher invite readers to make suggestions about future editions of *Catholicism on the Web*.

The Publisher also wishes to thank Linda Dickey for her advice and counsel.

P A R T   I

Catholic Organization

The Roman Catholic Church is immense—in its structure, in its variety of official and unofficial organizations, and in its people. The four chapters in Part I of this book describe the Web sites dedicated to the formal institutions of the Church, its religious orders, other organizations (some official, others not), and its people, including the souls in Purgatory and the saints in Heaven.

From the Vatican
To the Local Parish

The Catholic Church (from the Greek *katholikos*, "universal") is the worldwide Church that recognizes the Bishop of Rome, the Pope, as "the perpetual and visible source and foundation of the unity of the bishops and of the multitude of the faithful." (This description of the Pope is from the *Dogmatic Constitution on the Church*, in the documents of the Second Vatican Council.) There are approximately 1 billion Catholics worldwide, by far the largest distinct body of Christians on earth. The bishops who met in Rome from 1962 through 1965 spoke of the church as "The People of God," stressing that Christians live and act out of community. The structure of the church attempts to define, organize, and serve Catholic communities at many levels.

Chapter 1 offers examples of Web sites that serve Catholics at various church levels, from the Vatican to the local parish. The Vatican, the smallest sovereign state in the world (108.7 acres), is headed by Pope John Paul II and is administered by the sacred congregations of the Roman Curia, the central administrative organization of the church. At the next level, the Church is made up of archdioceses and dioceses, each headed by a local bishop, all working in union with the Bishop of Rome. However, to better allow the world's bishops to work on a regional or national level, episcopal conferences were formed at the Second Vatican

Council, and they, in a sense, mediate between the Vatican and the dioceses.

The Web sites in this chapter offer a sampling of these administrative bodies. I have chosen some for their special qualities and others because they typify similar sites springing up almost daily on the World Wide Web.

The Holy See

http://www.vatican.va

This is the Vatican's home page and is undoubtedly one of the most popular Catholic Web sites. The old-fashioned word *See* in its title refers to the site or seat or center of power and authority in the Church. Visitors are greeted with the Papal coat of arms and a picture of His Holiness Pope John Paul II. This is a rapidly growing site. No pope has used mass communications as successfully as Pope John Paul II has: his pilgrimages have been widely televised, his books and poetry translated and published in countless languages. However, the most recent Vatican foray into the world of modern communications has been its active involvement in the World Wide Web.

The Holy See is actively putting together a thorough database of church documents. It will include official documents organized to facilitate research under a search engine. Meantime, the site continues to provide the "Vatican Information Service," which provides news on Pope John Paul II and Vatican and other Church activities around the world. Begun in 1991, the Vatican Information Service is available Monday through Friday except for the month of August. Currently offered in English and Spanish, it deals primarily with the acts and nominations of the Holy Father; syntheses of his homilies and speeches; and presentations and communications relating to documents written by the Holy Father or other Vatican officials.

College of Cardinals

http://www.avenue.com/v/rccardn.html

Cardinals are chosen by the Pope to serve as his principal assistants and advisers in the administration of church affairs. Collectively, they form the College of Cardinals. Cardinals under the age of 80 elect the Pope when the Holy See becomes vacant; they are major administrators of church affairs, serving in one or more departments of the Roman Curia.

A cardinal's title, while symbolic of high honor, does not signify any extension of the powers of Holy Orders, which are conferred on all priests. In 1586, Pope Sixtus V set the maximum number of cardinals at 70, but this limit was abrogated by Pope John XXIII in 1958. In 1973, Pope Paul VI set a limit of 120 on the number of cardinals eligible to elect a pope. Though not previously required by legislation, with the promulgation of the 1917 Code of Canon Law, the title Cardinal could be conferred only on a priest.

This Web site lists alphabetically the cardinals of the Roman Catholic Church. Names are followed by nationality, date of birth, year of becoming cardinal, and current and past ecclesiastical positions. This list of the members of the College of Cardinals is current as of early 1995.

Canadian Bishops Conference

http://www.cam.org/~cccb/index.html

A conference of bishops is an association of the bishops of a nation or region. The idea grew out of the reforms of the Vatican Council and has been aimed at allowing the bishops of a local region to better deal with issues of a national or regional basis. The Canadian Bishops Conference, officially the Canadian Conference of Catholic Bishops, has been quick to use the Web, offering information in both English and French.

The site contains Canadian episcopal news, official public statements, organized by month and year. In May 1996, for example, you will find the text of the Canadian bishops' submission to the House of Commons committee studying Bill C-33, a law to amend the Canadian Human Rights Act Regarding Sexual Orientation, as well as a bishops' statement on the Canadian Catholic Organization for Development and Peace. Several of the statements the bishops have placed on their site deal with peace and justice issues. The Canadian bishops are generally viewed as moderate to progressive in their social views; and their site reflects these tendencies.

Catholic Church in Europe

http://communio.hcbc.hu/

This site offers a quick way to get in touch with English and non-English European Catholic news agencies and religious and lay groups, primarily of European background. Visiting this site, it struck me how the Internet is melting away traditional notions of national boundaries. This applies to Catholicism as well. This site, run on behalf of an organization called the Media Commission of the Council of European Bishops Conferences, is rich in information and resources. It connects the visitor with Catholics and Catholic organizations in more than 40 European nations. It also offers connections to the major European Catholic news agencies, religious orders, libraries, and religious movements, and it highlights a host of European and non-European Catholic links.

Bishops' Conference of England and Wales

http://www.tasc.ac.uk/cc/

This site aims to provide a general picture of the Catholic Church in England and Wales and offers what it calls a "jump-off point" to other dioceses and Catholic organizations on the Internet. While Catholics represent only a small minority of the population of England and Wales, they have had an influential place in the European church. The Benedictine, Cardinal Basil Humes of London, for example, is highly respected among the church's prelates.

After a brief introduction to the church of England and Wales, this site lists its 21 dioceses. A diocese is the local church in a particular region, and as such is complete in itself. However, for practical purposes and to facilitate communication and cooperation, most dioceses in the world form part of a bishops conference. The principal diocese in a province is called an *archdiocese* and its bishop carries the title of Archbishop.

This site also provides information about CAFOD, the Catholic international relief and development agency that assists the needy poor of the world. The site also draws attention to university Catholic Societies. British Catholics pride themselves for a tradition that respects scholarship.

Catholic Diocesan, Parish and Parishioner Listings

http://don.io-online.com/~catholic/section1.htm

This site is part of the Catholic Connection, a wonderful place to make contacts with all sorts of Catholics doing all sorts of good things in the Church. The Catholic Connection is maintained by R. Paul Gordon, to whom Catholics on the Net owe much gratitude for bringing them together. "Catholic Diocesan, Parish and Parishioner Listings" is pretty much self-explanatory. It provides names and links to people and places within Catholic dioceses and parishes. The list is active and growing. Alphabetically arranged, it is not difficult to find what you need here. The visitor finds no national boundaries on the list of dioceses, adding to the sense of the universal nature of the Catholic church. As the list grows, however, it may be necessary to find other ways—by nation or region—to divide the list.

Archdiocese of Dublin, Ireland

http://aoife.indigo.ie/~pcurran/dublin.html

With a Catholic population of just over 1 million, the Archdiocese of Dublin is the largest diocese in Ireland. A disclaimer on this site notes "this is an unofficial" Web site and that the "views and opinions expressed here do not purport to represent the views of the Archbishop or the Diocese." Not that anything controversial is offered. Visitors are treated to a colorful graphic of the crest of Archbishop Desmond Connell, which includes the Latin words *Secundum Verbum Tuum*, or according to your word, taken from Luke 1:38.

This site was created in April 1996; it offers information about the archbishop, houses of religious, and diocesan services and agencies. Email and regular mail address, telephone and fax numbers are provided for easy communication. Links appear to other Catholic resources, including the Vatican Web site. This site appears to be in its early stages, lacking the imagination of some other archdiocesan sites. Many U.S. Catholics, however, are of Irish heritage, and thus may want to keep their eyes on this location to watch it develop. Before leaving, visitors are asked to sign the archdiocesan guest book.

New Zealand Catholic Homepage

http://www.catholic.org/newzealand/

This is the official home page for the Catholic Church in New Zealand; it has been authorized by the New Zealand Catholic Bishops Conference through the National Office of Catholic. The site is still in its early stages of development. Many of the home page links have yet to be established. They will connect with all the various aspects of church life in New Zealand, starting with church agencies, schools, religious education, liturgy, workshop news, pastoral programs, and social justice matters. The site will also break down by dioceses and by issue, such as abortion, AIDS, aging, birth control, sexual abuse, marriage, pro-life, sacraments, and women.

It is always interesting to read statements by Catholics in other parts of the world. The driving moral principles are the same as anywhere in the church, but the circumstances and emphases are frequently different. The New Zealand bishops, on social justice matters, are generally a progressive group. I did notice when I visited the site that the first category to be developed in this young site was episcopal statements. A few sentences from one statement on crime and justice jumped out at me:

> From a Christian perspective no criminal justice system can afford to be built upon a philosophy of retribution, focusing primarily upon punishment flowing from feelings of revenge; a negative philosophy will produce negative results. ... We challenge this philosophy of retribution on the basis that it is negative and usually counterproductive. We believe it to be contrary to the example of Jesus in the scriptures and to the teachings of the Church.

I'm looking forward to hearing more from the New Zealand bishops.

Diocese of Eshowe, South Africa
http://www.shaka.iafrica.com/~gtl/eshowe.html

South Africa, still emerging from years of apartheid, is one of the more interesting nations in the world. The churches there, including the Catholic church, face many challenges of bringing together people and races. On the Eshowe diocesan Web page the changing face of the structure of Catholicism is apparent. Consider this diocese's explanation of its own recent evolution:

The Prefecture of Zululand was erected on 27 August 1921. Before that time it had formed part of Natal Vicariate. On 11 December 1923 it was raised to the status of a Vicariate under the title of "Vicariate Apostolic of Eshowe". With the establishment of the hierarchy in South Africa it became the diocese of Eshowe on the 11 January 1951. The diocese now comprises Zululand proper (with the exception of the districts of Ingwavuma, Ubombo and Hlabisa), and the four Natal districts of Vryheid, Paulpietersburg, Ngotshe and Babanango. It is bound on the East by the Indian Ocean, on the South by the Tugela River, on the West by the Tugela, Buffalo, Blood and Didusini Rivers, and in the North by the Pongola and Umfolozi Rivers.

How's that for a history and geography lesson?

A visitor to this Web site also learns that the total population of the diocese is 1,780,000, of which 70,000 are Roman Catholics. The site also features a photograph of the local bishop, Mansuet Dela Biyase, consecrated at Eshowe on June 28, 1975. Have a reason to contact him? His address, telephone, and fax numbers are posted, as are the names and locations of local religious orders and Catholic organizations. This site is still under construction. Ideas for development are requested. Somehow, I sense, these South African Catholics will find the way.

Episcopal Conference of Chile

http://www.puc.cl/vic/texto/

The World Wide Web contains information about the Catholic church throughout the world. Increasingly, this is going to allow Catholics to better realize and celebrate the universality of their church. A growing number of Catholic bishops are using the Web to publicize information about Catholicism in their nation. Since Chile is a predominantly Catholic nation, it should not be surprising that the bishops' conference of Chile has a Web page. Complete with an attractive map that locates this long and slender nation, more than anything else this site is a primer on the organizational structure of the Church in Chile. It also offers email and regular mailing addresses as well as telephone and fax numbers. This caution, however: visitors will need to read Spanish to absorb the site's full impact.

Chicago Archdiocese

http://www.archdiocese-chgo.org/

The Chicago Archdiocese Web site is probably the best developed archdiocesan site to date. In addition to plenty of information about the 2.3 million Roman Catholics who live in Cook and Lake counties in northeastern Illinois, the site features Chicago Cardinal Joseph Bernardin's major addresses. By episcopal standards, Bernardin is considered a moderate. In a church often divided on ecclesiastical issues, Bernardin is known for trying to find a middle path. He is a widely respected archbishop, and his speeches are worth seeking out. This Web site makes them available for the first time to a worldwide audience.

The site provides statistical information about the Archdiocese of Chicago. It offers a parish directory and lists archdiocesan ministry goals and the progress made in meeting these goals. A directory of archdiocesan agencies and departments is also available. Finally, for those interested, there is a map of the archdiocese.

Archdiocese of Los Angeles

http://www.la-archdiocese.org/

The Archdiocese of Los Angeles Web site, still relatively young, has a simple look, offering information from its communication, vocation, and justice and peace departments. The Catholic church in the United States, hurting for young people willing to enter the priesthood and religious life, has a new tool for reaching the young who may be interested in a religious vocation.

It is of interest, however, that one of the most developed aspects of this Web site is the information from the archdiocesan Office of Justice and Peace. The Justice and Peace page explains its mission in the following words:

> To educate the people of the Archdiocese of Los Angeles on the principles of Catholic social teaching and its application to contemporary local, national, and international issues; to advocate for public policy which affirms human life and human dignity and reflects a consistent life ethic; and to develop a constituency on social concerns.

The office lists justice and peace programs, offers links, introduces the archdiocesan staff, and highlights current justice and peace issues facing Los Angeles Catholics. At the top of the list in late 1996 was California Proposition 209, the November 5,1996, ballot initiative aimed at eliminating state affirmative-action programs and policies. Most Catholic church officials have voiced opposition to such initiatives.

Archdiocese of Philadelphia

http://www.archdiocese-phl.org/~diocese/index.html

The Archdiocese of Philadelphia's Web site in many ways is like most other archdiocesan sites. It opens with a collection of boxes the visitor can click to get to the following pages: History, Mission State, Geography, Statistical Information, Archbishop, Parish Information, Spiritual Renewal, Archdiocesan Offices, Vatican Web Site, Special Events, other diocesan Web sites, *Catholic Standard & Times*, and What's New.

If the visitor clicks on Archbishop a photograph of a smiling Archbishop Anthony Joseph Bevilacqua appears. He is dressed in cardinal red robes, and a biographical sketch is provided. On the same page the visitor can access important statements the cardinal has made or can hear him speak, if one's computer is set to receive voice transmission from the Web. (Voices and sound are now common on the Web, enhancing its communications abilities.)

What caught me the day I visited the Philadelphia home page was the flashing What's New box. Clicking on it took me to an online version of the archdiocese's weekly newspaper, *The Catholic Standard & Times.* The archdiocese is now putting up on the Web some of its news articles and features from the weekly publication—not only to spread archdiocesan news, but to push the publication itself. (Only some articles appear; to get the entire paper, you fill out a subscription form.) Here, then, is an archdiocesan communications site leveraging another of its communication vehicles. Good marketing, it seems.

Archdiocese of Atlanta
http://www.archatl.com/archatl.htm

Catholics may learn more about the history of their local church if the pages of this archdiocesan Web site become a prototype. The site offers historical thumbnail sketches of the archdiocese's history:

> From a simple log church in Locust Grove, Georgia, where the faithful worshipped in 1790, the Catholic population in North Georgia has experienced steady growth. By 1820 the Catholic population had grown to 1,000 in the Carolinas and Georgia, under the leadership of Bishop John England. At the time of the Civil War, there were 4,000 Catholics in Georgia alone, with parishes in Atlanta, Savannah, Macon, Columbus and Locust Grove. A new diocese, the Diocese of Savannah, was established in 1850 and headed by Bishop Francis X. Gartland. It included all of Georgia and parts of Florida. Post-war Atlanta had begun to rebuild. Along with the growth of the city came a growth in the Catholic population. ... In 1936, the Diocese of Savannah-Atlanta was established and the Co-Cathedral of Christ the King was erected. Bishop Gerald P. O'Hara, appointed Bishop of Savannah in 1935, was the last Bishop to serve the faithful of the entire state of Georgia. The Diocese of Atlanta was established in 1956.

The Archdiocese of Atlanta site also offers statistics about the local church as well as information about its bishops and priests. Articles from the official archdiocesan newspaper, the *Georgia Bulletin*, are also published. The emphasis here is clearly on local church matters, with a heavy emphasis on the appointments and activities of the local clergy. This note: During the Olympics, savvy travelers to Atlanta were able to learn from this site the times of masses and locations of parishes, helping them to attend Sunday mass.

Archdiocese of Baltimore

http://www.realinfo.com/pope/

The Archdiocese of Baltimore's Web site has church press releases, biographies, assorted information on the archdiocese, and more. It celebrates the October 8, 1995, visit of Pope John Paul II, including (for the audio-enabled) the sounds of his papal mass. One is welcomed to the site by a special message from Archbishop William Cardinal Keeler, who is obviously proud to have been chosen to host the pope. Much of the information on this page recalls the events that led up to the visit and details the visit itself. The Baltimore archdiocese has special significance in the history of the Catholic church because in 1789 the priests of the area elected John Carroll to be the first bishop of Baltimore, and in 1808 he became the emerging nation's first archbishop.

Archdiocese of Miami

http://www.safari.net/~miaarch/arch1.htm

The Archdiocese of Miami home page can be accessed in either Spanish or English. The archdiocese comprises Dade, Monroe, and Broward counties in south Florida, and the site covers normal archdiocesan matters, including information about the local archbishop, parishes, schools, ministries, and departments. As with most other archdiocesan sites, there is a featured section on the history of the archdiocese. The visitor learns that on August 13, 1953, Pope Pius XII announced that the Diocese of St. Augustine, which embraced all of Florida, had been divided and a new Catholic diocese was being created in Miami. Sixteen south Florida counties comprised this new ecclesiastical area and included 51 parishes, 81 priests, and 185,000 Catholics. That Miami was formed as an archdiocese as late as 1953 is an indication of the enormous demographic growth—and change—that has occurred in that part of the country in the past half century. Today the Archdiocese of Miami serves 1.2 million Catholics in 110 parishes with 430 priests, of which 245 are incardinated.

The site also allows the visitor to access the local Spanish-language archdiocesan newspaper, *La Voz Católica*, or its English counterpart, *The Florida Catholic*. Information is also available on the archdiocese radio stations.

Archdiocese of New Orleans
http://www.catholic.org/neworleans/archdiocese.html

More imagination shows up in this site than in most other archdiocesan sites. I especially liked the listing of volunteer possibilities for New Orleans Catholics. Many people like to get involved and to offer assistance but are uncertain how to take the first step. This site helps overcome this hurdle. "Come see the pastoral formation, the ministries, and the charitable giving opportunities we offer as we enter our 203rd year," this archdiocesan site calls out to "the faithful of Southeastern Louisiana." "In response to the number of requests that we have received from potential volunteers requesting more information on the opportunities available to them in the Archdiocese of New Orleans, we have developed the Volunteer Classifieds section of our homepage," the site explains enthusiastically. It then reveals its classifieds list of volunteer opportunities. Contacts, addresses, and telephone numbers are provided. While there is lots of other information about the New Orleans archdiocese on this site, its volunteer classifieds will likely be the most borrowed idea—one might hope.

Diocese of Lansing, Michigan
http://www.rc.net/lansing/lansing.html

A visitor to the diocese of Lansing's Web site is greeted by a welcome message and a grinning color picture of Bishop Carl F. Mengeling. Unfortunately, the large photograph slows the download process and one becomes tempted to move on. This site, then, may serve as an example of a mistake other Webmasters should avoid. That said, the page serves the visitor by locating the diocese up front, explaining that it is located in south central Michigan and noting that the diocese's key cities include Lansing, Ann Arbor, Adrian, Brighton, Flint, Jackson, Saline, and Ypsilanti. One then learns a brief history of the Lansing diocese (established in 1937) and its size (6,218 square miles) and population (1.6 million). The Lansing diocese has 94 parishes "serving nearly a quarter million souls." As is the case with many other diocesan Web sites, links are provided with parishes on the Internet. Also as in the cases of many other diocesan and parish sites on the Web, one reads these ubiquitous words: this page is still "under construction." Catholicism on the Web is changing not only by the month or week but by the minute.

Diocese of Des Moines, Iowa
http://members.aol.com/cathdiodm/index.html

Stop here to find the heartland. Des Moines, Iowa, has long had a reputation in the Catholic church for caring. This may stem from its strong agricultural roots, the uncertainty of weather and, thus, livelihood, and the recognition that people depend on each other to live and grow. This caring characteristic appears on the pages of this Web site. Introduced with the obligatory photograph of the local bishop, Joseph L. Charron, and his address, telephone, and fax number, the site goes on to publish the diocese's "latest news releases," including information that "Catholic Charities' domestic violence shelter in Council Bluffs" had recently been awarded $68,725 in grants. The visitor learns that "the Catholic Charities' domestic violence shelter opened in 1980 and has served nearly 3,000 women and children since its inception."

Remember the novel and motion picture, *The Bridges of Madison County?* Guess in whose diocese these bridges are located? And guess again: will you find colorful photographs of some of these bridges on these pages? And while we are at it, how about a heartland cookbook offering? There is variety here. Some might say that constitutes a sense of health. The *Catholic Mirror* is the name of the local diocesan newspaper. It offers to these pages articles from its own pages, filling out this Web site. And, of course, the diocese communications office gets its chance to provide statistical information about the local church. Also here is information concerning the bishop's weekly schedule and links to other Catholic sites.

Diocese of Erie, Pennsylvania
http://www.erie.net/~eriercd/

At first it struck me as odd that many diocesan Web sites place such a heavy emphasis on telling their precise geographical location. But upon further consideration, it occurred to me how much pride Catholics (or at least Catholic administrators) have in place, as a setting for the local church. Beyond the boundary of a given parish, the diocese defines church, grouping Catholics and drawing them together to be shepherded by the local bishop.

Thus, in the case of the diocese of Erie, Pennsylvania, a Web site visitor learns that this diocese is located in northwestern Pennsylvania, "bordered to the north by the shores of Lake Erie and Canada, as well as the Diocese of Buffalo. To the east by the Diocese of Scranton; to the south by the Dioceses of Altoona-Johnstown, Greensburg, and Pittsburgh. Our western neighbors are the Dioceses of Youngstown and Cleveland." And, so as not to get confused, a map of the diocese can also be viewed.

This site, like many other diocesan Web sites, introduces itself through a letter by the local bishop. In the Catholic church the local bishop sets the tone and pace of the diocese as no one else does. It seems this is also true with a diocesan Web site. Too much information on the local bishop up front can slow down a visitor who more often than not comes to the Web site for functional information—like the name and address of the head of a diocesan department or the address or telephone number of a local parish.

Diocese of Joliet, Illinois

http://members.aol.com/frjohnr/html/diocjol1.html

The Web site visitor to the Diocese of Joliet, Illinois, is greeted by a crude colored map and a series of statistics about the diocese. It's clear most diocesan Webmasters enjoy producing statistical information. Thus we learn that the diocese has 130 missions and has 162 "active" diocesan priests, 9 studying or working outside the diocese, 1 in a foreign mission, and 34 retired, sick, or on leave. One also learns that the Joliet diocese has 121 religious order priests, 118 permanent deacons, 788 sisters, 93 brothers, 62 elementary schools with 19,151 students, 8 high schools with 5,572 students, and 4 colleges with 8,249 students. The list could go on. Statistical information is provided for hospitals, homes for the aged and chronically ill, and much more. One hopes that one day this will be viewed as a primitive attempt at using the Web. But then, most of us are still novices.

The Joliet, Illinois, diocesan Web site offers names as well. The following list is provided:

> Bishop of Joliet: Most Reverend Joseph L. Imesch
> Auxiliary Bishop of Joliet: Most Reverend Roger L. Kaffer
> Moderator of the Curia: Reverend Joseph J. Tapella

Chancellor: Sister Judith A. Davies, OSF

Director of Administration: Mr. James Lynch

Finance Officer: Mr. Guy Sell

Missing in late summer were names, addresses, telephone numbers, explanations about the work going on in the diocese, its mission, stories about the faithful, perhaps some classified ads with a "help wanted" section. Links are provided to two vocation pages. One rarely encounters a diocesan Web site that does not emphasize the need for more priestly and religious vocations.

Diocese of St. Augustine
http://ballingerr.xray.ufl.edu/diocese.htm

The Catholic Diocese of St. Augustine, Florida, embraces 17 counties spanning northeast and north central Florida from the Gulf of Mexico to the Atlantic Ocean. The diocese was officially founded in 1870, but its history dates back to the sixteenth century. On September 8,1565, a small band of Spaniards celebrated mass on the shores of north Florida in preparation for starting a settlement. They named their new home St. Augustine, which became the oldest permanent settlement in the United States, and its Cathedral-Basilica serves the oldest parish. Records from as early as 1594 are preserved in the diocesan archives. Today, the diocese covers 11,032 square miles and serves 108,000 Catholics. This site has much statistical information on the diocese. One unique feature is to be able to read the email addresses of the last 20 visitors to the site; another is a week-by-week breakdown of site visits. The information on the diocesan Web site, other than these two features, is standard, showing parish information, mass schedules, offices and ministries, schools, clergy and religious, television masses, a map of the diocese, and links to other Catholic sites.

Diocese of Corpus Christi

http://www.goccn.org/diocese.htm

This diocesan Web site opens with color photographs of not one but two bishops! This is because Bishop Rene Gracida has a coadjutor bishop, Roberto Gonzalez. A coadjutor bishop is more than an auxiliary, or assistant, bishop. A coadjutor has the right of immediate succession. He is normally appointed for circumstances that are personal to the diocesan bishop, like age, health, or special responsibilities.

This site, like many other diocesan Web sites, pays special attention to the history of this Texas diocese. A visitor learns that the Catholic church

> has been visible in South Texas since European explorers arrived. In 1519, Captain Alonso de Pineda sailed into a bay and named it after the Feast Day of its discovery, Corpus Christi. Spanish missions provided a foothold for the conquest of the entire Southwest. ... Through the years, missionaries traveled on horseback, visiting as many ranches and settlements as they could reach. It was not unusual for bishops to travel in this fashion, taking as long as two years to cover South Texas on their confirmation tours. ... The Diocese of Corpus Christi has seen many changes through the years. Perhaps the most important change is in the size of the Catholic congregation itself. From its early beginnings of about 20 families, the congregation now numbers more than 330,920 who worship in 83 parishes.

While this site may pay attention to its history, it is not one of the more creative diocesan Web sites. There is little here, for example, to help a visitor understand what it means to be one of those 330,920 Catholics who worship in Corpus Christi parishes.

Diocese of Raleigh, North Carolina

http://www.raldioc.org/

The Diocese of Raleigh, North Carolina, official Web site is among the more versatile diocesan sites on the World Wide

Web. This becomes evident as a visitor quickly encounters the Catholic Employment Opportunities!!! menu. Increasingly, we will see dioceses getting into classified ads on their Web sites. It makes sense to post church jobs—as well as others—and it makes just as much sense for dioceses to allow their sites to benefit qualified Catholics looking for employment.

There is more, however, than job postings on the site of the Raleigh diocese, which encompasses 54 counties in the eastern half of North Carolina. For example, a visit earlier this year found information on World Youth Day, to be held in Paris in 1997. If youngsters will go, this is the time for schools to be explaining the opportunity to young Catholic students. I like to see local churches connected to the church universal. Posting World Youth Day information is an indicator that someone smart is in control. He or she grasps not only the connectedness of Catholicism, but also the potential of the Web itself.

On this site, of course, there is plenty of information about local parish mass schedules, news updates from the National Catholic news service, African-American ministry information, retreat centers, youth ministry programs, faith development courses, as well as religious vocation possibilities.

Diocese of Biloxi, Mississippi

http://www.datasync.com/~zeus/catholic.htm

Come to the deep south, where Catholics are few and far between but hearts are frequently warm and hospitable. When you are isolated you like to reach out, seeking visitors and guests. That may be why this diocesan Web site, in addition to basic information about diocesan administration, highlights the names and telephone numbers of its Catholic parishes. While it is still the case that most Catholics have never seen the World Wide Web, as the fastest growing element of the Internet, this may not be the case for long. I continue to marvel at the detailed images and bits of fresh information one finds on the Web. Among the greatest potential beneficiaries are people, in this case Catholics, who live in relative geographic isolation. The Web provides a sense and awareness of connection helpful to overcoming this isolation.

The Church of Saint Luke (Stroudsburg, Pennsylvania)

http://www.microserve.net/~fabian/

More often than not, parish Web sites are more fun than diocesan Web sites. They seem to take themselves less seriously, and they have a stronger community flavor. The site of the Church of Saint Luke of Stroudsburg, Pennsylvania, is no exception. It offers a "virtual tour" of the parish and can hardly contain the enthusiasm it has for its "special Christmas page."

As is the case with many of the hundreds, or thousands, of parishes now on the Web, the Church of Saint Luke is quick to share its history with visitors, who learn it was founded in 1968 "to serve the needs of the growing community of Stroudsburg and its environs." The visitor is told the parish is now meeting the needs of some 1,800 families, a considerable size for a Catholic parish.

Parish programs, directions to the parish, general office information, stewardship (parish giving), religious education, and youth ministry information is highlighted. Though a simple feature, to be able to glance at a parish site and learn the times of weekday and Sunday masses is often helpful. This is especially the case in a time of a priest shortage, when masses are not as regular as they may have been ten years ago.

Many parish sites offer links to Catholic resources on the Net, documents, files, and a host of other valuable information. There are many windows into this mansion, and once inside there is lots of room to roam.

Gesu Parish (Milwaukee, Wisconsin)

http://www.execpc.com/~gesupar/

This is a bright and lively parish Web site. Lots of color, and lots of information about the parish and its activities. The layout looks good as well, combining images and print. Gesu Parish, run by the Jesuits in downtown Milwaukee, has been connected with Marquette University for many decades. In 1994, however, the Wisconsin province of of the Society of Jesus decided to incorporate Gesu as an archdiocesan parish sponsored by the Society of Jesus. With the blessing of Milwaukee Archbishop Rembert Weakland, the Jesuits have continued to run the parish, serving both Marquette and local communities.

This Web site highlights the parish work and mission. The Jesuits' commitment to justice can be viewed in the words of the society's mission statement: "As the Society of Jesus, we are servants of Christ's Mission." The Society commits itself "to a radical life of faith that finds expression in the promotion of justice for all" and says that "the integrating principle of our mission is the inseparable link between faith and the promotion of the justice of the Kingdom."

Web links include the following: Gesu's Parish Council, Gesu staff, the parish vision, mass and confession schedule, "Have you thought of becoming Catholic?", a collection of Jesuit resources on the Internet, news, and a feature called "Our Favorite Links for Kids of All Ages." Visitors are invited to sign a guest book, and addresses and contact numbers are listed.

Historic Church of Saint Peter (Brownsville, Pennsylvania)

http://www.primepage.com/stpeter.html

"Step back in time nearly a century and a half to 1845, and imagine, if you can, 183 parishioners in a small western community laboring to build a stone church that, to this day, has not seen its architectural equal in the United States." With these words, the Church of Saint Peter opens its home page. There in full view of the visitor is an image of the church, standing on a hill located on the east bank of the Monogahela River. Its Gothic spire atop the rough-cut sandstone walls overlooks the town of Brownsville, Pennsylvania. The church is a pioneer American version of the English Gothic Revival parish church that flourished in the British Isles in the early 1800s.

This parish Web site is more of a historical guide, complete with photographs and historical texts. Instructions are provided for those who may wish to travel to Saint Peter. Mass schedule information is also provided.

St. Mary of the Visitation (Huntsville, Alabama)

http://fly.hiwaay.net/~stmary/

This is an award-winning parish, voted a top church site. It is a good example of what a parish can do with the Web to enhance parish life and extend the parish reach. The site has no fewer than 47 pages, including odds and ends on everything from directions to the parish by car to information on the local Catholic high school. A tip: I noticed myself attracted to the language on the site; it contained invitation after invitation beginning with these words: "We welcome you to St. Mary of the Visitation's web pages. We are a Catholic parish located in Huntsville, Alabama. We invite you to stay and read about our parish." Or "If you are contemplating a move to the Huntsville area, we invite you to make Visitation your parish home." Or later, "If you are interested in learning about the Catholic faith, we have regularly scheduled classes as part of our faith formation program."

St. John the Baptist Catholic Parish (Newburgh, Indiana)

http://www.pinncomp.com/stjohn/index.html

> On behalf of our parish community, I want to welcome you to St. John Parish. It is good to have you with us. We hope you will feel at home, and experience a sense of belonging if you choose to worship with us. We hope, too, that you will grow in your faith while you are a part of our parish family.

These are the words of greeting a visitor to the St. John Baptist parish Web site reads upon first encountering the site. The greeting is warm and appears extended to Web visitors as well as potential parish members. Is the Internet changing the way we approach the means of worship? Geographic location seems less important than the sense of community found. But how real is community in cyberspace? This is a question for which there appear to be different answers for different people. On the pages of St. John the Baptist parish site, a visitor senses Father Joseph L. Ziliak may be breaking new ground in defining community.

I like the feature on these pages called "the pastor's pitch," a kind of weekly homily. From the look of the pages on this site, I felt drawn to this parish. The weekly activities list reveals a vitally active parish life. This, in turn, makes for a Web site that lifts the spirit in cyberspace.

Padre Serra Parish (Camarillo, California)

http://www.rain.org/~serra/

The Los Angeles Archdiocese is one of the most interesting in the world. No other U.S. archdiocese comes close to its multicultural ethnic mix. One of the largest archdiocesan ethnic groups is Hispanic. This parish site proudly proclaims its

Spanish-speaking heritage, which goes back to the Spanish Franciscans who were among the first Europeans to settle along North America's western coast. The most famous of these Franciscans was Father Junipero Serra, after whom this parish is named. Though his alleged harsh treatment of native American Indians has made him a controversial figure in some parts of the church, he is generally revered by many Catholics. Pope John Paul II has proclaimed him "blessed," a step on the way to church-proclaimed sainthood.

Padre Serra Parish serves more than 1,800 families living in Camarillo, Somis, and Santa Rosa Valley in southern California. It was established by Los Angles Cardinal Roger Mahony in May 1988. This parish site provides information about many of the parish's programs, with an emphasis on adult religious education. The day I looked at this site the parish was proudly announcing that it had received a religious and architecture design award.

The site listed links to other Catholic sites, including the Los Angeles Archdiocese's home page and a local seminary and college.

St. Dominic's Catholic Church (Panama City, Florida)

http://www.wsnet.com/~gardneda/index.html

This is one of the more innovative parish Web sites. There is a lot of activity here. I especially liked the "Question of the Week" feature, aimed at helping Catholics brush up on church teachings. When I looked I found the following question asked and answered:

Q: What do Catholics believe about the Blessed Sacrament?

A: Catholics believe the Blessed Sacrament is the Living Eucharistic Christ containing the living substance of Christ's Body and Blood, Soul and Divinity. We believe that at the words of the consecration the substance of bread is converted into the Body of Christ. The accidental qualities of bread are still there, but there is no trace of the substance of bread.

Christ has become present under the external signs of what used to be bread. This is a great mystery, a mystery that our limited human intelligence cannot understand, but Catholics accept it as faith, because Christ said it [Matthew 26:26-49, Mark 14:22-25, Luke 22:19-20]. Some argue that it is against the laws of nature for this to happen, but we must remember that God is not limited by laws that He Himself established, and it is no created law of nature that is in operation here, it is God's own immediate work.

Visitors are asked to be interactive by posting questions, comments, or suggestions and are promised responses within three days. The site also features parish activities, Catholic links, a biographical sketch of Pope John Paul II, and the Stations of the Cross. Not bad for private meditation.

Mass schedules are posted, information on the nursery is also there. This parish is clearly wired. Ten o'clock Sunday mass is broadcast live on WMBB, Channel 13.

St. Helen Catholic Community (Portales, New Mexico)

http://www.enmu.edu/~martinet/catholic/sthelen.html

The parish of Saint Helen is located in the City of Portales, which sits on the eastern side of New Mexico in the Santa Fe diocese. One senses by the clear skies in the photograph of this modern parish that the living is clean in the highlands. Saint Helen is the only Catholic Church in Roosevelt County, the site tells the visitor. The parish currently has 913 registered households, a moderate number by today's standards. The friendly Catholics at Saint Helen tell the visitor that their home page is simply an attempt to share "a little of our ministry and activities." Information is provided about the parish's RENEW program, one of the best programs making rounds of the church today. (RENEW aims to reinvigorate Catholic faith life at the parish level.)

The site also features a black-and-white picture of the local archbishop, Michael J. Sheehan, that doesn't slow the download. (I found the use of some black-and-white images on these pages a nice change of pace.) Geography buffs will appreciate a map on the site that locates the archdiocese of Santa Fe.

St. Patrick's Basillica (Ottawa, Canada)

http://www.igs.net/~cyberchurch

Founded in 1855, Saint Patrick's, the oldest parish in Ottawa serving English-speaking Catholics, was completed and blessed in 1875. The interior "modern Gothic" design has been enriched by sacred paintings, stained glass windows, a Casavant pipe organ, marble altars, pulpit, communion railings, and statues. These traditional appointments to God's glory preserve an atmosphere for private prayer and public worship in the spirit of Vatican II. Saint Patrick's was elevated to the status of Basilica in 1995.

This is one of the more elaborate church Web sites. Visitors are treated to a brief biographical sketch of St. Patrick, along with information about the archbishop/rector, parish bulletins, times of masses and other services, community events, and links to other Catholic Web sites. Church documents and charitable organizations and associations are listed as well. Nice work from north of the border.

Our Lady of Las Vegas (Las Vegas, Nevada)

http://www.intermind.net/church/index.html

Temptation overcame me. When I stumbled across the Web site of Our Lady of Las Vegas, I simply had to stop and visit. Part of me expected the glitz and glamour of neon lights, but what I found was unexpected serenity, including a beautiful photograph of the parish church surrounded by trees under a rich blue sky. Another click of the mouse and I learned the diocese of Las Vegas was only recently established—in June 1995—by Pope John Paul II, and that the patrons of the diocese are the Holy Family and Sts. Peter and Paul. The diocese has twenty-six parishes, four missions, one Byzantine Community, one Cathedral, and one Shrine. It has seven Catholic elementary schools and one high school. The total population of the diocese as of 1994 was 1,493,000. Of this total, 260,106 are Catholic. And last but not least, it is shepherded by Bishop Daniel F. Walsh.

Paulist Center of Boston (Boston, Massachusetts)
http://www.wpi.edu:80/~bridget/pcc.html

The Paulist Center is a worship community of Christians in the Roman Catholic tradition in Boston, Massachusetts. It is not a geographical parish. (Technically, it is what is called a "semi-public oratory.") The Paulist Center draws on individuals and families throughout the greater Boston area who are attracted to the Center's ministries of worship, family religious education, social justice, and other activities. It is also the home of the Landings Program, a ministry geared to former Catholics whose early experiences with the Church may have left them bitter or alienated. As the name suggests, the center is affiliated with the Paulist Fathers, from whom the ordained ministerial staff is drawn. 1995 marked the fiftieth anniversary of the Paulist presence in Boston, and the twenty-fifth anniversary of the Paulist Center Community. The anniversary was celebrated, in part, by opening this site on the Web.

This site, like many others on the Web, says that it still represents "work in progress." Eventually, the site states, in addition to supplying information about the center and its activities and ministries, it will offer information about Christianity and spirituality on the Internet, will serve as a forum for the center and its online friends to exchange opinions and experiences, and most important will spread the good news of Jesus Christ.

The Paulist Center in downtown Boston is already a well-known Catholic institution. It speaks to some of the best Catholic instincts for education and service to the community, especially the marginalized and spiritually thirsty. Additionally, it has fine liturgies. Stop in when in the area. Worship times are, of course, listed on the site.

CHAPTER 2

Religious Orders

Religious orders and congregations are groups of Catholics living under a religious rule and most often professing the vows of poverty, chastity, and obedience. The terms also include associations of autonomous monasteries, such as the Benedictines. Traditionally, religious life dates back to the end of the third century, when groups of women and men ascetics retired to the Egyptian desert in search of the pure gospel life. There were also autonomous virgins or widows along with deaconesses within local Christian congregations in early Christian history.

This chapter contains sites from various religious orders, congregations, and monasteries. There are hundreds of such sites on the Web. I have chosen a sampling for their distinctive place in contemporary Catholicism, for their importance in Catholic history, or simply for the innovative ways in which they present themselves on the Web. Religious orders are understood best within the context of their own history. Their mission comes from the spirit of this history. Most continue to live out of these traditions. I have deliberately used the words of these religious, using their words as much as possible, to describe their missions and contemporary ministries. Their words, images, and views of the world help a visitor better understand their spiritual worldview. It is out of this that they live and fulfill their daily tasks.

The Order of Saint Benedict

http://www.osb.org/osb/

The Benedictine Order has a centuries old tradition of receiving guests. They have extended this tradition to the World Wide Web through this site. The Order is more properly a confederation of monasteries and congregations, men and women, adhering to the Rule of St. Benedict. Of the various Catholic religious orders, the Benedictines are noted for their local autonomy.

The Rule of Benedict constitutes the basic guide by which the Benedictines live. Written in the sixth century, the Rule has been passed down for some 1,500 years. Historians are relatively certain the Rule of Benedict was written by St. Benedict, the founder of the monastery of Monte Cassino. It was one of a number of rules by which the monks of Europe lived, gradually superseding all others, both because of its intrinsic excellence and moderation and because the emperor Charlemagne (d. 814) wished all the monasteries of his empire to be characterized by uniformity of observance under the Rule of St. Benedict.

The Rule contains a treasure of spiritual wisdom concerning the monastic movement in the Church. Its prologue and 73 chapters provide teaching about the basic monastic virtues of humility, silence, and obedience as well as directives for daily living. The Rule legislates a monastic life that has rhythm, measure, and discretion. Benedictine monks are not overdriven by austerities in fasting and night vigils. They do not own anything personally, but they have enough to eat and drink and clothe themselves. They work with their hands about six hours a day, but they also have leisure for prayerful reading and common prayer.

This site describes the Rule of St. Benedict, the order's history, and its monastic traditions and points to areas of further monastic interest.

Monte Cassino

http://www.osb.org/osb/gen/monte.html Monte Cassino

Having read that St. Benedict founded the monastery of Monte Cassino, I felt I had to visit the place—at least in cyberspace. Little did I expect what I found: one of the most breathtaking sights I came across on the Web, the view of the monastery overlooking Monte Cassino (http://www.osb.org/osb/graphics/mcas1.gif). Benedict founded this principal monastery of the Benedictine Order in 529, and it sits today in stately repose overlooking the city. Benedict and his sister, Saint Scholastica, the site states, are buried there. While it looks peaceful enough, it has not always been so. It was destroyed by the Lombards in about 585, by the Saracens in 884, by the Normans in 1046, by an earthquake in 1349, and by the Americans in February 1944. Most of the art collection, was destroyed in 1944, but many valuable manuscripts were saved. It was once again restored and reconsecrated by Pope Paul VI in 1964. (The monastery was designated an Italian National Monument in 1866, with the monks acting as guardians.)

Benedictine Sisters of Erie

http://www.bison.com/benedict/msb/index.html

The Benedictine tradition lives—and this site is fine evidence. This is the online representation of the 150 Catholic Benedictine Sisters who live together in community at Mount Saint Benedict Monastery on the shores of Lake Erie in northwestern Pennsylvania. "We lead an ordinary lifestyle of prayer and work, but do so for an extraordinary reason: we want to change the world," these Benedictines proclaim on their site. And they appear to be showing the world they do just that. This community has the reputation of being one of the most faith-inspiring and challenging in the United States today. And what is it they are working for? This is what the site says:

We want a world that is more compassionate, just and forgiving. We want a world where children can grow up without street gangs and guns. We want a world where there are no hungry and no homeless. We want a world where all people are treated with dignity and respect, where all creation is seen as sacred. We want a world that is centered in God. We gather three times a day to pray for the change of heart, the depth of spirituality needed for such a world. We work in a wide range of ministries to build such a world.

And to remind themselves they are not just dreaming, they quote the late anthropologist Margaret Mead, who wrote:

Never doubt
that a small group
of committed people
can change the world.
In fact, that is all
that ever has.

Among the ministries these women are involved in are the following:

- AIM: The Alliance for International Monasticism, the national office for AIM, a worldwide network of Benedictine and Cistercian communities founded to assist more than 175 monasteries in Latin America, Africa, and Asia.

- Benetwood Apartments: An apartment complex for low-income, handicapped, and disabled persons.

- Emmaus Ministries: A soup kitchen and food pantry as well as a knitting project for unemployed women.

- Glinodo Center: An environmental studies, summer camp, retreat, hospitality, and recreation center on the shores of Lake Erie.

- Inner-City Neighborhood Art House: A fine arts center for children and adults.

- Saint Benedict Child Development Center: An accredited early child care facility for economically disadvantaged children. It includes an East Coast Migrant Head Start program.

- Saint Benedict Education Center: A job training and educational center for people on public assistance. Classes are offered to low-income adults preparing for their GED or who need academic brush-up work prior to enrolling in job training.

- Sanctuary Committee: First organized in 1988, this group of Erie Benedictines serves as an outreach to Central Americans, offering them help in resettlement, reunification, and education.

Saint John's Abbey

http://www.osb.org:80/osb/sja/

Saint John's Abbey is a delightful Benedictine monastic community of men who follow the 1,500-year tradition of worship and work through daily prayer and service in ministries that include education, parishes, chaplaincies, and missions. The Rule of Saint Benedict places a strong emphasis on community living and hospitality under an abbot (Timothy Kelly) with common prayer at the heart of the day. About two-thirds of the community live and work at Collegeville. Unlike most Catholic religious orders, each Benedictine monastery is autonomous but grouped into congregations according to origin. Benedictine monasteries increase in number by starting foundations that later become independent. Saint John's has a history of leadership in liturgical development, pastoral ministry, and programs in religion, psychiatry, and ecumenical scholarship. It also has a reputation for monastic preservation and promotion of culture, exhibited in its Hill Monastic Manuscript Library.

The monks at Saint John's do well with their Web site. It opens with a sky view shot of Saint John's and the surrounding area. The pastoral setting is clear; the site is clean, with links to specific information readily at hand. A contact address and telephone number are prominently displayed. The site features the publication *The Abbey Quarterly*, which contains monastic information about Saint John's; the site also links to Collegeville institutions, parishes, and missions, Benedictine Oblates, monastic vocations, special programs at Saint John's, monks Web pages, and recent deaths in the community.

This home page announces Saint John's prayer schedule and explains how prayer fits into the Benedictine tradition. It says where the Abbey is located: on "2,400 acres of beautiful woodland and lakes ... about 10 miles west of Saint Cloud and 70 miles north of Minneapolis/Saint Paul, Minnesota." It includes an invitation: "All peoples are welcome at Saint John's for resting, visiting and renewing, for a little while or for a longer time," providing contact information. I had the urge to jump in a car to make the trip. Others visiting this site no doubt have the same desire.

Sisters of Charity of the Blessed Virgin Mary

http://www.adscape.com/bvm/

This Web site explains the values, purpose, and ministries of the Sisters of Charity of the Blessed Virgin Mary (BVMs). The site stems from a community of nearly 1,000 women religious based in Dubuque, Iowa. The BVMs, however, serve in 25 states and 3 foreign countries. Founded in Philadelphia in 1833 by Mary Frances Clarke, her four companions, and Rev. Terence Donaghoe, the order moved to the Iowa frontier in 1843 and began urban ministry in 1867 in Chicago. As more women joined, the young community began expanding into a cross-country educational network. The mission, however, remained constant: a sensitive, courageous, competent response to human needs.

The BVMs state their mission as follows:

We are women who have been touched by God's steadfast love. In response to that love we are moved to commit ourselves to a vowed life of faithfulness to the Lord, faithfulness to one another in community, faithfulness to God's people, especially the poor.

The BVMs state their core values as follows: "Impelled by the values of freedom, education, charity, and justice, BVMs today respond to critical human situations, especially among women and poor."

Their ministries find expression in a traditional commitment to education "and in ministries emerging from new needs in Church and society." The BVM site lists other ministries as staffing schools, diocesan offices, working with handicapped children and adults, assisting the sick and elderly, helping dependent people by counseling and spiritual direction as well as by working as nurses or pastors in hospitals.

This site, like other religious order sites, also invites visitors who might have an interest in religious life "to enter into the process of initial membership." There are several ways this can be done, as lay associates or as full members of the religious community. "Membership as a BVM associate," the site states, "offers the opportunity to develop a sense of community, deepen one's spirituality and be an integral part of BVM mission and ministry, while continuing to live within one's own lifestyle."

Salvatorians

http://www.sds.org/Eng.htm

The Salvatorian home page quickly addresses these questions: What are the Salvatorians? Where are they? What is their history? What is their mission? What makes them different? How do I become a Salvatorian? What are their Apostolates? And what other Salvatorian presence is on the Net? Pretty simple stuff. But the quick question and answer approach at the top of many home pages works well.

This Web site, like the other religious order Web sites, outlines the history of the Salvatorian development. The only way to make sense out of a religious order is to understand its history. It is in the history of a religious order that its "charism" is to be found. Its "charism" is its nature, its purpose, its way of being. These are tied to its founding circumstances. Tradition matters within Catholicism. Religious orders take their history seriously. They want to connect their current work with that of their past, especially their foundational purposes.

The visitor learns The Society of the Divine Savior, founded in 1881, is composed of Religious Priests and Brothers, some 1,200 members worldwide. Its women's counterpart, the Congregation of the Sisters of the Divine Savior, with 1,300 members worldwide, was founded in 1888.

Being a lay person, I liked the emphasis placed on explaining the growth of the Salvatorian lay apostolate work. Lay people are increasingly working with members of religious orders within an order's mission. The site states that Father Francis Jordan, founder of the Salvatorians, turned to lay people for help long before many other religious thought of doing so. He formed the Lay Salvatorians. The Lay Salvatorian signs a covenant embracing the Gospel counsels of chastity, poverty, and obedience in association with the Salvatorian Community. Like other Salvatorians, the Lay Salvatorians can carry out an apostolic ministry in a secular, ecumenical, or parish setting.

The Augustinian Order

http://www.geocities.com/Athens/1534/osa.html

The Order of St. Augustine, commonly known as the Augustinians, is one of the four great mendicant religious orders of the Middle Ages. It is commonly held that St. Augustine of Hippo (d. 430), one of the greatest theologians in the history of Christianity, wrote what is now known as the Rule of St. Augustine, a brief outline of principles governing life in a religious community. This Rule calls for unity of heart and mind in God. Augustine's theology on the primacy of grace marks the theology developed by Augustinians. Martin Luther was an Augustinian.

Tradition has it that monks and hermits, dispersed by the Vandal invasion of North Africa in the fifth century, fled to Europe, where they established monasteries, particularly in northern and central Italy. In 1244, Pope Innocent IV formed the Order of Hermits of St. Augustine by uniting several groups of hermits and ordering them to follow the Rule of St. Augustine. In 1256, Alexander IV joined other groups with the existing Order of St. Augustine and officially named them a mendicant order.

The Order spread rapidly throughout Europe, taking an active part in ecclesiastical affairs and university life, where the English Augustinians were known as the Austin Friars. Missions were established in Central and South America, Japan, and India. Augustinians were the first Catholic missionaries in the Philippines; they were instrumental in the founding of the University of Mexico.

The historical and concrete shape the Order has acquired over its history also has been a source of inspiration for Augustinians. The Order was apostolic from its beginning, following the model of fraternity lived by the Apostles and found in the early Christian community. It also carried out the mandate of the Church to proclaim the good news of the Gospel. Today, in addition to the parochial and missionary apostolates, the Augustinian Order conducts schools, colleges, and universities around the world.

This site outlines the history of the Order and places it in the modern context. It offers a list of Augustinian saints and blesseds, those considered on their way to official sainthood. Of course, there is information on this site about St. Augustine, including the most studied confession in Western history. The site also leads to a gopher directory with 13 entries, one for each book of Augustine's Confessions.

Carmelites

http://middletown.ny.frontiercomm.net/~ocarmvoc
/carmelites.html

The Carmelites describe themselves as a religious order of priests and brothers who minister throughout the world. There are two U.S.-based Carmelite Provinces, the New York–based Carmelites of the North American Province of St. Elias and the Most Pure Heart of Mary Province, based in Chicago. The Order states its primary mission as follows: "to follow Jesus Christ through prayer, fraternity, and prophetic service and presence in the spirit of Mary and Elijah." The Carmelites try to "develop and encourage a sense of contemplative service to all God's people, with special attention to the poor and to developing lay participation in the Church." The site offers basic information about Carmelite life and encourages those interested to write, call, or email the Order.

There is also ample information on this site about one of the most memorable Carmelites, St. Teresa of Avila. Born in Avila, Spain, March 28, 1515, she died in Alba on October 4, 1582. In 1528, when Teresa was 15, her mother died, leaving behind 10 children whom Teresa had to help raise. In her youth, she had the reputation of being quite beautiful and is said to have retained her fine appearance until her last years. Her personality was extroverted, her manner affectionately buoyant, and she had the ability to adapt herself easily to all kinds of persons and circumstances.

At a young age she began to wonder whether she had a vocation to be a nun. Toward the end of 1532, reading the letters of St. Jerome led her to the decision to enter a convent, but her father refused to give his consent. Her brother and confidant, Rodrigo, had just set sail for the war on the Rio de la Plata. She decided to run away from home and persuaded another brother to flee with her so that both might receive the religious habit. On November 2, 1535, she entered the Carmelite Monastery of the Incarnation at Avila, where she served as prioress. This duty she was loath to assume, and she had much opposition to face on the part of the community. However, with the help of St. John of the Cross, who served as a confessor for the nuns, she was able to bring about a great improvement in the spiritual condition of the community. Much more on Teresa and the mystic, St. John of the Cross, can be learned from this site.

Among the writings of St. Teresa, three can be indicated as the depositories of her spiritual teaching: her autobiography, the Way of Perfection, and the Interior Castle. This site introduces the visitor to all three.

De La Salle Christian Brothers

http://www.catholic.org/delasalle/

This is a Web site "devoted to coordinating the Internet presence of the De La Salle Christian Brothers, the many and various Lasallian educational institutions around the world, and the wide spectrum of activities and interests among those who maintain Lasallian connections." The site is taking suggestions and continues to develop.

The story of the Christian Brothers reaches from St. John Baptist de La Salle and a small group of teachers in seventeenth-century France to the Lasallian world of today, where 7,500 Brothers and more than 50,000 Lasallian educators teach more than 1 million students in 1,100 locations in 82 countries. The site allows the visitor to make contact with these communities. The United States–Toronto Region of the Christian Brothers includes 17 elementary schools, 48 secondary schools, 7 colleges and universities, 14 special education centers, and 6 retreat centers. Some of these

Lasallian schools have their own locations on the Internet; others are listed here. Both Lasallian schools in the United States and others around the world are listed on this site, many with direct links. The Japanese network of Lasallian schools is also highlighted.

Dominicans
http://158.36.79.4/op/

The Dominicans, sometimes referred to as the Order of Preachers, were founded as a religious order in 1216. The Dominican Family consists of communities of friars, enclosed nuns, apostolic sisters, and lay people. Throughout the Order's history, its special charism has been to serve the Lord and neighbors through preaching as St. Dominic did. This preaching is based on study, prayer, and community. The Dominicans have a reputation of reaching out to others. Thus, they can be found involved in ecumenical and interreligious work. "Dialogue," the Dominicans maintain, "is integral to the Order's mission." As friars, the Dominicans strive, their mission states, to live in community in the values of evangelical poverty, chastity, and obedience. From this center the mission of preaching, theological education, and the promotion of peace and justice flow.

This site, like other religious sites on the Web, offers a brief look at the history of the Dominican Order. It speaks about the life and traditions of the Dominicans, as well as the people who make up the Order and locations of Dominican communities. The site also offers a Dominican chat room. It lists key Dominican feast days, news of Dominican Order events, such as the International Meeting of the Dominican Youth Movement, in France, held in August 1996. The site shares a liturgical calendar, a Dominican library, a bookshop, email addresses, and a What's New category. The site appears in German, Spanish, French, Italian, and English.

Franciscans

http://listserv.american.edu/catholic/franciscan/

The Franciscan Order is the common designation of the Order of Friars Minor ("Lesser Brothers"), who follow the rule of life written by Francis of Assisi. In a broader sense, the term is used in reference to two other orders descended from Francis's original followers: the contemplative nuns known as the Poor Clares and the lay penitential movement later know as the Third Order. The Franciscans were founded by Saint Francis of Assisi (1182–1226) and Saint Clare of Assisi (1194–1253). Anglican Franciscans may join the Society of St. Francis, and other Protestants may join the Order of Ecumenical Franciscans.

Like other sites for religious orders, this one highlights the Franciscan Order's rich history and the life of its founder, St. Francis. It also links to pages that outline the mission and work of the various Franciscan religious groups, including the Secular Franciscan Order for lay people. The St. Francis Order rule calls for Secular Franciscans to be in the forefront in promoting justice by the testimony of their lives and initiatives. Following the example of Francis in his peacemaking, Franciscans are at work at the United Nations and around the world promoting peace, justice, and ecology. The site lists articles showing some of this work. One of the growing areas of Christian concern has been caring for the life of the earth or ecological concerns. Here the Franciscans stand out among the religious orders. The documents in this site reflect this concern.

St. Francis of Assisi, after all, is the patron Saint of ecology. Francis is deeply loved throughout the world; his simplicity and spirituality are examples for Catholics and non-Catholics alike. It is sometimes said that after Jesus himself, Francis is the most revered Christian. This site opens the visitor not only to the Franciscan Order but to the life and works of St. Francis; it makes for a worthwhile visit.

Jesuit Resources on the Web

http://maple.lemoyne.edu/~bucko/jesuit.html

The Society of Jesus, popularly known as the Jesuits, was founded by Ignatius of Loyola (1492–1556) and half a dozen companions who bound themselves by the vows of poverty, chastity, and special obedience to the Pope. During the course of its 400-year history, the Society of Jesus has had great influence in the church. Jesuits have been scientists and theologians, poets and philosophers, explorers and missionaries. This page attempts to collect the many links to the Jesuits and their works that appear on the Internet.

The categories of links on this page are many and lead to interesting discoveries: Jesuit Spirituality, Jesuit Retreat Houses, Jesuit Parishes, Jesuit Colleges and Universities, Jesuit Secondary Education, Jesuit Social Ministries, Jesuits and Lay Associations and Organizations, Jesuit Art, Jesuit Documents, Jesuit Publications, Jesuit Vocations, Jesuit Events, Jesuit Province home pages, Jesuit Individuals' home pages, Other Catholic Religious and Orders, and Resources.

Each of the religious orders, such as the Benedictines, Franciscans, and Dominicans, has a distinctive spirituality, a distinct charism, a distinct way of responding to the Holy Spirit. The items on this site are aimed at introducing the visitor to the Jesuit way of life.

Like other Web pages by religious groups, this one tries to gather interest in the Jesuit order. This page has listings of Jesuits throughout the world who can provide more information. The Jesuits are an international religious order. For administrative purposes, the Jesuits are divided geographically in regions known as Provinces. Some of these Provinces have created their own sites on the Web.

A number of Jesuits from around the world have put up their own home pages on the Web. The visitor is invited to browse through them.

Holy Cross Province of the South West

http://www.it.stedwards.edu/holycross/holycros.htm#toc

Since its beginnings, the Congregation of the Holy Cross has been dedicated to the mission of education. In the United States, this commitment has produced several colleges and universities. Fr. Basil Moreau, founder of the congregation, established the principle that Holy Cross religious "will not educate the mind at the expense of the heart." This concept, this site says, remains key to the education mission of Holy Cross "where respect and shared undertaking aim to be a hopeful sign of the kingdom."

This is how the congregation presents itself:

> We Stand with the Poor: Christ was anointed to bring good news to the poor, release for prisoners, sight for the blind, restoration for every broken victim. Our efforts, which are his, reach out to the afflicted and in a preferential way to the poor and the oppressed.
>
> We Must Be Competent and Courageous: The mission is not simple, for the impoverishments we would relieve are not simple. There are networks of privilege, prejudice and power so commonplace that often neither oppressors nor victims are aware of them. We must be aware and also understanding by reason of fellowship with the impoverished and by reason of patient learning.
>
> We Are Educators Wherever We Work: For many of us in Holy Cross, mission expresses itself in the education of youth in schools, colleges and universities. For others, our mission as educators takes place in parishes and other ministries. Wherever we work we assist others not only to recognize and develop their own gifts but also to discover the deepest longing in their lives.
>
> We Cross Borders: Our mission sends us across borders of every sort. Often we must make ourselves at home among more than one people or culture, reminding us again that the farther we go in giving the more we stand to receive.
>
> We All Serve the Mission: All of us are involved in the mission: those who go out to work and those whose labors sustain the community itself, those in the fullness of their strength and those held back by sickness or by age, those in their active assignments and those who are still in training.

We Pray: Periodically we review how well our ministries fulfill our mission. We must evaluate the quality, forms and priorities of our commitments as to how effectively they serve the needs of the church and the world. Our mission is the Lord's and so is the strength for it.

This Web site outlines the mission and work of the Congregations of the Holy Cross. It lists the Holy Cross provinces, districts, and vice-provinces, with mailing addresses provided. It also lists contacts with the Holy Cross Sisters. The site lists the universities and colleges of the congregations of Holy Cross in the United States. Of course, the most famous of these is the University of Notre Dame, in South Bend, Indiana, founded in 1842 and associated with the Indiana Province.

Immaculate Heart of Mary

http://www.marywood.edu/www2/ihmpage/

This is the home page of the Congregation of the Sisters, Servants of the Immaculate Heart of Mary, or IHMs. The IHMs are popular and widely known in the United States. They are involved in a wide variety of ministries. What unites them? This is how these religious women see their mission, in the words of their constitution, most recently written in 1992:

> We strive to serve in a joyful, loving, hospitable and self-emptying spirit, reflecting that humility and simplicity which present a clear and understandable witness to Christ, who welcomed everyone. In fidelity to that tradition we engage in the apostolic works of education, health care, social service and various pastoral and spiritual ministries. We are also called to incorporate a sensitivity and commitment to social justice in our ministry and to use every opportunity available to affect social structures.

The IHMs, founded in 1845 by a young Belgian priest and three young women who met in Monroe, Michigan, near Detroit, grew out of efforts to meet the needs of French-

Canadians, Irish, and Germans, many of whom suffered from alcoholism. Responding to those needs, Theresa Maxis Duchemin (cofounder) and two other young women came together and established a school. Today, 150 years later, this community consists of three autonomous branches of IHMs centered in Monroe, Michigan; Philadelphia, Pennsylvania; and Scranton, Pennsylvania, with a combined membership near 3,000.

In addition to outlining the history of the Order, this site speaks to their current ministries and hopes for the coming millennia.

Marionists

http://www.udayton.edu/~campmin/marianist.htm

William Joseph Chaminade (1761–1850) was a priest of the diocese of Bordeaux, France, during the French Revolution, when Christianity was all but destroyed and the Church left in structural ruin. Inspired by the Holy Spirit and dedicated to Mary, Father Chaminade, as this site tells the story, began forming service-oriented Christian communities of men and women (Sodalities) as a way to re-Christianize France. By their very way of life, these Sodalities attracted others and raised up new Christians.

Eventually some Sodalite members formed the nucleus of two religious congregations: for women, the Daughters of Mary Immaculate (founded by Adéle de Batz de Trenquelleon in collaboration with Father Chaminade in 1816) and for men, the Society of Mary (founded in 1817). The Society of Mary was established in the United States in 1849 in Dayton, Ohio. The Marianist Sisters were established in 1949 in Somerset, Texas.

Marianists have long lived in association with one another in ways that many in today's Church are just beginning to experience—small Christian communities. In fact, Marianist origins can be found in the community of Bordeaux Sodality in France. In that community, lay people, diocesan priests, and members of religious orders came together around a common vision and commitment and lived in a family spirit in order to deepen their faith, do good works, and invite others to life in Christ.

A brief comment about terms—Marianist Family and Family of Mary are used almost interchangeably now, but that wasn't always the case. The family is composed of both religious and lay members, and the term Marianist originally designated the men and women who were in the two religious institutes, the Society of Mary and the Daughters of Mary.

This site features the history, spirituality, personalities, and ministry of the Marionist "family." Vocations, telephone numbers, and contacts in the United States and other parts of the world are provided.

Oblates

http://puffin.ptialaska.net/~klayj/omi.htm

The word "Oblate" has the same origin as "oblation." It means a person whose life, by special dedication, is offered in service to the Lord. The Oblates began in 1816, when a young French priest, Eugene de Mazenod, formed a group of priests to revive the Faith that had suffered through the French Revolution of 1789. Soon other priests joined the group. In 1826, they received papal approval as a Religious Congregation under the patronage of Mary Immaculate. Later, Fr. de Mazenod became Bishop of Marseilles. At his death in 1861, 400 Oblates were working in Europe, Asia, Africa, and America. Today, about 5,000 Oblate priests and brothers work in 68 countries on every continent. There are four priorities that capture the Missionary Oblate vision:

- A commitment to carrying the gospel to others, with special preference for the poor and those on the margins of society.

- A recognition that the roles and responsibilities of lay people in the Church are significant, encouraging the leadership of the laity in all efforts.

- To work for justice and peace, striving to address the economic, political, and social structures that affect the lives of sisters and brothers worldwide.

- And a commitment to programs that foster the Order's renewal as missionaries in today's world, forming communities that give life and sustenance to one another.

This Web site, like that of most other religious orders, concentrates on the history of the Order, the life and spirit of its founder, its past and current missions, and offers contacts for those with possible interest in the Order.

Pallottines
http://www.dare.uni-essen.de/sac/welcome.html

This Web page is the unofficial Internet site of the Society of the Catholic Apostolate, otherwise known as the Pallottine Fathers & Brothers. The Society was founded in 1835 by Saint Vincent Pallotti, a Roman priest who became for his contemporaries an example of faith and genuine Christian spirituality. According to this site, the idea of St. Vincent Pallotti presents itself today, more than a century and a half later, in two parts: the interior part that consists of Pallottine Fathers and Brothers plus five other Institutes of Consecrated Life and the exterior part that includes different societies and groups of the laity that can be classified according to the form they cooperate with in the interior part. It is said that the Pallottine members strive to be a bridge between diocesan and religious priests. They make promises, not vows, of poverty, chastity, and obedience.

This site lists the Pallottine community's goals, its lay apostolate program, its ecumenical initiatives, missions, charity, social justice work, and media efforts. It also links with other Pallottine Web pages, including individuals' home pages. Visitors are invited to make contacts.

The Paulists

http://www.clark.net/pub/paulist/

The site asks: "Who are the Paulists?" It then provides a brief summary answer, courtesy of the University Catholic Center in Austin Texas. The Paulists are Roman Catholic priests who serve as missionaries in the United States and Canada. In 1858, five priests, each one a convert to Catholicism, were given permission to form a religious community that would work to spread the message of Jesus Christ to the people of this continent. From these small beginnings the Paulist mission expanded to the point where today they minister in 27 cities across the United States and Canada.

Their founding leader, Isaac T. Hecker, was steeped in the spirit of America through his participation in early labor movements and a time of spiritual searching in New England. His vision, rooted in the ongoing promptings of the Holy Spirit, has informed generations of Paulists as they try in his words, "to meet the needs of the Church in the modern age."

The stated mission of the Paulists is to work in parishes, in many larger cities, developing ways in which the parish community can be involved effectively in the areas of evangelization, ecumenism, and reconciliation. Paulists can be found at many of the larger secular campuses where their ministry helps challenge young Catholics both intellectually and pastorally to be effective and innovative Church leaders.

Paulists take pride in using modern means of communication. They are involved in television, radio, and cinema. They direct the New Jersey–based Paulist Press, the largest Catholic publishing venture in the English-speaking world. They design new approaches to evangelization and reconciliation in many areas of North America. They also are the organizers of ecumenical efforts in many cities.

Links are provided to the Paulist Directory, Photo Gallery, Paulist Communications, and Paulist Today.

Salesians

http://www.allencol.edu/salesian/salesian.html

This is the International Commission on Salesian Studies (ICSS) home page. It opens the Salesian world to the Web traveler. This home page is jointly sponsored by the ICSS and Allentown College of St. Francis de Sales. The ICSS assists the Oblates of St. Francis de Sales to carry out their mission to spread the spirit and charism of its patron St. Francis de Sales on a global level.

On December 8, 1602, during the ceremony in which he was ordained the Bishop of Geneva, Francis de Sales had a religious experience that was to set the apostolic agenda for the rest of his life. Later he described this experience to his spiritual friend and fellow saint, Jane de Chantal: "God had taken me out of myself in order to take me to Himself, and then He gave me back to the people. That is, He converted me from what I was for myself into what I was to be for them." In this action, Francis experienced in a special manner, according to this site, what is meant to be the single most important goal of every person: union with God for whom the human heart is created. He taught this truth to his people by preaching, by spiritual guidance, by catechizing, and by writing.

A major arena for Francis's apostolic zeal was the spiritual guidance of men and women from every walk of life. He was a master of this spiritual art. He respected the primary role of the Holy Spirit in guiding the life of each person, and he deeply regarded each one's unique dignity and inalienable freedom. These were principal characteristics of his spiritual guidance.

Francis died in Lyons on December 28, 1622, a still young but utterly spent man. Following the impulse of his religious experience in 1602, he had given himself throughout life to God in intimate prayer and had left God only to serve God's people by living among them as Jesus had. The phrase "as human as can be," which St. Francis de Sales wrote of himself, according to this site, is also wonderfully descriptive of the spirituality that bears his name. In this application, it would mean that his teaching articulates a way of living the full Christian life while enhancing rather than repressing a person's humanity.

This Web page opens the Salesian way of life in all its various manifestations: Salesian Resources, Libraries, Information Centers, and Other Resources. It provides many Salesian names, addresses, and contacts.

Taizé

http://www.almac.co.uk/taize/taize.html

For tens of thousands, especially the young, the name "Taizé" evokes authentic Christianity. It also evokes a certain style of chant that has become popular in churches, retreat centers, campus parishes, and seminaries. For some, the word also suggests gatherings that attract large numbers of young adults. Still others are aware that Taizé is in fact an ecumenical community of brothers located in a small village in eastern France.

Today the Taizé community is composed of approximately 100 brothers who come from different Christian traditions and more than 25 countries and every continent. They make a life commitment to live together as a "parable of community," a sign of the Gospel's call to reconciliation. Around the brothers, tens of thousands of people, mainly between the ages of 17 and 30, come each year to spend a week, returning to the roots of the Christian faith. They join in the community's worship three times a day, listen to Bible introductions on the sources of the faith, spend time reflecting in silence, and meet in small sharing groups.

Taizé began with one man, Brother Roger. In 1940, he came to what was then a semi-abandoned village in Burgundy, the regional origin of his mother's family. He was 25 years old, and he had come there to offer shelter to political refugees, notably Jews fleeing the Nazi persecution, and to work out a call to follow Christ in community. A few years later, he was joined by his first brothers, and in 1949, several of them committed themselves for life to celibacy and to material and spiritual sharing. Life at Taizé, following the monastic tradition, has always turned around three main axes: prayer, work, and hospitality.

Church leaders come to Taizé as well. On October 5, 1986, the community welcomed Pope John Paul II. As he said in his address to the young people present, "Like yourselves, pilgrims and friends of the community, the Pope is just passing through. But you pass through Taizé as you pass close to a spring of water."

Besides explaining the history and spirit of Taizé, this Web site offers careful instructions on how to travel to the community. It also offers monthly bible reflections, details of meetings in different countries, a daily meditation by Brother Roger, music from Taizé to sample, and addresses for further contact. The site is available in German, Spanish, French, Italian, Polish, Chinese, and English.

Daughters of St. Paul

http://bay.netrover.com/~pauline/

The Daughters of St. Paul is an international congregation of Catholic women religious whose aim is "communicating God's love through media technology."

In 1914, Father James Alberione began a mission of evangelization for the media age. One year after beginning the Society of St. Paul for priests and brothers he gathered the first Daughters of St. Paul. His idea was to form apostles consecrated in the Church for the proclamation of the Gospel with the means of social communication. Every new instrument of communication was to be adopted and put at the service of the Gospel.

From the start, Mother Thecla Merlo collaborated with Father Alberione. This frail woman guided the Daughters of St. Paul as the community grew throughout the world. Father Alberione's vision of the needs of the Church led him to found other religious congregations. Five religious congregations, four secular institutes, and the lay men and women of the Pauline Cooperators together form the "Pauline Family." Father Alberione died in 1971, and Mother Thecla Merlo died in 1964.

The Society of St. Paul (founded in 1914) was Father Alberione's first achievement. From it was drawn the inspiration for all the other foundations. The Daughters of St. Paul (founded in 1915) has the same specific purpose as the Society of St. Paul: "The glory of God and the salvation of souls by spreading Catholic doctrine through the apostolate of social communications: printing, cinema, radio, television, and all the other rapid and effective means in general."

St. Paul spirituality states that "the life I live now is not my own, Christ is living in me." To help them reach this union with Christ, the Daughters' lives encompass:

- A daily Hour of Adoration before the Blessed Sacrament
- Community participation in the Mass
- An additional half-hour of personal prayer for all the professed sister
- Meditation
- The Rosary
- Morning and evening prayer
- Monthly retreats
- A week-long annual retreat
- Valued periods of silence

This Web site tells the story of the Daughters of St. Paul and lists the many nations where they are active. It also offers a mail list and reference catalogue.

Secular Franciscans (Divine Mercy Region of Lower Michigan and Toledo, Ohio)

http://www.rc.net/org/dmercy/

This Web page is the work of a relatively new fraternity of the Secular Franciscan Order (SFO). It describes how it came into being and offers ample information on the history and work of the Order, also known as the Third Order of St. Francis. The Secular Franciscan Order is an organic union of all Catholic fraternities scattered throughout the world and open to every group of the faithful.

The Secular Franciscan Order is canonically recognized with a Rule of Life approved by the Pope. But it is an Order composed of lay men and women. Thus, it is to be distinguished from "religious" Orders, such as the other branches of the Franciscan family, as well as from other lay groups, such as the traditional confraternities and sodalities and the more recent small base communities.

The Order was founded by St. Francis—it is sometimes called the Third Order because he founded it after he founded the Friars and the Poor Clares. During the period 1210 to 1220, Francis and his brothers traveled throughout Italy preaching the Gospel. Many men and women flocked to join the Friars and the Poor Clares. Many others, however, wanted to embrace the Gospel life he preached but were tied to the world in some way—family, business, or feudal ties. St. Francis responded to them by organizing the Brothers and Sisters of Penance, perhaps using as his model the penitential orders that had come into existence in the preceding centuries.

Today, Secular Franciscans are men and women who would like to follow Jesus Christ in the footsteps of St. Francis of Assisi. They do so by professing a rule of life that reflects the Gospel call, the life and thought of St. Francis, and the particular role of laity in the Church and in the world. The three pillars of their life are the Gospels, the Rule, and the writings of Sts. Francis and Clare. The external obligations are few: to be an active member of a local fraternity, to wear a simple habit (usually a Franciscan Tau cross), and to pray the Office.

This Web site is the work of the Divine Mercy Region of Lower Michigan and Toledo. It had its origins in the spring and summer of 1992, when representatives from the 11 separate Secular Franciscan Provinces in the lower peninsula of Michigan began meeting with a representative of the National Fraternity to start exploring the process of regionalization. On October 31, 1993, all of the fraternities in lower Michigan and their brother and sister Secular Franciscans in Toledo, Ohio, were officially joined as the Divine Mercy Region.

This Web site not only tells their story, but also tells the visitor how to find a fraternity in his or her own region.

The Cistercians

http://www.osb.org/osb/cist/

The Cistercian order is an order of monks in the Benedictine monastic tradition. In 1098, 21 monks and Robert, their abbot, left the Benedictine abbey of Molesmes in Burgundy, France, to follow the Rule of St. Benedict to the letter, to sacrifice centuries of customs and devotional accretions for the sake of evangelical simplicity. At Citeaux, they established a new monastery. Simplicity governed everything, from their habits to the food they ate. Much of the Cistercians' spectacular growth can be attributed to Bernard of Clairvaux (1090–1153). The dominant figure of the early-twelfth-century church, Bernard articulated in sermons, letters, and treatises a theology of reformed monasticism that expressed the ideals of the Cistercian founders.

The Order continued to expand: by 1200 there were more than 500 houses; on the eve of the Reformation, the records showed 742. In time, geography began to defeat these model means of regularity, which were eventfully adopted by all other religious orders. The decline in the number of recruits had its effect, but most destructive was the practice of the ecclesiastical and secular powers to give the abbatial office to clerics who had no interest in the well-being of the monastery, only in its revenues, leaving the monks without guidance and financial means.

In 1892, Pope Leo sought to bring all the Cistercian houses back together into one Order. However, pastoral responsibilities and national loyalties made it impossible for the Common Observance houses, who were divided into many national congregations, to unite with the Strict Observance who were at that time largely French and who had opted for the strict monastic heritage of the Cistercian founders. Thus, the Pope recognized two Cistercian Orders, called today the Order of Citeaux and the Cistercian Order of the Strict Observance, popularly known as the Trappists.

This site connects with various Cistercian World Wide Web sites, including the Cistercian monasteries in France and Germany. The site also links with Cistercian Monks and Nuns in the United States, Cistercian Publications, the Abbey of Gethsemani, and other Cistercian sites, including the works of Thomas Keating and the late Thomas Merton.

St Benedict's Abbey (Atchison, Kansas)
http://www.benedictine.edu/Abbey.html

> Let them prefer nothing whatever to Christ, and may he bring us all together to everlasting life.
>
> —*Rule of Benedict 72: 11–12*

This site opens with the polite question: "May We Introduce Ourselves To You?" The visitor quickly learns that St. Benedict's Abbey, located in Atchison, Kansas, is home for 75 monks of the Order of St. Benedict. Atchison has been a home for Benedictine monks since 1857 when German-speaking men came from Pennsylvania to serve the early Catholic settlers in Kansas. They brought with them the Benedictine heritage, dating back to sixth-century Italy. The visitor to the site soon learns more about the historical St. Benedict, who only required that the monks "work and pray together, without defining the work." The prayer is the Liturgy of the Hours, or *lectio divina*, and the Eucharist. The work in Kansas has been identified with education and parish service.

The Benedictine monks are, along with the Benedictine Sisters of Atchison, cosponsors of Benedictine College, a four-year boarding and day school in Atchison. The monks also work in 22 parishes and missions in northeastern Kansas and have six monks on mission in Brazil.

The St. Benedict's Abbey home page also includes the testimonial of a young professional who wrote: "My wife and I want to recognize the degree to which the abbey community and college have positively blessed our lives— one of us as a student and the other a 15 year resident of Atchison and major supporter/admirer of the same entities. In a quiet, spiritual way, I can honestly say the abbey had a big influence on me as a young professional choosing a place to call home and entering my adult life."

The site, like other religious sites, but especially those of a Benedictine tradition, concludes with an invitation: "Come join us—for a day, for a college career, for a lifetime. Who knows the extent to which you will be attracted to Benedictinism? Young men who read this material may well be thinking about finding a community of men who value education, prayer, and service within the Catholic church." It adds the name and contact information for the vocation director at the abbey.

Mount St. Scholastica (Atchison, Kansas)

http://www.benedictine.edu/vocation.html

The visitor to the Mount St. Scholastica home page is greeted with the following meditation:

> To discover God is not to discover an idea but to discover one-self. It is to awaken to that part of one's existence which has been hidden from sight and which one has refused to recognize. The discovery may be very painful; it is like going through a kind of death. But it is the one thing which makes life worth living.

> —*Bede Griffiths, The Golden String*

It sets the tone to a site visit that is both reflective and creative, as clearly are the women religious responsible for the pages. Mount St. Scholastica in Atchison, Kansas, is home to some 247 Benedictine women who have lived there for 133 years. Located on 40 acres of rolling hills in a Benedictine environment, the community has an ideal setting for prayer and reflection.

Community members engage in a broad variety of ministries while living and praying together in large or small groups. Most live within the region around Atchison, particularly the Kansas City/St. Joseph/Topeka metropolitan areas and surrounding rural locales. A number are also engaged in ministry within the monastery, either in some form of active service or through the prayer and suffering of their infirmity.

The site relates that on November 11, 1863, at 11:00 P.M., seven Benedictine Sisters arrived in Atchison, Kansas, from Eichstatt, Germany—by way of Pennsylvania and Minnesota. Upon their arrival, they opened St. Scholastica Academy and a long history of educational opportunities for young women and men from all over the midwestern United States became a reality.

The site contains much information, and it links with a number of Benedictine sites and other good Catholic sites, many of them of a generally progressive nature.

St. Mary's Abbey (Morristown, New Jersey)
http://www.osb.org/osb/sma/sma.html

When I came across the St. Mary's Abbey, a Benedictine monastery in Morristown, New Jersey, and began to skip through its site connections, it was the St. Mary's Abbey Retreat Center that jumped out at me. An often over-looked service that monks provide—one that is desperately needed in our hectic modern world—is a spiritual retreat. Curiously relatively few people take advantage of the opportunities a retreat provides to refresh physical, psychological, and spiritual health.

This site invites the visitor to come on a retreat. Nearly every monastery offers retreats. At St. Mary's (in the words of the monks), the retreat center "exists to share your spiritual journey and to serve you in your pilgrimage." The imagery, of course, is life as a journey. And that is the way the monks see it, moving from Creator to return to Creator. The opportunity is to recognize the spiritual nature of the trip. This is precisely what the monks at St. Mary's beckon the traveler to understand.

The directed retreats are for those "who would like to spend an extended period of time with God in prayerful silence." Retreatants meet with a spiritual director each day "to discuss how God is working within them and to discover the direction in which God is leading them." They also have the opportunity to pray with the monks in the Abbey church. Aside from retreats, the monks offer days of individual prayer and recollection "for any person who would like to take time away with God in quiet reflection in the atmosphere of the Abbey grounds and to join in prayer with the monks."

The site offers basic information, even the fact that "linens are provided upon request" and "delicious meals are served in the spacious abbey cafeteria." The abbey is located in the Diocese of Paterson, and the monks serve in the Archdiocese of Newark, the dioceses of Paterson, Metuchen, Trenton, and Wilmington, Delaware.

Claretian Missionaries
http://http1.brunel.ac.uk:8080/depts/chaplncy/cmfs.htm

This Claretian site explains that Anthony Claret was first and foremost a missionary. He preached, taught, organized, and counseled through Spain, the Canary Islands of Africa, Cuba, and beyond. He became a prolific author. His Christian concern for compassion and justice motivated him to struggle for the freedom of slaves in Cuba, to found credit unions for the poor, and to work to help people "to know the freedom and peace to which God calls each human being."

The site also offers explanations about who the Claretians are: men and women, single and married, who seek to share the Good News throughout the world. The visitor learns that as priests, brothers, and lay people, Claretians follow in the spirit of their founder, St. Anthony Claret. They are especially available to those in need. Claretians aim "to be present especially to the poor, to youth and families, and to the unchurched."

The site lists the various Claretian ministries. These include youth ministry work, social justice work, foreign mission work, and publishing. Besides youth ministries in their parishes, Claretians work on college campuses and sponsor volunteers who work in summer programs for children. Claretians also work with refugees, the homeless, and those needing health care and housing. The Claretian's of the USA Eastern Province work with Claretians from England to staff and support a mission in remote jungle areas of Izabal, Guatemala. Finally, Claretians continue to be very active in the field of publications. Two of their best-known magazines are *U.S. Catholic* and *Salt of the*

Earth. They also publish a wide variety of newsletters and pamphlets. The Claretians operate the U.S. Catholic Bookstore in downtown Chicago.

This site links with other Claretian sites, including some in England and Canada. The site allows visitors to subscribe to the Worldwide Claretian Listserver and offers other contacts for further information.

The Sisters of Saint Joseph of Florida, USA

http://ballingerr.xray.ufl.edu/sisters.html

This site has a special flavor, combining black-and-white pictures with text as it explains the vision, mission, and work of a local religious congregation. Nothing too fancy, but the pictures and text tell a moving story of commitment to the needy. Since photographs are not in color, the visitor does not have to wait unduly for downloading.

I learned that the Sisters of Saint Joseph of Florida are a religious congregation of Catholic women "called to live the Gospel of union and reconciliation. ... For us, service means a consistent effort to promote union among our neighbors and with God ... In whatever form we minister, we find ourselves called to be healers in situations of pain, ignorance, and dissension." The site then invites the visitor to "come with your unique talents to work with us to heal a world so in need of reconciliation."

This site is one of a few active sites that appear on a list of congregations belonging to the Federation of the Sisters of Saint Joseph of the United States.

Federation of the Sisters of Saint Joseph of the United States of America

http://www.nd.edu/~csjus/home.html

This Web home page is the official home page of the Federation of the Sisters of Saint Joseph of the United

States of America (CSJ/SSJ), a voluntary union of all Sisters of Saint Joseph of the United States who claim a common origin in the foundation at LePuy, France.

The site is not particularly attractive, but it is functional. I found the wording stiff but it provided the necessary information. The site states that the purpose of the federation is promoting the following ends:

- To support in all Sisters of Saint Joseph.

- To integrate a continuing exploration of the CSJ/SSJ charism by an approach that looks toward its living expression as well as its historical roots.

- To collaborate in programs that facilitate the understanding and interpretation of the CSJ/SSJ charism as it affects the life and ministry of the members.

- To provide the members with a sense of belonging to a movement greater than one's own congregation.

- To link leaders and members of CSJ/SSJ congregations through the direction of a Governing Board.

This page is an example of how the Web, without fanfare, can unite various religious groups by providing basic information—in this case about the Federation.

Archabbey of Pannonhalma

http://www.osb.hu/eng/e_cimek.html

This site, the Archabbey of Pannonhalma, a Benedictine Archabbey, is an example of the increasing number of European religious communities that can be found on the Web. I thought it would be fun to choose one from a nation most Americans do not frequently visit, but that is easily accessible on the World Wide Web. The Archabbey of Pannonhalma is located in Hungary. The Web site takes the visitor on a tour of the Archabbey and surrounding grounds which Pope John Paul II visited in September

1996. Read a bit of the description provided, which appears with helpful photographs:

> The classicist tower of the basilica can be found at the axis of the complex. The cupola with its columned gallery rises above its rigid lines, and bears the gilt Hungarian double cross as seen in the country's coat-of-arms. Left of the basilica the Baroque library (another classicist structure) can be seen; to the right the Baroque wing built in the early 18th Century. The gymnasium built in 1940 is attached to this core on its southern side. From here we will proceed to the basilica. ...

It is difficult to overemphasize the importance of St. Benedict in the monastic tradition. On the occasion of the 1964 dedication of the rebuilt monastery of Monte Cassino, Pope Paul VI proclaimed St. Benedict the principal, heavenly patron of the whole of Europe. The title piously exaggerates the place of Benedict, but in many respects it is true. St. Benedict did not establish the monastery of Monte Cassino to preserve the learning of the ages, but in fact the monasteries that later followed his Rule were places where learning and manuscripts were preserved. For some six centuries or more the Christian culture of medieval Europe was nearly identical with the monastic centers of piety and learning.

This site features links to sites that tell the history of the Archabbey of Pannonhalma, the life of St. Benedict, and the Rule of Benedict in English and Latin. The site also offers links to other European monastic sites and the Hungarian Catholic Bishops Conference—and more.

Mount Athos

http://www.media.dbnet.ece.ntua.gr/athos/uk/general/top.htm

This Web site is a special treat. It lists "in hierarchical order" 20 Greek Orthodox monasteries on Mount Athos, situated in the entire third, eastern, and most beautiful peninsula of Halkidiki, called the peninsula of Athos. It is the only place in Greece that is completely dedicated to prayer and worship of God. For this reason, it is called the Holy Mount. The Holy Mount is about 50 kilometers long and 8 to 12 kilometers wide. The natural beauty of the peninsula is extraordinary. The Mount Athos that dominates is a huge cone, a naked, treeless crest that seems to lance the sky; its slopes are fully covered with ancient evergreens. All these help to create an area of incomparable natural beauty.

The Holy Mount is a self-governed part of the Greek state, subject to the Ministry of Foreign Affairs in its political aspect and to the Ecumenical Patriarch of Constantinopole as regards its religious aspect. It has been divided into 20 self-governed territories. Each territory consists of a cardinal monastery and some other monastic establishments that surround it (cloisters, cells, cottages, seats, hermitages). All the monasteries are communes (of a convent nature), which means there is common liturgy, prayer, housing, nourishing, and work among the monks.

This site is breathtaking. Photographs appear with descriptions and information about the monasteries, their histories, and activities. For those who will not one day make it to Mount Athos, this site is the next best thing.

Inkamana Abbey, Vryheid, South Africa
http://www.shaka.iafrica.com/%7Egtl/inkamana.htm

The Catholic Church is growing in Africa faster than on any other continent. This site in its own way tells the story of this remarkable growth—from missionary territory to abbey in less than 100 years.

This is the site of Inkamana Abbey in Vryheid, South Africa, and among other things it describes how Benedictine monastic life got here. It was in 1887 that Pope Leo XIII entrusted the Benedictines with the Apostolic Prefecture of South Zanzibar, in what was then German East Africa. One mission station after another was established, from Dar es Salaam on the coast to the deep interior of the country. The most important of these, Peramiho and Ndanda, became abbeys in 1931. The abbots of the monasteries also served as bishops for these mission dioceses. This region is now the southern part of Tanzania and comprises four dioceses, with local bishops, priests, and religious.

The work of the Benedictine missionaries has also taken root in Zululand, South Africa. Since 1922, the monks there have preached the Gospel in the diocese of Eshowe. The missionary monks undertook work there among the semi-nomadic people of the Kerio valley, Kenya, in 1972. In the monastery erected in Nairobi in 1978, monks from Europe and Africa pray and work together in the same priory.

As for the Inkamana Abbey, the site states it is situated on the shores of the Klipfontein Dam outside Vryheid (Northern Natal). The monastery was founded as a mission station on August 3, 1922, and was given the status of a Priory on October 10, 1961, and a Conventual Priory on June 21, 1968, and was made an abbey on February 25, 1982. Inkamana Abbey has grown into a major monastic and educational center where Priests and Brothers from South Africa and overseas work and pray together. Supported by the Benedictine Sisters of Tutzing, it runs a fully established school for boys and girls and exercises an apostolate for guests who share the prayer and community. As of January 1, 1995, the community consisted of 20 priests, 19 brothers, 8 monks with temporary professions, and 1 oblate.

Russell Neville's Monastic Den

http://www.efn.org/~russelln/

This site shows how a person's personal interests can be put to good use on the Web. This monk's page is one of the more popular Catholic Web sites. Russell Neville begins by asking a straightforward question: "Why monks?"

He answers, saying "so many pages on the web seem to exist without purpose or reason. Being in a reactionary state of mind, I wanted to have a reason for my specialization." The visitor learns that Russell, in the course of writing a book, learned "a bit about monks, monasteries, abbots, cloisters, scriptoriums, and various other tidbits." Instead of letting all the research hide between the pages of an unpublished work, he began a monk page to share his findings.

So we have "Russell Neville's Monastic Den." However, Russell quickly offers a disclaimer: "As any experienced web traveler knows, the information one finds is only as accurate and valid as the person who posts it. In other words, much of what one finds is slanted, misleading, or flat wrong. I have tried to compile information from reputable sources and cite those sources, if possible."

Besides assembling an interesting set of links to colorful and informative monastic Web sites, Neville reveals a flair for having fun along the way. Included in his links, for example, is St. Benedict's Beer label! We all needed that, right? This site is clean and colorful and worthy of a visit.

Abbey of the Genesee

http://web.lemoyne.edu/~bucko/genesee.htm

I was skipping through some monastic Web sites when I came across this one. There is much that is similar on these pages to other Benedictine sites on the Web. The life of Benedict can be found, as can the Rule in all its glory. Links with Benedictine sites and much on the history of monasticism, including how the Cistercians grew as a reform movement and flourished, are available. A unique feature, however, is the simple entries that appear under What's New every several days. Here the ordinary life of the monks' community is shared with the world at large. What comes across is the natural—not the supernatural—world, making the monks more human. Therefore, we can feel more like them, or rather, we could be like them if we prayed more and centered our lives, as they do, on Ultimate Reality. What do these "ordinary" entries, these news accounts, look like?

The visitor learns, for example, that one day last July, "volunteer fire departments from several nearby towns responded in great numbers to the alarm (at the abbey) but could not save the garage nor its contents which included two cars and an apartment. Thanks be to God no one was injured! At the moment the cause remains undetermined."

Also, this news flash: "Cake and ice cream, followed by a little after dinner speech marked the occasion of Fr. Thomas Bond's celebration of his 90th birthday on Thursday, July 18th. Even at this age Fr. Thomas rises at 2:10 each morning and follows the full daily schedule. He invited us back in ten years for his 100th birthday when he promised a really BIG party!"

And this: "There was cause for rejoicing Sunday, June 30th. Our postulant, Br. Malachy (formerly Jim Greenawalt) received the novice's habit and entered into the novitiate on that day."

Priestly Fraternity of St. Peter

http://www.crnet.org/fssp/fsp_html.htm

Sometimes I think Catholicism is best viewed as a raucous family. I picture parents, brothers and sisters, uncles, aunts, grandparents, and in-laws all at a large Thanksgiving table discussing—no, make that heatedly arguing—the issues of the day. In many ways, this member or that is divided. Tension rises; tempers can flare. They don't all share a common vision. But they share deep bonds, much history, and love—and they keep returning to the table because they are family and they need each other.

It is helpful to consider this imagery when thinking about Catholicism today. Catholics have become divided, especially since the Vatican II, when enormous change began to occur in the church. Most Catholics accept conciliar change, but for some it continues to be painful. These family members feel too much tradition has been sacrificed.

Liturgy has been one area of church division. While most Catholics have adapted to the new liturgies, including mass in the vernacular with the priest facing the faithful, others have not. Some Catholics became so upset with the liturgical changes following the council that they left the church. The most notable breakaway was led by the late French prelate, Archbishop Marcel Lefebvre. He attended the Council but refused to sign some of the documents. Disenchanted with the postconciliar direction, he opened a traditionalist seminary in Switzerland in 1970. He split with Rome in the 1970s and was excommunicated in 1988 for ordaining bishops without papal authority. That was the year Pope John Paul II, in an effort at reconciliation with disaffected Catholics, approved the formation of a fraternity of priests in the framework of the traditional liturgy of the Roman rite, the Priestly Fraternity of St. Peter.

This fraternity site outlines its history, its numbers, and its works. The fraternity is relatively small, with some 60 priests and 115 seminarians. Its international headquarters is situated at the Marian shrine of Wigratzbad, near the Bavarian town of Lindau, Germany. Wigratzbad is also where the Seminary of St. Peter trains European candidates for the priesthood. The fraternity also operates out of North America. Beginning with an apostolate in Dallas, Texas, in 1991, it operates in a dozen or more U.S. dioceses and others in Canada. Besides offering information on the fraternity, the site offers contact information including addresses, telephone numbers, and an email address.

St. Benedict's Monastery (St. Joseph, Minnesota)

http://www.physics.csbsju.edu/osb.sisters/

The Sisters of St. Benedict of St. Joseph, Minnesota, are a community of nearly 450 women who follow the Gospel and the Rule of Benedict. Through prayer, work, and community, they "listen and respond to the needs of the church and the world." The community's monastic roots go back to St. Walburga's Abbey in Eichstatt, Bavaria, from where in 1852 Benedicta Riepp led Benedictine women to Pennsylvania and then in 1857 to Minnesota. Today, close to 200 of the community members live in St. Joseph. Many of the community elderly live in nearby St. Cloud in two centers that are extensions of the motherhouse. Others are in rural and urban areas—from St. Cloud to Recife, Brazil—where they live out their monastic call. Adjacent to the monastery is the College of Saint Benedict, which began in 1913 and in which the sisters continue to serve as faculty, staff, and administrators.

St. Benedict's Monastery has been the founding community for independent Benedictine houses in several other locations in Minnesota and other parts of the United States, including Kansas, North Dakota, Washington, Wisconsin, and Utah. Monastic houses founded outside the United States are located in Japan, Taiwan, Puerto Rico, and the Bahama Islands. These Benedictine women have been involved in education, health care, and parish ministry. Some Sisters now serve as writers, researchers, artists, liturgists, musicians, spiritual directors, consultants, and counselors.

As with other Benedictines, hospitality remains an important part of the community's life and service. Guests join them in daily worship (Liturgy of the Hours and/or Eucharist); as participants in workshops, courses, and retreats; as scholars-in-residence; and for spiritual direction. This site tells of the mission and work of this community. It offers a tour of its monastic spaces including its chapel. It gives information on retreats, publications, and how laity can get more involved in working with these women. It also lists and depicts the various art forms these women are involved in—some impressive and creative presentations.

Franciscans International

http://listserv.american.edu/catholic/franciscan/cord/grady.html

This site presents the work of Franciscans who, since 1990, have been present as a nongovernmental organization (NGO) at the United Nations. The Franciscans explain that they belong at the U.N. as an NGO "because they have a deep concern and reverence for creation" and because "they are involved in peacemaking, and care enormously about the poor."

Historically, the nongovernmental organizations and its members, both known as "NGOs," have enjoyed a special relationship with the United Nations. The drafters of the United Nations Charter foresaw the necessity of a nongovernmental balance against the preponderance of governmental delegations at the U.N. Article 71 of the Charter ensures the existence of NGOs under the aegis of the U.N. Economic and Social Council. Most of the nearly 1,700 NGOs are international in their membership and, because of this, bring to bear an important balance vis-á-vis the member states—the scope of NGO concerns cross national boundaries.

The spirit of Francis of Assisi permeates the Franciscan movement through the ages, so that today it is possible to view the characteristics of the saint operative within the membership and work of Franciscans International. The values embraced within its aims and structures and modeled by its governance and members testify that "being an NGO" can be an authentic form of Franciscan ministry.

Membership in Franciscans International includes persons from every continent and 137 countries (as of 1994). Current individual, active members number more than 17,000 with the potential of 1.2 million, the worldwide Franciscan population. The work of Franciscans International is evangelical, attempting to model for the United Nations a way of being a community that transcends national boundaries and sovereignties and, of greater importance, regards every human being of equal worth and the earth a common good.

This site explains the purpose of Franciscans International and how its work fits into the Franciscan mission. It links with U.N. and U.N. Development Program documents. It connects with other Franciscan sites and tells the visitor how to connect with Franciscans International.

Abbey of Gethsemani
http://www.monks.org/abbey-pg.htm

This is the site of probably the most famous Catholic monastery in the United States. It gained its notoriety from being the monastic home of one of the nation's most famous twentieth-century converts and monks, Thomas Merton. The following, taken from the site, is an example of the contemplative writings of Merton, author, peace activist, and ecumenist:

> The contemplative life must provide an area, a space of liberty, of silence, in which possibilities are allowed to surface and new choices—beyond routine choice—become manifest. It should create a new experience of time ... one's own time, but not dominated by one's own ego and its demands. Hence open to others—compassionate time; rooted in the sense of common illusion and in criticism of it.

—The Asian Journal

Merton, baptized in 1938, astonished his friends by entering the Trappists three years later. He lived at part of the Gethsemani Trappist community until his accidental death in 1968 while traveling in Thailand. But the site does not focus on Merton; instead it addresses what it is to be a Trappist monk today.

This site explains: "Trappists are a kind of Cistercian; Cistercians are a kind of Benedictine; Benedictines are a kind of monk." The site explains monastic origins: It was around A.D. 300, the visitor learns, that Christians began to seek solitude as a means of drawing closer to God. Some lived as hermits, others lived in communities where silence and a simple lifestyle helped them focus on God. Shortly after A.D. 500 in central Italy, St. Benedict wrote a rule for monks living in community.

The site offers schedules, practices, and accommodations at Gethsemani. It also offers directions on how to get there. There is a guest house, and the site can be used for contacting the monks to make reservations. The Gehsemani site finally offers the visitor the opportunity to connect with the Trappist mission, the abbot, and says what steps are required to become a monk.

Holy Cross Abbey
http://www.presstar.com/fruitcak/aboutabb.html

This site opens with an image of an inviting fruitcake. Making and marketing fruitcakes has been one of the traditional means by which monks have supported themselves over the years. The Web provides another marketing opportunity. The monastery gift shop and information center are easily accessible.

This site, similar to other monastery sites, offers information on the history and mission of these Trappist Cistercian monks, located by the Blue Ridge Mountains in the Shenandoah Valley of Virginia. The images of the monastery and its surroundings are worth the trip to this site. However, the site offers more; it integrates pictures of the monks with text that explains their work, prayer life, and communal living. The visitor sees, for example, the Holy Cross bakery and learns the role of work as prayer. The visitor is invited to enter into the texture of monastic life where monks rise long before dawn for the night Office of Vigils, followed by a period of silent prayer. The hours before the morning Office of Lauds and mass are given to Scripture and other spiritual readings, personal prayer, and meditation. The monks' prayer day is explained, hour by hour.

Holy Cross Abbey is one of 12 Cistercian monasteries for men and 5 monasteries for women in the United States. They trace their lineage back to the Abbey of Citeaux in France where the order began in 1098. In the United States, the three earliest monasteries were Gethsemani in Kentucky; New Melleray in Iowa; and Saint Joseph's Abbey, originally in Rhode Island and now in Spencer, Massachusetts.

The site offers information on how to contact the monastery, the time of retreats, prayer services, Cistercian publications, and, on the Monastery Fruitcake page, where and how to purchase the delicious delights.

Abbey of Our Lady of the Holy Trinity

http://www.travelassist.com/mag/a15.html

The Abbey of Our Lady of the Holy Trinity—also called the monastery East of Eden—sits in a quiet, rural setting about five miles southeast of Eden, Utah. It is home to 33 Catholic monks who belong to the Order of Cistercians of the Strict Observance. Peacefully coexisting with their Mormon neighbors, they live on a 1,850-acre farm in Huntsville, northeast of Salt Lake City. Here the monks find the seclusion and natural beauty conducive to their simple life of prayer and manual labor.

They support themselves by raising about 300 cattle and poultry and offering three types of honey (creamed, fruited, and liquid), as well as wheat, plain, and raisin bread. Visitors can buy honey and bread in the small shop or by contacting the monastery. A small and growing mail-order business makes the creamed, fruited, and plain honey available to those too far away to visit. About 750 acres of irrigated fields produce around 50,000 bales of alfalfa a year, as well as barley, wheat, and pasturage.

The monks have placed on their Web site the instructions for making their wheat bread. Of course, I called up the recipe and printed it; it looks tempting. I imagine more than a few visitors to the site have done the same. The story is told that when a visitor to the monastery asked for the monk's bread recipe he was told: "Start with 94 pounds of whole wheat flour, add 30 pounds of unbleached white flour. ..." Not to worry. The monks have reduced the whole wheat portion to eight cups.

The site states that from Monday through Saturday the monks sell their bread and honey in their small store. On Sunday the store is closed, but visitors are still welcome to join in any of the five public daily services at the monastery—just east of Eden.

Hill Monastic Library

http://www.csbsju.edu:80/hmml/

This site opens by reminding the visitor it only takes a minute to destroy history's greatest ideas. Throughout history, manuscripts have been threatened by fire, flood, theft, and civil disturbance, the site states. Shortly after World War II—a war that had been a catastrophe for manuscripts—Pope Pius XII asked Father Colman Barry of Saint John's Abbey in Collegeville, Minnesota, about the future fate of manuscripts. When Father Colman assumed the presidency of Saint John's University, he had already envisioned a plan in which Saint John's Abbey would microfilm the documents housed in Europe, store the microfilms at Collegeville, and make them available to researchers.

In 1965, this proposal was presented to the Louis W. and Maud Hill Family Foundation. The executive director of the Hill Family Foundation, A. A. Heckman, recognized the enormous possibilities inherent in this proposal to preserve on microfilm the classical and medieval handwritten cultural heritage of Western civilization—every text and book written before the invention of printing—and agreed to provide initial funds.

Since its founding in 1965, the Hill Monastic Manuscript Library has sent teams of researchers and technicians to film more than 25 million pages from nearly 90,000 volumes in libraries and archives throughout Europe, the Middle East, and north Africa. Today, it represents one of the largest and most comprehensive archives of medieval and Renaissance sources in the world.

This site explains the history and purpose of the library. It lists its hours, offers travel and accommodation information, tours, and registration. It also links to pages that include library resources, sights and sounds, events and programs, a library gift shop, and a guest book for visitors to sign.

Charlie the Carmelite

http://www.carmelnet.org/chas/

This site is the work of Carmelite Brother Charlie, who lives with the Mount Carmel High School Community in Chicago. He likes being a Carmelite and has put together a lively package of Carmelite links that offer the visitor an interesting cyberspace look at Carmelite spirituality and ministry. "My pages," says Brother Charlie, "are sort of a Carmelite family album containing images and documents of the men and women of the Carmelite Order—the work that they do, where they live, what they believe—all, of course, from my point of view."

Brother Charlie sees to it that Carmelite links are current on his pages. On this site, the visitor can find a host of interesting Carmelite connections, highlighting history, rule, and current work. These links include:

- A library for the Lay Carmelite Order.
- Selected writings of and about Blessed Titus Brandsma, Carmelite martyr.
- Los Santos Carmelitas, the lives of Carmelite Saints.
- An image gallery of Carmelite saints and sites.
- Links to Carmelite foundations, documents, and personal home pages.

Also included are links to:

- The Carmelites in the United Kingdom.
- Caravan Fan Page at Mount Carmel High School (Chicago, Illinois).
- Carmel High School (Mundelein, Illinois).
- Carmelite Resources—links to Carmelite home pages and email addresses of Carmelites.
- The (Discalced) Carmelite Home Page (Teresian Carmel in Austria).
- Numerous writings by John of the Cross and Teresa of Avila.

Once again, this site is an example that one person can do much to make a difference on the Web when he or she simply follows a passion.

Maryknoll

http://www.academic.marist.edu/maryknoll/

Maryknoll is a New York–based missionary society. Established in 1911 as the Catholic Foreign Mission Society of America by the Bishops of the United States, responsibility for its development fell to two diocesan priests, Fr. James Anthony Walsh of Boston and Fr. Thomas Frederick Price of North Carolina. They were commissioned to recruit and send U.S. missioners abroad.

Maryknoll's first missioners left for China in 1918. In ensuing years, Maryknoll Sisters expanded throughout Asia, but their work was interrupted by the Second World War. Many Sisters were detained for the duration while others were deported; two lost their lives. After the war, new works were accepted in Latin America, Africa, and the Marshall and Caroline Islands in the Pacific.

In 1932, a Maryknoll cloister was established as an integral part of the congregation. These Sisters devote themselves exclusively to prayer and penance for the missions. Later, Maryknoll Sister cloisters were set up in New Mexico, southern Sudan, Guatemala, and Thailand.

After the Second Vatican Council, Christian justice surfaced as a world issue, and Maryknoll Sisters, with other religious communities, made an option for the poor. Maryknoll Sisters Maura Clarke and Ita Ford were among four churchwomen killed in 1980 by the military in El Salvador because of their ministry to the poor and oppressed. Sisters also responded to the needs of refugees in El Salvador, Guatemala, Somalia, Sudan, Thailand, Mozambique, and Vietnamese in Hong Kong and earlier in Saigon. Today there are about 700 Maryknoll priests and Brothers serving in 27 countries around the world, principally in Africa, Asia, and Latin America. Maryknoll Sisters currently number nearly 750 members from 22 nations and serve in 31 countries worldwide.

This site explains the Maryknoll history, mission, and ministries; it provides contact information and facts about the Maryknoll Lay Missioners and Lay Affiliate programs, among the more successful lay-religious endeavors. Lay missioners make a three-and-a-half-year renewable commitment to working with the poor, oppressed, and marginalized overseas.

Retirement Fund for the Religious

http://www.missionnet.com/~mission/cathlc/retrelig/fund.html

As a matter of justice, this site deserves attention. Women and men religious have given so much of their lives to so many for so long that their many acts of generosity can be taken for granted. In recent years, decades of generosity caught up to the U.S. religious. As many face retirement, they run into some cold truths: Their ranks are not being replaced fast enough to produce adequate care-givers and, having worked for little or nothing, they have put nothing aside for retirement. In light of all this, special efforts have grown in the past decade to raise money for needy religious orders to help them provide dignity for their elderly. This site is best viewed as part of this effort. It lists four reasons for giving:

- More than 45,000 women and men Religious have reached the age of 70 and beyond.
- The majority of Religious still actively serve others. Those who are not physically able to serve do so through their prayers.
- Current sources of retirement funds—Social Security benefits, retirement savings, and grants from the Retirement Fund for Religious—do not cover skyrocketing health and living expenses for elderly Religious.
- Ninety-six percent of donations to the Retirement Fund goes directly to support women and men Religious. Less than 4 percent goes toward administrative and promotional costs.

This site, then, is a "thank you" for all that the religious have done and continue to do. It gives information on giving and supplies information regarding bequests. More than 600 congregations across the country receive grants from the Retirement Fund for the Religious.

Congregation of the Sacred Heart

http://www.sscc.org

The Congregation of the Sacred Hearts of Jesus and Mary is a worldwide religious community founded in France in 1800. Its members are sometimes called the Picpus Fathers because the first foundation was on Picpus Street in Paris. The Sacred Hearts Community aim is to witness and proclaim the Love of God as found in the hearts of Jesus and Mary. The congregation states that it accomplishes this by living as a "vowed family of brothers and sisters who support, strengthen, and serve each other in a reparative communion of prayer and ministry centered in Eucharistic celebration and adoration." This call directs the congregation, it states, to serve the mission of the church and the needs of all people with emphasis on the poor and unevangelized.

The search for the origins of the religious community brings one face-to-face with two historic persons, Peter Coudrin, the Good Father, and Henriette Aymer, the Good Mother. These two people were profoundly affected by the French Revolution and the cruelty that resulted from religious persecutions. They witnessed widespread hate and brutal injustice in their society. On Christmas Eve in 1800, in the shadow of the guillotine, they founded a community of men and women dedicated to spreading the good news of God's unconditional love as manifested through the Hearts of Jesus and Mary, to making reparation through adoration of the Blessed Sacrament and through the work of renewal. The members of this new community were soon engaged in a variety of apostolates: schools, especially for the poor; the direction of diocesan seminaries; and parish missions. In 1827, they were the first Catholic missionaries to go to the islands of the Pacific. The congregation carries on the work today with more than 3,000 priests, brothers, and sisters.

Francisan Custody of the Holy Land

http://www.christusrex.org/www1/ofm/TSmain.html

This site describes the history and current work of the St. Franciscan Friars who work to maintain a Christian presence in the Holy Land. One of the largely untold stories of the modern Christian era is the diminished presence of Christians in the Holy Land, where Muslims and Jews play increasing social and political roles. This site provides valuable information about the area, including information on key Christian locations, including:

- The Church of the Holy Sepulchre
- Christian Mount Sion
- The Nativity Church at Bethlehem
- Church and excavations at the Dominus Flevit
- The tomb of the Virgin Mary
- The Church and excavations at the Annunciation—Nazareth

The site highlights the Franciscan presence in the Middle East. The visitor learns, for example, that the Franciscan Order dates back to the thirteenth century, when it was founded by Francis of Assisi (Italy) and began to reach out to the Muslims. St Francis himself visited the region in order to preach the Gospel to the Muslims, seen by him as brothers and not as enemies. The mission resulted in a meeting with the Sultan of Egypt, who, records show, was surprised by the unusual behavior of the man. The Franciscan mission in the Middle East has been rocky, reflecting the history of the area itself. This is one of the more interesting religious sites on the Web. Much history here, and much for any contemplative Christian to think about.

CHAPTER 3

Organizations

Catholics gather within the church for a seemingly unlimited number of reasons. The most common is to find community within a Christian worshipping environment. The local Catholic parish is the primary building block of Catholic identity. However, Catholics also come together to promote ideas, causes, missions, or to simply more effectively serve one another or the needy among them. Some of these groups of Catholics, or Catholic organizations, are local; others are regional while still others are national in scope.

The list that follows is a sampling of Catholic organizations active in the church today and using the World Wide Web to further their missions. I've selected a cross section of these organizations, looking primarily to those that are interesting and are making novel uses of the new Internet technologies. Encountering Catholic organizations on the Web is to be reminded of the great diversity of identity and interest that exists in the Catholic church.

Caritas Christi

http://www.HealthReport.com/

The term *networking* can mean various things. Generally, it involves putting people together to fulfill a common task; this requires information. In the nonprofit sector, it helps to find low-cost ways to network quickly. To this end, the World Wide Web has been a major boost to many organizations. This Web site is an example. *Caritas Christi* is using the Web to network for better health care in the common-wealth of Massachusetts.

Caritas Christi is involved in a number of different projects including providing assistance to some 20,000 fishermen and their families who do not have access to affordable health care. *Caritas Christi* has also taken a firm public stance to preserve health care, coming out strongly against the entrance of publicly traded, investor-owned interests in the acute-care hospital market in Massachusetts.

The site, among other things, lists the various *Caritas Christi* health care providers in Massachusetts, offering information on how to contact them.

Friendship House

http://www.friendshiphouse.org

Friendship House is one of the many Catholic community-based organizations living out the Gospel message in the world today. Some of these organizations are finding their way to the Web to spread their message of hope. An interracial apostolate since 1938, originally founded in Toronto, and in Chicago since 1942, Friendship House shelters the homeless, the alcoholic, and the addicted. Its aim throughout its ministries is to work for interracial justice.

At the Chicago-based Friendship House, Catholic worship services are in English, Polish, and Spanish and precede meals on weekdays. Members of the organization are involved in job, shelter, and treatment referrals as well as helping the needy with clothing and food. Friendship House also gets into advocacy work on behalf of the homeless and addicted. The group feeds between 60 and 120 people each day.

This site provides addresses and telephone numbers for contacting Friendship House. Since most of the work is done by a volunteer staff and the work is supported by donations, it is necessary to spread the word about the group to ensure its survival. The Web becomes an effective means to achieve this necessary end.

Catholic Alumni Clubs International
http://www.clark.net/pub/cac/

This site is as simple as it is effective. It is for Catholics who want to meet Catholics. A Catholic Alumni Club is an organization of single Catholic professional men and women. Its purpose is to provide a friendly setting for single Catholics to meet and develop friendships with people who share their faith. Meanwhile, this site is run by Catholic Alumni Clubs International, an association of local Catholic Alumni Clubs. Its purpose is to host an annual national convention, encourage the development of local CACs, facilitate communication between local clubs, and represent the interests of single Catholics at a national level.

The site explains that CACI is divided into four regions: West, Midwest, East, and South Central. The different regions sponsor regional weekends during the year, where members of different local CAC clubs come together to meet friends from other areas of the United States. Each summer nearly 300 members gather for a national convention. Some of the previous conventions have been held in San Diego, Hawaii, Vancouver, Montreal, Williamsburg, Florida, and the Bahamas. During a convention, participants enjoy sightseeing, sporting events, dinner-dances, liturgies, seminars, and parties.

While CAC is not a matchmaking organization, the site notes, it does provide ample opportunities to socialize and date, and many marriages result from these interactions. CACs allow those who do not feel called to marriage to pursue their interests with other Catholic singles; there is no pressure to marry. When you join CAC you have the opportunity to participate in activities sponsored by the local and regional clubs and the national organization.

Membership in a local CAC is open to all men and women who meet the following requirements: single, Catholic, free to marry in the church, two- to four-year college degree or equivalent, or a registered nurse. This site is a means of contacting local clubs. Club names, addresses, and email are provided.

Catholic Charismatic Center
http://www.garg.com/ccc/articles/

Charismatic renewal in the Catholic church intensified following Vatican II in the mid-1960s. Groups in North America have flourished. The renewal movement claims to be inspired by the charisms (gifts) present in some of the early Christian communities and associated with the feast of Pentecost. These charisms include words of wisdom, words of knowledge, healing, prophecy, and speech in new languages. According to the *Encyclopedia of Catholicism* (HarperCollins), since the late 1960s the claim to, and emphasis on, charisms has become increasingly common among Catholics and is more generally accepted by the leadership of the Church.

Catholic Charismatic Center is the charismatic renewal focal point on the World Wide Web. This site lists all sorts of articles, meditations, testimonies, and prayers aimed at fostering the charismatic renewal. The site also contains charismatic news, a directory of charismatic organizations, a calendar of events, and a schedule for meetings. Additionally, the site connects with other Christian Web sites of interest to charismatics. Charismatics will find much to their liking on this page; it will help others better understand the charismatic renewal movement.

Catholic Civil Rights League of Canada

http://www.io.org/~ccrl/

This site is an example of how the Internet breaks down national borders. The work of this Catholic Canadian civil rights organization is not much different from that of similar U.S. Catholic groups that work on behalf of civil rights and religious freedom. While specific issues may differ, a common theological and philosophical foundation unites Canadian and non-Canadian Catholic groups—and they can support and learn from each other.

The stated mission of the Catholic Civil Rights League of Canada, a nonprofit organization, is "to inform public policy and public opinion with light from religious faith and reason." The organization promotes the search for truth in society through sound education, open communication, and respectful dialogue.

It affirms:

- The traditional family to be the only secure basis on which a society can be built.
- Parents to have primary responsibility for the education of their children.
- The protection of all human life from conception to natural death.

It opposes discrimination against Catholics in the workplace on the basis of their beliefs.

The league's goals are:

- To assist in creating conditions within which Catholic teachings can be better understood.
- To cooperate with other individuals, groups, and institutions in mutual efforts to further the understanding and protection of religious rights.
- To defend the legitimate civil rights of Catholics and others in Canadian society.

- To counter defamation against the Catholic Church and its members as well as other religious bodies and their members.

The site outlines the league's beliefs, functions, and goals; it lists the executive board, supplying contact information. The site is accessible in both English and French.

Cursillo Movement

http://www.sound.net/~eering/

The Cursillo Movement is a renewal program that began in Spain in 1949. It focuses on Christ as the center of spiritual life and human activity. The movement was borne out of an idea to teach Catholics the importance of Christ in one's life and has grown into an international movement. The Cursillo strives to motivate Christians to take interest in the existing activities of families, parishes, and communities.

This is the home page of the Kansas City/St. Joseph, Missouri, Cursillo Movement. But what is the Cursillo? A *Cursillo* is a three-day learning and sharing experience of living in a Christian community. The word *Cursillo* is Spanish, meaning "a short course." Cursillo is an abbreviation of the full title, *Cursillo de Christiandad*, which means "a short course in Christian living." During the three days of a Cursillo, a person not only hears talks on what it means to be a Christian today, but experiences the joy and energy of building and being part of a Christian community. It is aimed at refreshing the spirit and building community.

The "retreat" portion of the Cursillo lasts only from the opening night until breakfast the following morning, during which time silence is observed. Thereafter, there is much informal talk, some singing, joking, laughter, and prayer. The atmosphere of a Cursillo is joyous. During the three days, a number of talks dwelling on living one's daily life as a Christian are given by the laity and clergy.

This site lists Cursillo groups. A telephone number is also provided for further contact, or the visitor can fill out an on-line application.

St. Anthony of Padua Chapter
http://www.netaxs.com/~rmk/Cath/fall94.html

In October 1984, Pope John Paul II granted permission for the mass to be offered again in Latin with approval of the local bishop. The Latin mass had virtually disappeared in the church following the reforms of the Second Vatican Council, which closed in 1965. In a second letter, "Ecclesia Dei" (July 2, 1988), the pope expanded his earlier directives, calling for the rite's "wide and generous application." The Letter was issued on the personal initiative and authority of the pope himself. Most U.S. bishops, having worked to integrate the Council reforms into their dioceses for two decades, were lukewarm to the idea of reintroducing the Latin mass. They feared it would be used as an anticonciliar rallying point, causing further dissension in their dioceses. Some of these fears may have been exaggerated. Pertinent excerpts of *Ecclesia Dei* are as follows:

> To all Catholic faithful who feel attached to some previous liturgical and disciplinary forms of the Latin tradition, I wish to manifest my will to facilitate their ecclesiastical communion by means of the necessary measures to guarantee respect for their rightful aspirations. In this matter I ask support of the Bishops and of all those engaged in the pastoral ministry of the Church.
>
> By virtue of my Apostolic Authority I Decree ... respect must everywhere be shown for the feelings of those who are attached to the Latin liturgical tradition, by a wide and generous application of the directives already issued some time ago by the Apostolic See, for the use of the Roman Missal ... of 1962.

The letter thrilled some conservative Catholics; church moderates and progressives merely accepted it as one more directive from a pope long known for his strong conservative inclinations. In the wake of the two directives, local

Catholic groups grew up to ensure that the traditional Latin rites were implemented in dioceses across the nation. The Philadelphia-based St. Anthony of Padua Chapter of the International Ecclesia Dei Association is such a group. It began in 1993, it states, to promote the traditional Latin mass, and to put into action "the spiritual works of mercy." The group uses this Web site to network its members, providing information about meetings and about these papal directives.

Traditional Latin Mass

http://www.netaxs.com/~rmk/trid.html

This home page by Rick Kephart intends to support the use of the traditional Latin language as the language of Roman Catholic worship and prayer. This page, the love of one person, lists "Catholic items" (including Kephart's collection of prayers in Latin and many other languages, and a WAV file of a kindergarten class praying in Latin). On this site, there is also a page of links to other Catholic resources on the Internet, many of them conservative in nature. And there's information on this site about the Traditional Latin mass.

The Latin Mass Directory, also in this site, is a catalogue of all Latin masses licitly celebrated in the United States and Canada. The site invites additions, corrections, or deletions. Information is also provided about the Latin Liturgy Association, including information on how to join it. The Webmaster makes it clear that this site is in union with the pope and is in no way promoting rebellion or schism. "Many of the problems in the Church could be resolved by restoring the Tridentine Mass," the site states. "But there are right ways and wrong ways of dealing with the problems in the Church!"

National Association of Hispanic Priests of the USA

http://www.christusrex.org/www1/NAHP/NAHP-index.html

The National Association of Hispanic Priests of the USA is a Houston-based association of priests offering support to Hispanic priests. Established in 1990 as a nonprofit corporation, it has some 120 members in 42 dioceses. This is still only a fraction of the estimated 2,500 U.S. Hispanic priests. The association hopes this site will help reach some of these priests.

The site explains the purpose and activities of the association, stating that one of its primary functions is the organizations of an annual convention. It is during conventions that the priests get to know one another better and to share personal and professional bonds. Recent convention themes have been the Hispanic Priest and the Family, Hispanic Priest and Immigration and Hispanic Priests and Sects.

The association's stated goals are to:

- Promote similar groups.
- Offer regional retreats, workshops, and courses of continuing education.
- Conduct a professional study of Hispanic priests and seminarians.
- Offer support to Hispanic seminarians.
- Promote vocations to the priesthood among the Hispanic community.
- Work for more Hispanic U.S. bishops.
- Work for the promotion of social justice among Hispanic priests and the faithful.

The site states that the association wants to collaborate with U.S. bishops in facilitated Hispanic priestly ministries. It also wants to work with the laity and bishops in implementing the National Plan for Hispanic Ministry. The site offers names, addresses, and telephone numbers as well as email addresses for expanding contact and the mission of the association.

National Federation for Catholic Youth Ministry

http://www.parentsoup.com/cgi-bin/genobject/bpd0306

Of all the Catholic groups in need of support and attention, none seems to have greater needs than teenagers. Peer pressures, insecurities, the lure of a materialistic culture, all make teens vulnerable. Catholic youth groups need support. It is good to see their number growing on the Web.

The National Federation for Catholic Youth Ministry, Inc., is an organization that strives to meet the needs of youth, according to this web site, through a network that includes the National Conference of Bishops, the Catholic Committee for Girl Scouts, and local churches. The federation's stated purpose is:

- Maintaining a vision for Catholic youth ministry.
- Supporting diocesan youth leaders.
- Providing leadership and support to youth and adults.
- Offering a forum for youth to raise issues affecting their needs in relation to the church.

The NFCYM sponsors many programs, conferences, and retreats for teenagers. This site provides information so that teens and others can contact the federation. To this end, the site lists an address and telephone number. The site also has a bulletin board to foster communication, a chat area, and a page for feedback.

Life Teen

http://www.lifeteen.org/

God knows how difficult it is to be a teenager. And God knows how difficult it is to reach teens with the Christian messages that Christ matters and they are loved. Take these core messages and add a lively celebration of the Eucharist, put them into youth community, and you are beginning to outline the Life Teen youth program. It is just over a decade old, and its coordinators make the claim that it is "the fastest-growing, most dynamic youth ministry program around!"

As the organizers of the program explain on this site, Life Teen's ministry is about setting the environment so that teenagers can encounter Jesus. Phil Baniewicz, Life Teen National Director, states in a letter:

> You will see that the Mass is the central part of the Life Teen program. Therefore, our liturgies need to be alive and done with good quality, especially music. Jesus is present in the Eucharist (the Body and Blood), and leading teens to this experience is the most important thing we can do in youth ministry. … I know it is very difficult to explain what a Life Teen Mass is like, so I will just encourage you to go see one for yourself.

To this end, the site supplies a list, by state and parish, of all the nation's Life Teen programs. It also provides testimonials by teens and information on developing a parish-based program. This is done, in part, through program tools sold by Life Teen on the Web site.

The site, while complicated and at times difficult to follow, contains links to other teen ministries as well, including a World Youth Day and Catholic Youth Ministries page, which contains directories of teen programs and activities. These Catholic links enhance the visit.

Teen ministry efforts need to be encouraged. Let's hope Life Teen remains as successful as it claims to be in reaching this young and vibrant audience.

Interfaith Alliance

http://www.intr.net:80/tialliance/index.html

The Interfaith Alliance describes itself as a nonpartisan, interfaith organization committed to three main goals: (1) promoting the positive role of religion as a healing and constructive force in public life, (2) encouraging the renewal of values within families and communities, and (3) providing people of faith with an alternative voice to that of the radical religious right. The Interfaith Alliance believes that religion best contributes to public life when it works for reconciliation, inspires common effort, promotes concern for the less fortunate, and upholds the dignity of all human beings. It affirms both the plurality of religious voices and the strength that diversity brings to national life. It challenges any candidate or political organization that explicitly claims to speak for all people of faith.

This site grew out of a response to Ralph Reed's and Pat Robertson's radical right wing messages, including attacks on Catholic social teaching and on positions taken by the U.S. bishops over the years on behalf of freedom of speech, press, and religion. To numbers of people it appeared that in the name of Christianity the radical right had begun to preach intolerance. This intolerance appeared to many as a threat not only to the basic values embedded in the U.S. Constitution, but also to the human dignity of each individual, a dignity that stems from being a son or daughter of God and a member of the human family.

This site was created by the Interfaith Alliance and contains press releases, a quarterly newsletter, its position on various issues, membership information, and links to other sites with similar interests. One feature on this Web site is "What are the bishops saying?" which offers Catholic perspectives on timely social issues. While this site is not explicitly Catholic, many Catholics, supporting freedom of speech and freedom of religion, have become active in the Interfaith Alliance.

Apostolate of Roman Catholic Homeschoolers

http://www.rc.net:80/org/arch/

This is the site of the Apostolate of Roman Catholic Homeschoolers (ARCH), established in 1993 and located in Houston, encompassing southeastern Texas. It grew out of the realization that there were many homeschoolers in southeastern Texas and that they were facing similar needs. First was the need for a central organization to disseminate information and coordinate area-wide activities. It was for this reason ARCH and its satellite groups came into being. Some 100 families are now involved in the program.

What does ARCH do? First, it offers support for Catholic homeschool families in their religious, educational, and social endeavors by maintaining a central information source on activities. Second, it provides each member a newsletter with federal, state, and local information that keeps Catholic homeschoolers up to date on events of interest to them. Third, it coordinates area-wide activities such as curriculum fairs, conferences, spelling bees, choir, language, art classes, and an annual homeschool kickoff mass. Fourth, it offers discounts to members at local bookstores and merchants. Fifth, it researches and watchdogs state and federal legislative actions that have an impact on Catholic homeschooling families. And sixth, it maintains a curriculum library for members interested in various curriculums.

While some of the information on this site is particular to Texan families, much of it is of a wider interest. First, because homeschooling continues to grow across the United States and second, because this site is an example of how the Web can be used by groups of dispersed families who need to stay in touch with one another for social or religious support.

The site provides information on homeschooling as well as contact names and addresses for those seeking further information.

Knights of Columbus

http://www.nd.edu/~knights/supreme/history.html

This is the site of the Knights of Columbus, one of the most widely known Catholic organizations in America. Founded by Father Michael J. McGivney, the Knights of Columbus, a fraternal society, was incorporated in New Haven, Connecticut, in 1882. McGivney, concerned with the plight of widows and their families, emphasized the insurance feature of the society. Because Christopher Columbus symbolized the Catholic foundations of the New World, the Knights proudly proclaimed him their patron. Over the years, the ceremonial aspects of Knights' activities were aimed at winning back young Catholics who had become attracted to the Masonic organizations.

The Knights are known for their loyalty to the pope and each year contribute a large sum to the Peter's Pence, a papal charity. With more than 1.5 million members and more than $20 billion in insurance in force in 1992, the Knights contributes nearly $100 million annually to charitable projects and almost 200 million hours of volunteer work. In recent years, some knights have criticized their national leadership, charging them with receiving excessive salaries. The leadership has countered that their salaries are comparable to those of other executives in large insurance agencies.

This site gives the history of the Knights, the structure of its order, membership programs, initiations, and degrees. It gives information on insurance programs, school and vocational programs, student loans, and service programs. The site also links to other Catholic sites of interest to the Knights of Columbus, including antipornography campaigns, the St. Peter's Basilica restoration project, and the Vatican film library.

Worldwide Marriage Encounter

http://www.scri.fsu.edu/~sollohub/wwme/wwme.html

The purpose of this site is to spread the word about Marriage Encounter, a movement aimed at revitalizing a couple's marriage through increased communication and a deeper awareness of the faith life that binds couples together in love.

Marriage Encounter is designed to give married couples the opportunity to openly and honestly examine their lives together and to share their feelings, hopes, disappointments, joys, and frustrations.

The emphasis of Marriage Encounter is on communication between husband and wife, who spend a weekend together away from the distractions and the tensions of everyday life, to concentrate on each other. It's not a retreat or a marriage clinic. Nor is it group sensitivity. It's a unique approach aimed at revitalizing marriage. This is a time for a couple to be alone together for an entire weekend, to rediscover each other and focus on their relationship.

Marriage Encounter presents God as a focus for successful marriage. There are many faith expressions of Marriage Encounter weekends—Catholic, Jewish, and several Protestant denominations. While the weekend may be presented in a given faith expression, each is open to couples from other orientations.

During the weekend, a series of presentations are given by a team of married couples and a religious in the particular faith expression (priest, rabbi, minister). Each presentation allows the couple a rare opportunity to look at themselves as individuals, then to look at their marriage and relationship to one another, and finally to look at their relationship to God and the world.

The site gives information about a Marriage Encounter weekend, including how to sign up. Other Marriage Encounter links are also on this site. Many thousands of married people can attest to the success of a Marriage Encounter weekend, including this author.

National Association of Catholic Families

http://homepage.interaccess.com/~dfroula/nacf.html

This is a site for a Catholic family organization whose purpose is to support each other and to proclaim the official teaching of the church, especially the church's teaching that life must be protected from the moment of conception to the moment of death. The organization sees itself as responding to Pope John Paul II's call to support family life.

In the eyes of the association, it exists to "give one another mutual, moral, spiritual and social support in a culture which is now at war with our values." The site states that this is achieved by "linking committed Catholic families locally, nationally and internationally." It states that it is "answering the Holy Father Pope John Paul's call for families to be what they are."

The work of the NACF, the site states, is based on the Catechism of the Catholic Church, *Familiaris Consortio*, The Holy See's Charter of the Rights of the Family and *Evangelium Vitae*. The emphasis on these documents, which Pope John Paul II has seen as central in the war to protect families from a secular culture, reveals the association's generally conservative nature and bias. While most Catholics recognize the frequent conflict between Catholic values and those of the wider culture, conservative Catholics are more prone to see the church as being fundamentally at war with society.

The association uses the site to inform Catholics about the association, family-related news developments, and association programs, including Family Days and Family Weekends. During these gatherings, the Holy Father's Prayer for Families is said and a priest or a parent gives a talk on some aspect of Pope John Paul's teachings on the family. The site also has information on the association's quarterly publication.

The association began in the United Kingdom but has spread to other parts of the world, including the United States. Contact information is available on the Web site.

Serra International
http://www.rc.net/org/serra/

That the church in the United States faces a growing priest shortage has been acknowledged for at least two decades by virtually all familiar with its proceedings. While the numbers of Catholics rises, now at about 60 million, the numbers of priest has steadily fallen since the early 1970s. Even more alarming for Catholics, seminaries hold only a fraction of the candidates they held a generation back. The priest pinch is already being felt throughout the nation. The prognosis goes from bad to dismal.

The origins of the current crisis first began to show when thousands of priests in the late 1960s and early 1970s began to petition Rome to be dispensed from their vows so they could leave their priestly ministries. Most who left— some say close to 90 percent—eventually married. Some 20,000 priests have dropped out in the past 25 years. The most critical aspect of the priest shortage involves the seminaries; many have closed for lack of candidates, while others have consolidated. In the early 1960s, rectors could turn down candidates, taking the best among the applicants.

This site, by Serra International, is attempting to face the vocation crisis. Serra is named after the Franciscan missionary, Junipero Serra, founder of many of the California missions. It was founded in 1935 in Seattle Washington by a small group of Catholic lay men who saw the need to foster vocations to religious life, both by recruiting vocations and by supporting those religious in their active careers.

As of 1995, there were 607 active clubs with more than 23,00 members in 31 countries. Most clubs meet twice a month at either lunch or dinner meetings. Many clubs also have a mass before each meeting. The short meeting programs are used to plan activities to support vocations and to enrich the spiritual lives of the members through fellowship and by having qualified speaker guests on spiritual matters.

This Serra club home page offers contact names and addresses, and it connects with other Serra clubs in different parts of the nation.

Catholic Health Association of Wisconsin

http://www.execpc.com/~chaw/

The Catholic Health Association of Wisconsin (CHA-W) consists of 38 Catholic hospitals, 35 Catholic long-term care facilities, 14 Catholic systems, 22 religious congregations, and 5 Catholic dioceses that guide and/or sponsor these health care facilities in Wisconsin. Founded in Milwaukee in 1920, the stated purpose of the association is to "collectively influence the direction of health care in Wisconsin by facilitating the development of responsible leadership in the advancement of the collaborative use of the membership's resources, just social policy, and spiritual and ethical decision making."

This site explains the mission of the association and aims to help it in networking the various health care agencies. It sees itself as a force for better health care and especially for seeing to it that ethical practices and just policies are followed in the health care field. To this end, one area of concern for the association—reflected on this site—is the fostering of living wills. The site offers information on living wills, documents prepared by the able-minded to offer care guidelines in the event they cannot offer instructions at a later date.

In recent years, many ethical questions have arisen regarding health care. This site explores some and offers its own moral perspectives. Some of the ethical issues considered include nutrition and hydration issues, physician-assisted suicide, physician obligations concerning life-sustaining treatment, and changing health care delivery physicians.

Volunteer Opportunities Directory

http://helios.njit.edu:1962/RCC/Help_Wanted/CNVS/res_out.html

I have a fondness of voluntary agencies; I have worked in several. Not only do they make a difference in improving the quality of life for many needy, they also teach rich life lessons. Virtually any volunteer who ends an assignment comes back to say he or she got more out of it than he or she put into it. Voluntary agencies are great teaching and missionary agencies as well.

The Franciscan Mission Service is on this rich list. It provides Catholic lay women and men with opportunities to serve in Franciscan missions overseas. The lay persons sent under the auspices of Franciscan Mission Service give witness to the Gospel by living the Word, breaking the Bread, and living in solidarity with the local mission community. Upon their return, the lay missionaries are called to continue that mission as witnesses of their Third World experience to North Americans.

This directory lists many Catholic voluntary agencies at work throughout the world. The various volunteer groups explain their work, living arrangements, and stipends. This site plays a useful role on the Web. My hope is that the number of voluntary agency names on this list continues to grow and that many young people find this site and become inspired to respond to its call.

UNDA USA

http://www.catholic.org/orgs/unda/

This is the site for the National Catholic Association for Communicators. It tries to bring together men and women who work to communicate gospel values through today's media. UNDA USA is a national network of broadcasters, directors, public relations personnel, independent producers and syndicators, and other media professionals. This national network provides an opportunity to share the hows and whys of communication with other professionals striving to spread the Good News.

Actually, UNDA USA is part of UNDA-International: The International Catholic Association for Radio and Television. UNDA-International was founded in 1928 by a group of European broadcasters looking to associate, assist, and encourage one another in what was at that time a brand new apostolate. Twenty years later, a similar affiliation was being formed in the United States. The Catholic Broadcasters Association (CBA) began as a way of uniting American Catholic communicators in one strong national organization that shared ideas, resources, expertise, and a common vision. It was out of these roots that UNDA USA was formed in 1972.

As an organization, UNDA USA attempts to provide the opportunity to be professionally invigorated by other communicators. Having the same dreams and aspirations, members learn from each other. Benefits come from the interaction and challenge of others in the field of church communications. UNDA offers workshops, conferences, and seminars as well as sharing information on media research and new technology, technical training, and education.

A national organization specifically for Catholic communication professionals, UNDA USA has members in almost every state. Through its regional chapter meetings, UNDA USA members gather and work with other professionals on local communications issues and concerns and exchange ideas with the UNDA USA organization itself.

The annual General Assembly provides an opportunity for professional development, spiritual renewal, and social contacts. At the General Assembly/Convention, UNDA USA members come together with industry professionals and church leaders to discuss the impact and influence of the media on church and social concerns.

Besides giving more information on UNDA USA and its goals, the site offers names, addresses, and telephone numbers for further contact.

Catholic Engaged Encounter

http://www.catholic.org/engaged-encounter/

Catholic Engaged Encounter (known as CEE) is an international organization that was founded in 1975 to offer marriage preparation to U.S. Catholics. It is an independent, voluntary organization funded by donations. CEE currently claims that several thousand members now work in most U.S. dioceses and overseas. Couples who work in the program come from every walk of life, from the highly trained professional to the unskilled, but they all have one thing in common: "they believe in their marriages and commitment they made on their wedding day."

The Engaged Encounter staff introduces couples preparing for marriage to a communication technique they can use to foster deeper knowledge of each other. "Each couple," the site states, "comes to realize that marriage is a sacrament and a vocation, and that God and prayer are essential to a fruitful marriage." The Engaged Encounter program involves an intensive weekend during which each couple is offered the time and opportunity to question, examine, and deepen their relationship with each other and with God. Couples are challenged to explore their relationships.

The Engaged Encounter team usually consists of two married couples and a religious who give a series of carefully prepared presentations. Teams counsel those in the program to see marriage as a sacrament that should not be entered into unadvisedly or lightly. After each presentation, couples answer questions individually in writing. Their answers are then read by future spouses, and private time is allowed for the couple to discuss their answers.

This site explains what an Engaged Encounter weekend is like and highlights the needs and fruits of open communication within marriage. Topics covered during a weekend include self-awareness, human sexuality, communications, decision making, natural family planning, vocations, and sacraments. The site offers Encounter information and can be viewed as part of a larger movement within the Catholic church and other religions to pay greater attention to marriage preparation.

CHAPTER 4

People

The Catholic Church teaches that all share one spirit through baptism, becoming one in the Body in Christ. This includes the living, the souls in purgatory, and the saints in heaven. Catholics call this the communion of saints. Sensing these connections, Catholics often pray to saints to intercede in heaven. Saints, then, are not only holy people who have lived exemplary lives; they are like friends—soulmates—who help out on one's spiritual journey. Saints play large roles in the Catholic psyche.

This chapter celebrates "people connections" that Catholics hold dearly. It looks at Web sites of declared and undeclared saints, of famous people and not-so-famous people, all part of that communion of saints. A delightful finding I had browsing Catholic Web sites was to see how many Catholics continue to look to holy people to inspire their lives. Not all the people in this chapter are or will be declared holy by the church, but they are people who have and continue to shape it during its journey through time.

Catholic People on the Net
http://www.cs.cmu.edu/Web/People/spok/catholic/people.html

This site is an all-purpose "people" page. It connects to Catholics and Catholic saints in numerous ways: writings of saints, writings about saints, indexes of saints, lists of special saints—all can be found on this site. One learns, for example, that certain religious orders have a special fondness for certain saints, including their order's founder but also other order members who lived holy lives. This site, for example, offers a Franciscan calendar of Saints. It also offers an Irish calendar of saints. Want more information on Mary, the Mother of God? This site links to a number of Mary sites, including a page on Our Lady of Fatima and another on Medjugorje, the town where some say Mary continues to appear. This site also offers special resources for clergy and religious; it has lists of popes, bishops, priests, and deacons. There is a link to a page that tells Catholics how to place pages on the Web. Catholics of all stripes appear on this site. It is one of the more fun-filled sites on the Catholic Net.

St. Augustine
http://ccat.sas.upenn.edu/jod/augustine.html

This site opens with an image of the oldest surviving portrait of Augustine, from the Lateran in Rome in the sixth century. It sets the scene for a rich look into history.

Christians generally view St. Augustine, bishop of Hippo in Roman Africa from 396 to 430, as the greatest thinker of Christian antiquity. He is credited with fusing the religion of the New Testament with the Platonic tradition of Greek philosophy. At the age of about 45, he wrote the *Confessions,* the story of his own sensuous youth that ended in his conversion to Catholicism a dozen years earlier.

Augustine, born in 354, showed promise from an early age of being a bright student. By 19, he traveled to study at Carthage, where he was influenced by Manicheans who viewed existence in starkly dualistic terms, that is, as a conflict between light and dark substances with the human soul caught up in the struggle. The Manicheans claimed to be the true Christians. Some practiced deep asceticism, preaching that the redeemed Christ enabled imprisoned particles of light to escape from darkness. The philosophy influenced but did not satisfy Augustine's spiritual quest.

At about age 28, he moved to Milan, Italy, where he began to hear the bishop of Milan, Ambrose, the most eminent Catholic churchman of his day, preach his sermons. This was Augustine's first intellectual exposure to Catholicism. In the seventh book of the *Confessions*, Augustine explains how he finally found God—the "changeless light," at once imminent and transcendent. The discovery was more than the conclusion of a reasoning process, he wrote. It was a mystical experience. While Catholics view Augustine as one of the greatest of all church teachers, he has come under increased criticism in recent times for his excessive sexual pessimism. Augustine eventually came to see human nature as corrupted and totally dependent on the grace of Christ.

For starters, this site contains both the Latin text and English translations of Augustine's *Confessions*. It contains many other significant Augustine works, including a short text from his commentary on the Sermon on the Mount. The Rule of St. Augustine can also be found here. There is much research information on this site including Augustine the African, a short biographical sketch. The influence Augustine has had on Christianity has been enormous. This site both introduces the man and sets the stage for further scholarly research.

St. Thomas Aquinas

http://www.epas.utoronto.ca:8080/~loughlin/index.html

This is the home page of Stephen Loughlin, a graduate student at the University of Toronto. His field of study is medieval philosophy, with a particular interest in matters involving psychology. His thesis, he states, concerns "the doctrine of passion in the writings of Thomas Aquinas, particularly in determining the psychological mechanisms involved in the evocation of an emotion."

This site looks at the thinking of Aquinas. It contains lots of information and links to other sites with Aquinas material. This thirteenth-century Dominican is best known for the *Summa Theologica*, considered the greatest achievement of Scholastic theology. Aquinas bridged Aristotle's thought with Augustine's, attempting to show how reason and revelation enhanced each other. He departed from the Augustinian tendency to be suspect of all pleasure, viewing it as natural insofar as it was governed by reason.

Roman Catholic thought was for centuries very heavily influenced by Thomism and Scholasticism. By the early nineteenth century, many Catholic scholars were abandoning this approach to moral reasoning, but Pope Leo XIII in 1879 installed Thomism as the Catholic philosophy and theology. Scholastic thought sees human reason as the key to unraveling the mystery of the divine. Closely associated with this approach to theological pursuit has been the natural law theory. The Catholic tradition has insisted that its moral teaching is based primarily on natural law and not primarily on faith or scripture. This emphasis on the rational recognizes that such teaching can and should be shared by all human beings of all faiths and no faith, for natural law is the law that governs all of nature, human beings, and the animal world.

This site outlines Aquinas's life; it offers a general bibliography and connects to other sites for medievalists.

St. Francis of Assisi

http://www.powerup.com.au/~pwinter/francis.htm

Even a quick glance at the Web reveals page after page of St. Francis of Assisi biographies. I scanned a few, looking

for one that captured the spirit of the remarkable man—
probably the most popular saint in the Roman Catholic
Church. None quite satisfied me; they tend to come across
as too saccharine. I offer this one and let you be the judge.

> Franciscan was a reformer. He felt the truths of Christianity
> could be found in simplicity of lifestyle and service to the poor.
> He felt the need to be close to nature, seeing it as the art work
> of God. His influence has been lasting. Ecologists have been
> the latest group to find his spirituality empowering, a relief
> from the wider (and harmful) Western attitude of "conquer-
> ing" nature. Francis, on the other hand, taught that one must
> find one's place within the web of life. There are more than a
> few who believe today that the world's many environmental
> problems will not find solutions until the human family adopts
> a different attitude toward nature, beginning with simpler
> lifestyles spawned by an awareness for the sacredness of all of
> life. In this sense, St. Francis of Assisi becomes all the more rel-
> evant to the world today. He was proclaimed the patron saint
> of ecology in 1980.

This site offers the life story of St. Francis, about the
Franciscan life and about the Capuchins, a brand of
Franciscans.

St. Anthony
http://listserv.american.edu/catholic/franciscan/anthony
/anthony.html

I must admit to a special fondness for St. Anthony, considered a miracle worker and patron of lost objects.
Traditional Catholic devotion holds that prayers to St.
Anthony help the petitioner find lost objects. Having regularly misplaced important personal belongings, at age 12,
when I was to choose a confirmation sacrament name, I
took the name Anthony.

The site contains a brief sketch of St. Anthony and
Anthony devotions, meditations, and prayers. St. Anthony
was born in Lisbon, Portugal, near the end of the twelfth
century. He joined the Canons Regular of Saint

Augustine, but, shortly after ordination to the priesthood, he transferred to the Friars Minor to devote himself to spreading the faith among African peoples. He had his greatest success, however, preaching in France and Italy and converting heretics. His sermons are notable for their learning and gentleness.

The story and tradition of devotion to St. Anthony of Padua began almost with the moment of his death on June 13, 1231, this site tells the visitor. Since then, popular piety and devotion to him has taken many forms. After Vatican II, confusion arose regarding devotion to St. Anthony. "The emphasis on St. Anthony as a miracle worker and finder of lost articles overshadowed the true nature of devotion to the saint," the site states. "To a great extent prayers in his honor lacked a solid scriptural and liturgical foundation." This left the church with a dilemma: how to recapture the true meaning and value of St Anthony without damaging the devotion and piety of the people who find great consolation in him as they live their lives in our troubled times. The devotions on this site attest to St. Anthony's continued popularity.

This site was composed and compiled by Franciscan Frances M. Cardillo, Department of Biology at Manhattan College, Riverdale, New York, on the occasion of the eight-hundredth anniversary of the birth of St. Anthony of Padua. Nice way to celebrate a birthday!

Hildegard von Bingen

http://tweedledee.ucsb.edu/~kris/music/Hildegard.html

This site celebrates one of the most remarkable women in Catholic history, Hildegard of Bingen (1098–1179). At a time when few women wrote, Hildegard produced major works of theology and visionary writings. When few women were accorded respect, she was consulted by and advised bishops, popes, and kings, the site tells the visitor. She used the curative powers of natural objects for healing and wrote treatises about natural history and medicinal uses of plants, animals, trees, and stones. She founded a convent, where her musical plays were performed. Although not yet canonized, Hildegard has been beatified, and she is frequently referred to as St. Hildegard.

Revival of interest in this extraordinary woman of the middle ages was initiated by musicologists and historians of science and religion. It continues as Catholic women increasingly look back into a church history recorded by men to rediscover feminine identity. "Her scientific views," the site states, "were derived from the ancient Greek cosmology of the four elements—fire, air, water, and earth— with their complementary qualities of heat, dryness, moisture, and cold, and the corresponding four humors in the body—choler (yellow bile), blood, phlegm, and melancholy (black bile)." Human constitution was based on the preponderance of one or two of the humors. Hildegard's writings are also unique for their generally positive view of sexual relations and her description of pleasure from a woman's point of view. They might also contain the first description of a female orgasm.

This site has a thorough bibliography, where visitors who may be encountering Hildegard for the first time can look to learn more about this twelfth-century mystic.

St. Joan of Arc
http://www.netsrq.com/~dbois/joanarc.html

Joan of Arc (1412–1431) has her own Web page because she has been deemed one of the 100 "Most Influential Women of All Time" by the Carol Publishing Group. This Web site is, then, a subsite of another—but it draws attention were attention is due.

The site shares with the visitor a biographical sketch of this remarkable woman's life. It states that Joan of Arc, also called the Maid of Orleans, is patron saint of France. A national heroine, she led the resistance to the English invasion of France during the Hundred Years' War.

When Joan was about 12 years old, the site tells the visitor, she began to hear "voices" of St. Michael, St. Catherine, and St. Margaret, believing them to have been sent by God. These voices told her that it was her divine mission to free her country from the English and help the dauphin gain the French throne. They told her to cut her hair, dress in a man's uniform, and pick up the arms. That's what she did.

By 1429, the English, with the help of their Burgundian allies, occupied Paris and all of France north of the Loire. Resistance was minimal due to lack of leadership and a sense of hopelessness. Henry V of England was claiming the French throne.

Joan convinced the captain of the dauphin's forces and then the dauphin himself of her calling. After passing an examination by a board of theologians, she was given troops to command and the rank of captain. At the battle of Orleans Joan led the troops to a miraculous victory over the English. Later, Joan persuaded the dauphin that he should be crowned Charles VII.

In 1430, she was captured by the Burgundians while defending Compiegne near Paris and was sold to the English. The English, in turn, handed her over to the ecclesiastical court at Rouen to be tried for witchcraft, heresy, and wearing male clothing, which was considered an offense against the church. Joan was convicted and on May 30, 1431, she was burned at the stake in the Rouen marketplace.

In 1456, a second trial was held and she was pronounced innocent of the charges against her. She was beatified in 1909 and canonized in 1920.

Bernadette of Lourdes

http://www.catholic.org/mary/berndtte.html

Some venerated Catholics have their own home pages; Bernadette of Lourdes is an example. The Church considers

Lourdes a holy shrine. Tens of thousands make pilgrimages to this site each year, many seeking physical miracles or simply answers to personal prayers. The story of Lourdes is also the story of Bernardette; it is told on this site.

Bernadette was the oldest of six children. Born January 7, 1844, she was baptized the next day in a parish church and given the name Marie Bernarde. Because of her small stature, she was always referred to by the diminutive form of the name, Bernadette. She was a weak child, suffering even then from the asthma that would cause her so much suffering that later, in the convent, she would beg the nuns to tear open her chest so she could breathe.

Later in life, she became a Sister of Charity of Nevers. Bernadette (in religion, Sister Marie-Bernarde) spent the latter part of her life at the convent. She sought God in the silence of the cloister. She lived in the convent for 13 years, spending a large portion of this time ill in the infirmary—when a fellow sister accused her of being a "lazybones," she was to have said that her job was "to be ill."

Eighteen times in the year 1858, the Blessed Virgin Mary is believed to have appeared in apparitions to Bernardette. Although by the end of that year the apparitions of Our Lady at Lourdes were over for Bernadette, their message and mission were never to be forgotten. Bernadette silently offered all her sufferings, internal and external, for the benefit of "poor sinners."

This site tells the Bernardette story, including the story of each apparition. It explains the message of Our Lady of Lourdes, placing this veneration in the context of Catholic history.

Sister Faustina Kowalska

http://www.cais.com/npacheco/mercy/faustina.html

Sister Faustina Kowalska, as the visitor to this site learns, was a Polish nun who is said to have received a series of private revelations from Jesus beginning in 1931. It is said that she received a vision of Jesus with rays streaming from his heart, in which Jesus told her to have the image painted and include the words "Jesus, I trust in You!" He also told her to begin writing a diary so that others—even the greatest of sinners—might know and trust in His Mercy.

In these visions, Jesus was to have told Sister Faustina about ways that individuals could respond to His Mercy, and was to have given special promises to those who observe the special devotion that He revealed to her. This became known as the Devotion to the Divine Mercy. The devotion began to spread, slowly at first, and then it gained in popularity throughout eastern Europe until Sister Faustina's death in 1939.

Following her death, Fr. Joseph Jarzebowski, a Polish Marian priest, appealed to Jesus's Divine Mercy to help him escape from the Nazis, vowing to help spread the Divine Mercy devotion if he escaped. Father Jarzebowski did escape, and he arrived in America in May 1941, where he began spreading the Devotion of Divine Mercy in Marian communities in Detroit and Washington, D.C. By 1953, an international center for the Divine Mercy Devotion was completed in Stockbridge, Massachusetts, and that center has distributed more than 25 million pieces of Divine Mercy material each year. In 1966, the beatification process was begun for Sister Faustina, culminating thus far in her beatification (the first step toward sainthood) in 1993. Sister Faustina's diary has become the handbook for the Devotion to the Divine Mercy.

This site details the story of Sister Faustina, the message of Divine Mercy, and the Response of Trust and Conversion. It is one of many Web sites that highlight one person's spiritual journey in an effort to spread the good news, encouraging others to do the same. This spirituality focuses on the unlimited mercy and forgiveness of Jesus. Receiving God's mercy, however, also means being merciful to others. This, too, is at the core of what Sister Faustina had to say in her personal diary.

Mary's Place

http://www.ate.uky.edu/~mlpetry/

This is an example of a site being used by a Catholic to help herself and others to overcome physical barriers, in this case barriers stemming from a physical disability. "We all have our own limitations to contend with," states Mary. "I have a physical disability." Mary goes on to say her disability is of the spine and that it limits her movements. While this may slow her down a bit, she makes up for it by moving about on the Web. She offers her mail and email addresses, inviting responses. She also lists interesting sites she has found on the Net. At the top of her lists are the Disability Hotline Numbers, Disabled Hotline Home Page, Respect the Disabled, and a poem, "I'm Fine."

Gandhi

http://www.maui.com/~lesslie/gandhi.html

The nonviolence taught through word and action by Mohandas K. Gandhi has had such an influence on so many Catholics that I felt this Web page belonged in this chapter.

This page contains an essay by Richard Attenborough on the life of Mohandas Gandhi. Very briefly, the visitor learns that Gandhi, born in 1869 to Hindu parents, entered an arranged marriage when he and his wife both were 13 years old. His family eventually sent him to London to study law, and later he traveled to southern Africa where he worked to improve the rights of the immigrant Indians. It was there where he developed his creed of passive resistance against injustice, *satyagraha*, meaning truth force.

Back in India, he led the long struggle for independence from Britain. When Muslim and Hindu compatriots committed acts of violence, whether against the British who ruled India or against each other, Gandhi fasted until the fighting ceased. Independence, when it came in 1947, was not a military victory, but a triumph of will. To Gandhi's despair, however, the country was partitioned into Hindu India and Muslim Pakistan. In January 1948, at the age of 79, he was killed by an assassin as he walked through a crowded garden in New Delhi.

This site is laced with inspiring quotations. Consider these:

> "Nonviolence is the greatest force at the disposal of mankind. It is mightier than the mightiest weapon of destruction devised by the ingenuity of man."
>
> —*Gandhi on nonviolence*

> "Gandhi was inevitable. If humanity is to progress, Gandhi is inescapable. He lived, thought and acted, inspired by the vision of humanity evolving toward a world of peace and harmony. We may ignore Gandhi at our own risk."
>
> —*Dr. Martin Luther King, Jr.*

> "Generations to come will scarce believe that such a one as this ever in flesh and blood walked upon this earth."
>
> —*Albert Einstein*

> "Gandhi murmured, "Hey, Rama (Oh, God)." A third shot rang out. ...

Dorothy Day
http://www.cais.com/agf/ddaybio.htm

Bibliography of Dorothy Day and Catholic Worker Movement
http://www.cais.com/agf/daybib.htm

The first of these sites is a first-rate essay by Jim Forest on Dorothy Day. It was prepared for *The Encyclopedia of American Catholic History*, published by the Liturgical

Press. Forest, once a managing editor of *The Catholic Worker* newspaper, is the author of *Love is the Measure: A Biography of Dorothy Day*, published by Orbis.

The second Web site serves as a bibliography of Day and the Catholic Worker Movement. It was compiled by Anne Fullerton, a graduate student at the School of Library and Information Science at Catholic University of America. She states its purpose is to acquaint scholars with the range of resources available on Day and the Catholic Worker movement. While not exhaustive and restricted to English-language materials, it appears to be the most comprehensive collection of materials on the subject. Day's works are housed at Marquette University in Milwaukee, Wisconsin.

Dorothy Day (1897–1980) was arguably one of the most influential Catholics of the twentieth century. After the birth of her only child, Tamara, she abandoned her Bohemian lifestyle in Greenwich Village and converted to Catholicism in 1927. She and her friend, Peter Maurin, cofounded the Catholic Worker movement in New York. Their purpose was to live simply and nonviolently and to serve the poor. Important to Day and Maurin were reflections on the social and political currents of their time. Day's belief centered on Christian personalism, a philosophical orientation that stresses the value and dignity of each person.

The list of books on this site is impressive. Also noted on the site are periodical entries and articles from newspapers. Many of the Catholic Worker communities in the United States publish their own newspapers or newsletters. The best-known and longest running one is *The Catholic Worker* (36 East First Street, New York, NY 10003).

Firewatch
http://140.190.128.190/merton/merton.html

Firewatch is dedicated to distributing information on the works of Thomas Merton and religious contemplation in general. This group is affiliated with the Merton Research Consortium, a loosely coupled association of groups, centers, institutes, and organizations with an interest in the contemplative life.

Thomas Merton is one of the nation's most influential twentieth-century converts and monks. He was baptized in 1938, to the astonishment of his friends. Three years later, he entered the Trappists to live at Gethsemani, a Trappist community near Louisville, Kentucky. During the next 20 years, he wrote prolifically on a vast range of topics. While his earlier books dealt with religious matters, his later writings ventured into controversial issues connected with social problems and the Christian response to these problems including race relations, violence, war, and economic injustice. He is widely regarded as a spiritual master and a man who embodied the quest for God and human solidarity in the modern world. He died an accidental death on December 10, 1968, while traveling in Thailand.

Besides featuring Merton, his works, and his monastic life, this site links with a host of other Catholic sites, beginning with the Abbey of Gethsemani. It also links with a number of other monastic sites and spiritual centers.

Merton Research Institute

http://webpages.marshall.edu/~stepp/vri/merton/merton.html

The stated purpose of the Thomas Merton Research Institute in Huntington, West Virginia, is to foster, encourage, advance, and communicate research on contemplative life. The site explains the institute's goals, fellows program, media requisitions, agreements, sponsorships, and funding.

The site also features the Merton Archive and answers questions about Merton-L, the email list sponsored by the institute. Merton-L, according to the site, is "a forum for substantive discourse on research and scholarly inquiry to create and develop knowledge about contemplative life within and across multiple traditions, disciplines, and professions." The site goes on to say that the descriptions of varieties of personal, mystical, and/or contemplative experiences and practices are a basic aspect of such discourse.

The name Merton-L was chosen in honor of Thomas Merton. "Though his life, thought, and writings are important to this forum," the site states, "the scope of Merton-L encompasses the totality of contemplative life."

The site also links with Research on Contemplative Life: An Electronic Quarterly, FireWatch (Merton server at Saint Mary's College of Minnesota), the International Thomas Merton Society, and the Internet Interfaith Consortium.

The Merton Research Institute is headed by Dr. Ermel Stepp, executive director. His mail, email, and telephone numbers are listed on the site.

Pope John XXIII's Writings

http://listserv.american.edu/catholic/church/papal
/john.xxiii/john.xxiii.html

Millions of Catholics remember Pope John XXIII with great fondness. He was, by instinct, conservative, but he saw the need to usher renewal into the church. Pope John XXIII called for the opening of the Second Vatican Council, but he did not live to see it through. One American bishop, seeing Pope John on the balcony overlooking St. Peter's Square shortly after he was elected pope, remarked that the short heavyset prelate looked more like a pizza maker than a pope. Because Pope John called for the council he will go down in history as one of the most influential—perhaps the most influential—Catholic of the twentieth century. His writings, which have been gathered on this site, convey his simplicity, gentleness, and deep spirituality. While written decades ago, they have a timelessness all their own.

Patron Saints

http://www.catholic.org/saints/patron.html

This site aims to explain the idea of patron saints. It also offers a thorough list of patron saints. First, the question is asked: What is a patron saint?

"Patron saints are chosen as special protectors or guardians over areas of life," the site states. These areas can include occupations, illnesses, churches, countries, causes—anything that is important. The earliest records show that people and churches were named after apostles and martyrs as early as the fourth century. Recently, popes have named patron saints, but patrons can also be chosen by other individuals or groups.

Today, patron saints are often chosen because an interest, talent, or event in their lives overlaps with a special area. For example, the site tells the visitor, Francis of Assisi loved nature and so he is patron of ecologists. Francis de Sales was a writer and so he is patron of journalists and writers. Clare of Assisi was named patron of television because one Christmas when she was too ill to leave her bed she saw and heard Christmas mass—even though it was taking place miles away. Angels can also be named as patron saints. A patron saint can help when one follows the example of that saint's life and when one asks for that saint's intercessory prayers to God.

Devotion to saints is an expression of the Catholic doctrine of the communion of saints, a belief that even death does not break the bonds that tie Christians together.

This site allows the visitor to find the patron saint of a particular area and provides an alphabetized list of patronages with the names of the saints attached. It also provides an email address for patron saints to be added to the list. Some examples:

Actors	Genesiu
Animals	Francis of Assisi
Archers	Sebastian
Bakers	Elizabeth of Hungary
Broadcasters	Gabriel the Archangel
Housewives	Anne
Young girls	Agnes

Catholic Online Saints Pages

http://www.catholic.org/saints/saints.html

Want to know more about saints? This site answers many of the questions a visitor might have. Saints are important to Catholics. However, the whole idea of saints and sainthood raises questions for many—Catholics and non-Catholics.

This site answers some important questions: How does the Church choose saints? When did the Church start honoring saints? Is keeping statues or pictures of saints idolatry? Do Catholics pray to saints? Is there a Feast day for every day of the year?

The visitor learns that *canonization*, the process the Church currently employs to name a saint, has only been used since the tenth century. For hundreds of years, starting with the first martyrs of the early Church, saints were chosen by public acclaim. By the year A.D. 100, Christians were already honoring other Christians who had died and asking for their intercession. In taking the long look, the Church discovered that there was little proof that many "saints," including some very popular ones, ever lived. Christopher, for example, was one of the names that was determined to have a basis mostly in legend.

This site also lists saints' feast days by month and provides an alphabetical listing of popular saints.

L.P.H. Book of Saints

http://www.netaxs.com/~rmk/saints.html

The L.P.H. Resource Center site has a different perspective on saints. The center started in 1992 when it was decided that it would be good to have a place where local homeschoolers who were Catholic could get together with other Catholic homeschoolers, have some fun, and learn subjects that were often difficult for parents to teach.

One of the activities during the center's first year was assembling a "Saints Book." Every morning, two or three children would get up in front of the group to tell a story about a saint. These were taped and later transcribed. This site, then, might be called "Saints Through Children's Eyes." Two examples follow:

St. Barbara

Her father believed in false gods but she believed in God. So her father made a tower and put her in there. And then her father took her to a judge and she had a choice: either to believe in the false gods or else be beaten, and so she got beaten. And then later her father took her up to a mountain and he found her praying to God to ask her father to believe in Him. Then her father killed her because he didn't want that. Her feast day is December 4.

—Lucy

St. Agnes

St. Agnes was only 12 years old when the soldiers seized her. In those days they killed all Christians. One day they saw St. Agnes being good so they went to kill her. She was led to the pagan goddess Miriva in Rome. But instead she raised her hands and made the Sign of the Cross. They put handcuffs on her and they slipped right off her wrists. And then the soldiers dragged her on the roads on the streets and people laughed at her. After that she was offered a rich young man's hand in marriage, but she refused. She said, "I belong to my Savior alone." And then one strike of his sword killed that little girl. Agnes means Lamb. She was gentle and pure. Her feast is January 21.

—Daniel

Chief Seattle's Letter

http://www.nidlink.com/~bobhard/seattle.html

Chief Seattle, Chief of the Suquamish Indians, wrote a letter to the American government in the 1800s that revealed a Native American spirituality in such devastating contrast to the stereotypes Western settlers had of "red skins" that it continues to move people throughout the globe. At the core is a belief, indeed a profound understanding, of God in all things. When I came across this letter, I realized immediately I wanted to place Chief Seattle in my people chapter.

Too long to recite in its awakening fullness here, I include these verses taken from the site:

The President in Washington sends word that he wishes to buy our land. But how can you buy or sell the sky? the land? The idea is strange to us. If we do not own the freshness of the air and the sparkle of the water, how can you buy them?

Every part of the earth is sacred to my people. Every shining pin needle, every sandy shore, every mist in the dark woods, every meadow, every humming insect. All are holy in the memory and experience of my people.

We know the sap which courses through the trees as we know the blood that courses through our veins. We are part of the earth and it is part of us. The perfumed flowers are our sisters. The bear, the deer, the great eagle, these are our brothers. The rocky crests, the dew in the meadow, the body heat of the pony, and man all belong to the same family. ...

This we know: the earth does not belong to man, man belongs to the earth. All things are connected like the blood that unites us all. Man did not weave the web of life, he is merely a strand in it. Whatever he does to the web, he does to himself.

One thing we know: our God is also your God. The earth is precious to him and to harm the earth is to heap contempt on its creator.

When the last red man has vanished with this wilderness, and his memory is only the shadow of a cloud moving across the prairie, will these shores and forests still be here? Will there be any of the spirit of my people left? ...

Mother Teresa

http://www.fn.net/~bbrown/sr/mother.html

Mother Teresa, aside from the pope, may be the best known Catholic in the world.

She was born Agnes Gonxha Bojaxhiu in 1910 in Skopje, Yugoslavia, to Albanian parents who settled in Skopje shortly after the beginning of the century. In 1928, she became a nun and traveled to Dublin, Ireland, to join the Sisters of Loreto, a religious order founded in the seventeenth century. After studying at the convent for less than a year, she left to join the Loreto convent in the city of Darjeeling in northeast India. On May 24, 1931, she took the name of "Teresa" in honor of St. Teresa of Avila, a sixteenth-century Spanish nun. In 1929, Mother Teresa was assigned to teach geography at St. Mary's High School for Girls in Calcutta, south of Darjeeling. At the time, the streets of Calcutta were crowded with beggars, lepers, and the homeless. On a train back to Darjeeling in 1946, Mother Teresa felt the need to abandon her position at St. Mary's to care for the needy in the slums of Calcutta. In 1948, Pope Pius XII granted Mother Teresa permission to live as an independent nun. That same year, she became an Indian citizen and founded a religious order of nuns in Calcutta, India, called the Missionaries of Charity.

Through this order, she has dedicated her life to helping the poor, the sick, and the dying around the world, particularly in India. In 1971, Pope Paul VI honored Mother Teresa by awarding her the first Pope John XXIII Peace Prize. The following year, the government of India presented her with the Jawaharlal Nehru Award for International Understanding. In 1979, she received her greatest award, the Nobel Peace Prize.

This site offers a talk Mother Teresa gave at a National Prayer Breakfast in Washington, D.C. in February 1994. It shares with the visitor a sense of this remarkable woman's outlook and spirituality.

Benedictine Sister Diana Seago

http://www.benedictine.edu/diana.html

I enjoy reading personal Catholic home pages. There is often enough on them to feel you are making a new acquaintance. The best manage to convey a sense of values and personality. In this category, I would place the home page of Benedictine Sister Diana Seago, who lives at Mount St. Scholastica in Atchison, Kansas. Opening her page, the visitor encounters the following exchange from "A Jewish Tale."

> A young woman once said to an old woman, "What is life's heaviest burden?"
> And the old woman said, "To have nothing to carry."

Sister Seago, it appears, does not mind carrying things. At the top of her list is the responsibility for raising money for Benedictine College at the Mount. She is director of planned giving there. She goes on to say that in her spare time she reads poetry; does crochet; plays the harmonica, guitar, hammered dulcimer, and mountain dulcimer—and writes a little poetry. She also likes to fish and recall with fondness her "best fishing experience" ever off the shore of Two Rivers, Wisconsin, on Lake Michigan, when she caught a 32-pound rainbow trout. "It was a beauty!"

Personal home pages appear to work best when the author does not take him- or herself too seriously. It is possible to share one's spirit on the Web. Seago does this simply by writing about her habits of work and play. I also found Seago's related links of considerable interest. If I feel I know someone or share something with a person, I begin to value his or her ideas, in this case, recommendations for other interesting Web sites.

Recommended Seago links include, under Heroines and Heroes, Hildegard of Bingen, Dorothy Day, Chief Seattle, Oscar Romero, and Sojourner Truth; under A Woman's Perspective, Early Music by Women Composers, A Celebration of Women Writers, Women's Web Links, Women's Wire, Women's Studies, and Centers and Black Women's Spirituality Page; under Other Links of Interest, *Pax Christi*, Sojourners Online, Bread For The World, Labyrinth Medieval Studies Home Page, Jacques Gaillot—Bishop of Partenia, Russian Icons, Celtic Christianity, and North American Time Zones.

Jesuit Home Pages

http://maple.lemoyne.edu/~bucko/sj_pers.html

More and more Jesuits around the world have put up on the Web their own home pages. This site doesn't do more than invite the visitor to browse through them and learn about the many varied works that the Society of Jesus does. I enjoy the Jesuits. They seemingly always have a strong sense of purpose and are good at what they do. Traditionally, this is a religious order of educators, and their educational inclinations show on this site. So, too, do a lot of other personal interests. This sites takes you to individual home pages that can take you in a seemingly countless number of different directions, a journey I enjoyed. This page is the work of Jesuit Father Raymond A. Bucko of the Department of Sociology and Anthropology at Le Moyne College, the Jesuit College of Central New York.

Rob's Lonely Catholic Youth Page

http://www.geocities.com/Heartland/3905/youth.html

This page is significant not so much for what it is but for what it augurs on the World Wide Web: Catholics reaching out to other Catholics looking to share their faith. This page was composed by a "young Catholic," who wonders aloud if others are out there who sometimes feel "no one else really cares." If so, he wants to let them know they are not alone. "Sometimes being a Christian (especially Catholic) in today's world," he states, "can be pretty rough—sometimes it seems like the whole world is against us."

Alas, he wants to fight discouragement and begins by offering the following quotation from Scripture. It reads:

> Trust in the Lord with all your heart,
> and do not rely on your own insight.
> In all your ways acknowledge Him,
> and He will make straight your paths.

—Proverbs 3: 5–6

He then writes that if someone needs to talk, he is available. Rob offers his email address, adding that he is neither a priest nor any sort of professional counselor; "I'm just a guy who knows what it's like to feel alone."

Finally, he offers some Catholic links—starting with directories—to spark some extra life. He adds some youth pages, "Funky Friar" pages, and some other Catholic pages. Within a year, thousands more Catholic Robs will be helping people make connections on the Web. It's coming.

Fr. Al Bitz's Homepage
http://www.majesticweb.com/albitz/pages/intro.html

In this people chapter, I am including some individual Catholic home pages composed by members of the faithful who in some way see their work as helping to spread the faith. Father Al Bitz's home page is one such example. First an introduction is in order.

Father Bitz tells us he is pastor of three rural Catholic parishes in central North Dakota: St. Boniface in Wimbledon; St. Mary in Courtenay; and St. John in Kensal. He has pastored in cities of North Dakota, including 10 years in Fargo. Since becoming pastor of these rural parishes in 1994, he has also worked in "support ministry" to the bishop in Siberia and has served on the national committee that sponsored the First International Conference to Assist the Catholic Church in Russia, Belarus, and Kazakhstan. That gathering took place in Colorado Springs and Denver, Colorado, in June 1995.

Father Bitz uses this home page to speak a bit about his work, to post parish liturgy schedules, weekly reflections, his mail and email addresses, and to link the interested to other Catholic sites. In rural North Dakota, where parishes are many miles apart, he is using the Web to enhance communication. Surely, this use of the Web in such a rural ministry is still in its infancy. As more people get hooked up, communications will only increase. Father Bitz may live quite inconspicuously in North Dakota, but the man is a pioneer.

Ingrid Shafer's Homepage

http://192.146.206.5/www/faculty/shaferi/index.html

This page has been developed by an interesting Catholic scholar at the University of Science and Arts of Oklahoma. Ingrid Shafer explains that teaching for her is more than a job, "it is a vocation, a calling, a consuming passion." It allows her, she states on the site, "to challenge and encourage men and women of all ages to discover the life of the mind, and in the process grow in knowledge, discernment, and humaneness."

This site tells Shafer's story and her approach to education. For some 30 years already, she states, she has been deeply concerned about the post-Enlightenment tendency among intellectuals in the West "to shatter and compartmentalize knowledge" with the result "of turning higher education into a loose confederation of separate departments designed to produce (much like factory assembly lines) graduates who knew a great deal about certain carefully circumscribed areas and practically nothing about anything that was not directly relevant to their major."

Teaching at USAO, she states, has allowed her to break from those habits. She now shares the USAO dream. "Whenever I teach one of the World Thought and Culture courses ... I realize that we are doing education for the future—that right here in Chickasha, Oklahoma, we are developing ways of healing the disease of intellectual fragmentation and tunnel vision through interdisciplinary dialogue." Then she adds: "But now I also follow my dream beyond the borders of Oklahoma, both physically and in cyberspace."

This is one of the reasons that Shafer cites for being on the Internet—the development of discussion forums, including a Web site for the Association for the Rights of Catholics in the Church (Chapter 11, Renewal Groups). She calls the association "an organization dedicated to encouraging openness to change, compassion, rationality, ecumenical dialogue, and respect for democratic values in the Catholic Church." Shafer claims today's moral challenge within the Church is "to overcome deeply entrenched habits of absolutism, dualism, and rigidity," and do so without sinking into the morass of lazy "everything goes" totally relativistic rejection of all standards.

With a lot going on in her life, Shafer has also made a major effort to study the works of Catholic novelist and sociologist Father Andrew Greeley. This site gives voice to one of the more interesting Catholics on the Web today.

PART II

Catholic Ideas

Part II of this book focuses on Web sites concerned with the ideas that have shaped and continue to shape the Church. Chapter 5 deals mainly with Church history, and points to a large number of source documents for those interested in the Catholicism's intellectual heritage. Chapter 6 contains more recent teaching sites, including those that are official—part of what is called the *magisterium*—as well as "unofficial" sites. Chapter 7 explores educational sites, Chapter 8 Catholic periodicals, books, and other publications with a Web presence, and Chapter 9 Web-specific Catholic resources.

CHAPTER 5

History

Catholicism is steeped in history—a 2,000-year history. It is virtually impossible to understand the Catholic faith without knowing Catholic history. This is in part because the Church believes in the development of Catholic doctrine and especially the key role that tradition plays in Catholic life. Thus, Catholicism grows out of more than the study of Scripture; the church teaches doctrine that grows also out of the deliberations of the magisterium, which includes bishops and theologians. These deliberations, in turn, grow out of the experiences and beliefs of the Catholic faithful. Catholic history, then, documents not only the lives of Catholics through 20 centuries, but the development of the faith itself.

The Historical Jesus

http://marie.az.com/~mrosen/

During the last decade, there has been a remarkable renaissance in Jesus scholarship. The Jesus debate has spilled over into the public arena and initiated a national conversation about the historical and religious significance of Jesus. What began as an academic exercise has fast become a media sensation. Scholarly books about Jesus are suddenly making the best-seller lists. Cover stories have appeared in *Time, Newsweek,* and *U.S. News & World Report.* And television specials have aired on both sides of the Atlantic. The age-old question "Who is Jesus?" has become the spiritual query of seekers everywhere.

This site probably provides the best study on the Internet of the historical Jesus. There are many answers to the question, "Who was Jesus?" For the past 200 years, scholars have conducted a search for Jesus's true words, deeds, and identity. Through this search, a variety of portraits of Jesus have emerged. Some see him as a countercultural cynic sage dedicated to radical egalitarianism, others as a charismatic prophet, sage, and healer who called his fellow Jews to a new ethos of compassion. Still others hold to the traditional view of Christianity and believe that Jesus was and is the Son of God who came to save humanity from its sin. This page sees itself as "dedicated to giving the visitor information and resources to decide who the real Jesus was."

The site links to the historical Jesus authors, articles about Jesus, Jesus at 2000, the Jesus Seminar, Jesus texts, and other miscellaneous documents concerning Jesus.

The Ecole Initiative

http://www.evansville.edu:80/~ecoleweb/internet.html

This site, the copyrighted work of Anthony F. Beavers, contains many useful links to Web sites dealing with early church history. The site states that the Web file may be copied only on the condition that its entire contents, including the header and copyright notice, remain intact. Rather than reprint the entire file here I would rather simply say that I found this file to be thorough and a good starting point for anyone interested in early church history. Some links are quite scholarly; others are interesting to those simply dabbling in the church history. A very nice addition to the Web. Thank you, Anthony F. Beavers.

Guide to Early Church Documents

http://www.iclnet.org/pub/resources/christian-history.html

This guide appears under the auspices of the Institute for Christian Leadership. It is the copyrighted work of John Brubaker and Gary Bogart, who do not want it reproduced and/or distributed unless it is kept fully intact. Since the file is far too large to reproduce here, I will not begin to list the many sites on this list. Suffice it to say that the presentation of the site list is clean and clear and presented neatly in chronological order. There are scores of sites on this list, many of them leading to even more sites and all dealing with canonical documents, creeds, the writings of the Apostolic Fathers, and other historical texts. This home page has won several Internet awards. I recommend it highly.

Two Thousand Years of Catholic Writings

http://www.cs.cmu.edu/Web/People/spok/catholic/writings.html

Just to read the words of this site's title is an inviting experience. Moreover, the page captures the flavor of the works of significant Catholic authors through 20 centuries. In doing so, it begins to tell a wider story about a church that has helped shape Western culture. Historians or simple history buffs will be especially attracted to this site. This listing shows authors in roughly chronological order. Starting with Scripture and on to the Didache (the teaching of the 12 apostles), to St. Clement of Rome (pope from 92 to 101), to the early church Fathers and through the centuries, this site also provides a service by matching authors with dates and showing how they have fit into church history.

Selections for the basic writings of St. Augustine of Hippo (354–430) are generously cited, as are the works of many other Catholic authors including St. John of the Cross (1542–1591), John Henry Cardinal Newman (1801–1890), and the twentieth-century popes. Edith Stein's (Blessed Teresa Benedicta, 1891–1942) "The Hidden Life: Hagiographic Essays, Meditations, Spiritual Texts" is on the list. There is also a link to the Catholic Encyclopedia (1913), where work continues to put the entire edition online.

Medieval Sourcebook

http://www.fordham.edu/halsall/sbook.html

Historians teaching medieval history almost always want to combine a textbook, a sourcebook, and additional readings. Textbooks, as an ever-evolving form, are probably worth the cost, but sourcebooks are often unnecessarily expensive. Unlike some modern history texts, the sources used for medieval history have been around a long time. Many were translated in the nineteenth century, and, as a rapid review of any commercial sourcebook will show, it is these nineteenth-century translations that make up the bulk of the texts. Many of these nineteenth-century texts are now available on the Internet. The goal of this site is to construct an Internet Medieval Sourcebook from available public-domain and copy-permitted texts.

The Internet Medieval Sourcebook is part of ORB, the Online Reference Book for Medieval Studies; Paul Halsall is the ORB sources editor. The Sourcebook is in two parts. The first is made up of fairly short extracts appropriate for use in a classroom, derived from public-domain sources or copy-permitted translations. The second is composed of the full documents or Web links to the full documents. It is specifically designed for teachers to use in teaching.

Summa Theologica

http://www.knight.org/advent/summa/summa.htm

The Summa was the crowning work of St. Thomas Aquinas. He and St. Augustine have shaped Catholicism as no other church fathers since the time of the Apostles. It is fitting that a Web site be dedicated to the *Summa Theologica*. This file is presented with permission of EWTN Online (formerly the Catholic Resources Network), from which the entire work may be downloaded.

Dominican Friar and Doctor of the Church, St. Thomas Aquinas lived ca. 1225–1274. His theology has acquired a quasi-official status through repeated formal endorsements by various popes. Aquinas believed that human beings could draw closer to God through human reason. The *Summa Theologica* was a systematic attempt to achieve a reasoned faith. The Summa breaks down into several parts: the first deals with God, humanity, and the relations between the two; the second deals with human acts, habits, and law; and the third deals with the work of the savior Jesus Christ in the world. St. Thomas Aquinas died before completing the *Summa Theologica*. The remainder of the Summa, known as the Supplement, was probably compiled by Fra Rainaldo da Piperno and was gathered from St. Thomas's commentary on the Fourth Book of the Sentences of Peter Lombard.

Documents of the Council of Trent

http://listserv.american.edu/catholic/church/trent/trent.html

Trent was the nineteenth and one of the most significant of the Roman Catholic Church councils. Beginning in 1545 as a reaction to the Protestant Reformation, Trent lasted 18 years and solidified Catholic teachings for four centuries. Trent marked a major turning point in efforts of the church to respond to the Reformation; it shaped the counter-Reformation.

The council met during three separate periods (1545–1547, 1551–1552, and 1562–1563) under the leadership of three different popes (Paul III, Julius III, and Pius IV). All of its decrees were formally confirmed by Pope Pius IV in 1564. In the area of religious doctrine, the council refused any concessions to the Protestants and solidified Catholic dogma. It directly opposed Protestantism by reaffirming the existence of seven sacraments, transubstantiation, purgatory, the necessity of the priesthood, and justification by works as well as by faith. Clerical celibacy and monasticism were maintained and decrees were issued in favor of the efficacy of relics, indulgences, and veneration of the Virgin Mary and the saints. Tradition was declared equal to Scripture as a source of spiritual knowledge, and the sole right of the church to interpret the Bible was asserted. This site publishes Trent documents by session.

Second Vatican Ecumenical Council

http://webzone1.co.uk/www/jcrawley/v1.htm#Church

This site offers a brief history of the Second Vatican Council, the most important Catholic event in modern history. Opened under Pope John XXIII in 1962 and closed by Pope Paul VI in 1965, Vatican II, as it has come to be called, ushered in a spirit of renewal in the Catholic Church. It did nothing less than change how tens of millions of Catholics view themselves and their church.

This site considers the council, its context, and its documents. The First Vatican Council was adjourned in 1870, following the solemn definition of papal infallibility. Only a part of its task had been accomplished, but it was destined never to meet again. Pope Pius IX died in 1878, and five popes came and went before the Second Vatican Council was proclaimed by Pope John XXIII.

Pope John announced his intention of summoning the Ecumenical Council in January 1959, within three months of his election as pope. Meanwhile, 10 commissions had been formed to prepare draft decrees to be debated in the Council. At first, 70 decrees were proposed, but gradually their number was reduced to 17. When asked to reveal his intentions for the Council, Pope John reportedly said he simply wanted to let fresh air in the Church.

The Second Vatican Council opened October 11, 1962. More than 2,500 bishops were present at the opening mass—the greatest gathering at any Council in the history of the Church. Pope John did not live to see the Council through. Cardinal Montini, the archbishop of Milan, succeeded him as pope and saw the Council through to its end in 1965. For those Catholics who lived through the Council years, this site will bring back warm memories; for those too young to remember, it will provide insights into their Church's history. A very nice site to find on the Web.

Pope John's Opening Speech to the Council

http://www.christusrex.org/www1/CDHN/v2.html

On October 11, 1962, the first day of the Second Vatican Council, Pope John XXIII delivered an address in St. Peter's Basilica. It is one of the most important addresses in modern Church history. Like many Catholic documents that can be found on the Web, this address has its own Web page. Because of the importance of the Council and Pope John's important place in church history, I have included this speech on this historical list. In his address, Pope John spoke of the roles of other church councils and the origin of this Council. In his speech to the assembled bishops at St. Peter's Basilica, his boundless optimism and hope shined through.

Documents of Church Councils

http://catholic.net/RCC/Indices/subs/councils.html

This site is self-explanatory. Throughout Catholic Church history, there have been 21 ecumenical councils. Most have had some lasting impact on the Church. The two most widely discussed councils have been the Council of Trent (1545–1563) and the Second Vatican Council (1962–1965). The documents of these councils and others can be accessed through this site. The list of Vatican II documents introduced to the visitor include the following:

- *Sacrosanctum Concilium* (Constitution on the Sacred Liturgy)
- *Inter Mirifica* (The Means of Social Communication)
- *Lumen Gentium* (Dogmatic Constitution on the Church)
- *Orientalium Ecclesiarum* (Eastern Rite Catholic Churches)
- *Unitatis Redintegratio* (Decree on Ecumenism)
- *Christus Dominus* (The Pastoral Office of Bishops)
- *Perfectae Caritatis* (Renewal of Religious Life)
- *Optatam Totius* (Decree on Priestly Training)
- *Gravissimum Educationis* (Decree on Christian Education)
- *Nostra Aetate* (The Church and Non-Christian Religions)
- *Dei Verbum* (Dogmatic Constitution on Divine Revelation)
- *Apostolicam Actuositatem* (The Apostolate of Lay People)
- *Dignitatis Humanae* (Declaration on Religious Freedom)

- *Ad Gentes* (The Church's Missionary Activity)
- *Presbyterorum Ordinis* (Ministry and Life of Priests)
- *Gaudium et Spes* (The Church in the Modern World)

United States Catholic Historical Society
http://www.catholic.org/uschs/

In 1884, John Gilmary Shea founded The United States Catholic Historical Society for "the appreciation and preservation of American Catholic Heritage." For more than a century, the Society pursued its mission by publishing scholarly texts, conducting seminars and lecture series, and funding research projects. Today, the New York–based Society continues to fulfill its mission with the publication of *The U.S. Catholic Historian*, a historical journal of the church in America, which can be found in university libraries throughout the world. In addition to the journal, the Society publishes scholarly works on the history of American Catholicism. The last such work was an analysis of Italian immigrants and their relationship with Archbishop Corrigan, a nineteenth-century ordinary of the Archdiocese of New York. In addition to publishing, the Society conducts the National Catholic History Awareness Program. This program distributes educational materials and organizes activities for dioceses to use in Catholic schools, parish programs, and adult education classes.

This site introduces the Web visitor to the Society and its works. It also publishes works (subject/author index) from *The U.S. Catholic Historian* as well as documents on Church history, Catholic archives, news about the Society, information on how to join the Society, and the guidelines for Society governance. Visitors are invited to send email to the Society for more information.

Jesuits and the Sciences

http://www.luc.edu/libraries/science/jesuits/jessci.html

Since the mid-sixteenth century, the Society of Jesus has been known for its teachers; in fact, the Jesuits are called "the society of teachers." The Society has also been known for having within its ranks some of the most notable scholars of the times. Saint Ignatius Loyola, the Web visitor is told, considered the acquisition of knowledge and the performance of mundane labor as spiritually profitable tasks, and this fostered in the Society an action-oriented, utilitarian mentality sympathetic to scientific study.

This site introduces the Web visitor to some of these scholars, with a specific focus on science. The purpose of this site is to show the link between the Jesuits and the advancement of the sciences during the past 450 years. The time span is broken down into six scholarship periods. The result? A rather remarkable presentation of academic endeavor by these men.

Christian Classics

http://ccel.wheaton.edu/

This site, coming out of Wheaton College (Illinois), is called the Christian Classics Ethereal Library. And what, in heaven's name, is the purpose of such a library? Its stated purpose is to build up Christ's church by addressing fundamental questions of the faith. This is accomplished, the site states, by presenting one of the most complete listings of Christian classics ever assembled on the Internet. It is indeed thorough. There is a mind-boggling amount of classical Christian literature to be found here.

This explanation from Webmaster Harry Plantinga: "If you read a variety of the books on this list, you will come to realize that while the greatest Christian authors from various traditions, those evidencing humility and holiness, those obviously having been taught from above, agree for the most part on fundamental issues, they also disagree at times on important points. Apparently it is possible to be holy and pleasing to God and still to have some wrong or skewed beliefs." Wheaton College has provided a server for this site and the Internet connection as well. The site is the love of Plantinga, a professor of computer science at Wheaton. This is obviously a popular Web site, with mid-1996 hits running at about 120,000 per week, from roughly 12,000 different people.

Diotima
http://www.uky.edu/ArtsSciences/Classics/gender.html

This Web site, the work of two women, Suzanne Bonefas and Ross Scaife, is intended to serve as an interdisciplinary resource for those interested in patterns of gender around the ancient Mediterranean and as a forum for collaboration among instructors who teach courses about women and gender in the ancient world. Diotima includes course materials, the beginnings of a systematic and searchable bibliography, and links to many online articles, book reviews, databases, and images.

Newcomers to the pleasures of classical Greek literature may be interested to know that the name for the site was borrowed from a tantalizing passage in Plato's Symposium, where Socrates claims to be passing on to his friends what he himself had learned about Eros from a woman named Diotima, who "in this matter was very wise, and in many others as well."

I include this site in this historical list because of the importance women's studies have taken on within the Church, particularly those aimed at understanding the social and cultural settings of the ancient Mediterranean. Catholic women have entered many scholarly fields in recent decades, including those of Church history, philosophy, and theology. The result is that they are bringing new insights into these disciplines. Understanding the roles of women in ancient and classical society inevitably adds to an understanding of the ways the Church has traditionally viewed gender questions.

U.S. papal visit

http://www.cua.edu/www/pbaf/pope.htm

This site, dedicated to the October 4–8, 1995, visit by Pope John Paul II to the United States, is especially useful to historical buffs and others. It details the visit more thoroughly than any other site. Further, it was constructed by historians at the Catholic University of America. All of Pope John Paul's talks made during the visit can be found here, as well as colorful photographs and an hour-by-hour presentation of the visit's major papal events. We find, for example, this summary by the pope of his visit on returning to Rome.

> Dear brothers and sisters, during my recent visit to the United States of America, I celebrated the Eucharist with the Catholic communities of Newark, Brooklyn, New York and Baltimore. The United States, as a nation of rich ethnic and cultural diversity, is being challenged to strengthen those truths and values on which the country was founded and without which a genuine democracy cannot prevail. Throughout my visit, I was impressed by the efforts of America's Catholics to promote a true civilization of love. At Newark, I recalled that America has been, from the beginning, a society marked by hospitality to the newcomer and to those in need. Today that same tradition needs to be affirmed with regard to the unborn, the elderly and the marginalized. In Brooklyn, I spoke of the need to strengthen family life in openness to the mystery of God and his plan, while, at the Mass in New York's Central Park, I encouraged young people to respond to the truth and love of Christ and to bear witness to their faith by building a society worthy of the human person. Finally, at Baltimore, I urged America's Catholics to work for the renewal of their society in light of the Gospel and to recognize that authentic freedom is fulfilled in truth. May the United States remain ever faithful to its calling as a nation of freedom, virtue and openness to life! As the dawn of the third Christian millennium approaches, I pray that America's Catholics will continue to serve Christ and to proclaim the Gospel of hope with the generosity and dynamism that they have always shown.

Clearly the trip had an impact on the Pop as well.

CHAPTER 6

Teachings

I enjoy the image of a large family sitting around a table at a special banquet and over dinner each member is talking heatedly about the way he or she looks at the family and the wider community. No two persons see things precisely the same way, but all keep talking, at times debating. And while things get heated up, somewhere beneath the apparent conflicts are deep familial assumptions of love and fidelity. Raucous, at times, but the food keeps getting passed from one to another. Even anger, because the discussion matters. Yet when all is done, after the meal is finished and dessert served, all can agree on one thing: They will all gather again on the next special occasion. In my mind, this is the image of the Catholic Church trying to figure things out, trying to understand, trying to teach and learn theology and truths, trying to pass the faith on to the next generation. It's never neat, never easy, but all agree it is worth the effort.

This chapter stresses those Web sites that attempt to teach and pass on the faith. In the Catholic Church, not all voices are considered equal. Official teachings come from what is called the *Magisterium*. In the Catholic tradition, each bishop with pastoral responsibility has authority regarding the teaching of Christian doctrine in his diocese. The whole episcopal college is the bearer of the supreme magisterium, which it exercises both when dispersed throughout the world and when gathered in an ecumenical council. The pope, as head of the episcopal college, can exercise the supreme teaching authority that resides in the college. Most sites in this chapter deal with efforts by the magisterium to teach the Catholic faith.

Ecclesiology

http://honey.acu.edu.au/~yuri/ecc/index.html

Ecclesiology is a discipline involving the study of the Church itself. How one defines *church* inexorably leads to how one defines church mission. Catholics today are divided, and these divisions are in no small amount the result of different definitions and images of church. This Web site, coming out of Australia, is fascinating in that it explores the different images traditional and progressive Catholics have of their church.

This Web site offers an introduction to Ecclesiology and church history. In one of its most fascinating features, it compares and contrasts images of church before and after the Second Vatican Council of the 1960s, when differences among Catholics became increasingly exacerbated.

As this site explains, the church before Vatican II was identified with the kingdom of God and was considered a perfect society. The Catholic Church was frequently described as the one true Church. Outside the Church there was no salvation. Conversion was needed; other Christian churches were seen as lacking ecclesial character. Certainly, outside Christianity, other religions were deemed as having no salvific value. The Church was a teacher. It is engaged in a monologue—teaching the world. An emphasis was given to the sacrament of ordination. Through Holy Orders, the charismatic power to teach, preach, forgive, sanctify, dispense divine graces, and govern was given to the Church. Catholic life was generally devotional. The lay person was expected (in the words of Cardinal Octaviani) "to pray, to pay, and to obey."

After the Council, the Church began to see itself as the pilgrim people of God, and as sacrament and mystery. The

Catholic Church is now seen as the heart of the one true Church; salvation is not seen as the exclusive possession of the Catholic Church. The Church recognizes that divisions exist within itself and in the wider Christian community. Therefore, ecumenism is important. The Church must become involved in dialogue, which necessitates not only speaking to the world but also listening to it with sensitivity. The Church is based on baptism and on the priesthood of all. It is charismatic and must reflect its collegial character. Catholic life is sacramental and scriptural: People belong to the Church in different ways and in different degrees. Laws are less important. Theological pluralism flows from the reality of cultural pluralism in the world.

Finding a way to accommodate both images of church, building on both in the twenty-first century, is the greatest ecclesial challenge facing contemporary Catholics. This site spells out that challenge.

Mater et Magistra

http://listserv.american.edu/catholic/church/papal/john.xxiii/
j23mater.txt

Pacem in Terris

http://listserv.american.edu/catholic/church/papal/john.xxiii/
j23pacem.txt

Populorum Progressio

http://listserv.american.edu/catholic/church/papal/paul.vi/
p6popp.txt

These three encyclicals—the first two by Pope John XXIII and the third by Pope Paul VI—share a revolutionary openness to the world and a sense of the refreshing idealism that swept through the Church during the 1960s. All three encyclicals outlined paths to social progress and peace, and all three revealed a Church breaking out of centuries of defensive institutionalism into new and undefined territories.

They revealed a Church not only interested in saving souls, but also in feeding them. A student of Catholicism cannot hope to understand the spirit of the Catholic Church in the 1960s without reading these three papal documents.

The first, *Mater et Magistra* (Mother and Teacher), was promulgated in 1961 and was addressed to the people of all nations. The second, *Pacem in Terris* (Peace on Earth), promulgated in 1963, argued that world peace is possible and can be found in the natural order. This meant that the road to peace is planted in the hearts of all people and is discernible by all. The third, *Populorum Progessio* (The Progress of Peoples), promulgated in 1967, aimed the Church's attention "at the development of those peoples who are striving to escape from hunger, misery, endemic diseases and ignorance; of those who are looking for a wider share in the benefits of civilization and a more active improvement of their human qualities; of those who are aiming purposefully at their complete fulfillment." (Incidentally, it is the practice of Catholic encyclicals that their titles are taken from words contained in the first sentences of the documents.)

Laborem Exercens

http://listserv.american.edu/catholic/church/papal/jp.ii/jp2labor.txt

Undoubtedly, this 1981 encyclical by Pope John Paul II, *Laborem Exercens* (On Human Work) has been the pontiff's most dramatic foray into the social and economic arena. In it John Paul offered a framework of analysis for the socio-political-economic questions of the day. The Pope devoted this document to addressing the vast subject of the reality and meaning of work. Always attempting to emphasize the symbolism of his writings, Pope John Paul II released this document on the ninetieth anniversary of Pope Leo XIII's *Rerum Novarum* (Of New Things), the first social encyclical of the modern age. Pope John Paul II's *Laborem Exercens* became the *Magna Carta* for the Polish Solidarity movement during the 1980s and helped ignite the revolution in Poland that eventually brought down Communism there—and later throughout all of Eastern Europe. This, then, is one of the most important Church documents of the twentieth century.

The Millennium
http://listserv.american.edu/catholic/church/papal/jp.ii/jp2-3rd.html

Catholic leaders have become increasingly focused on the Third Millennium. One of the earliest statements on the subject came out of the Vatican in November 1994, in a papal statement entitled *Tertio Mellennio Adveniente* (The Coming of the Third Millennium). The Pope addressed the document to all Catholics, setting out themes for the Church to develop as the millennium approaches. Many programs that have sprung from this document are being implemented as the year 2001 draws near. (For purists like myself, the new millennium does not begin until the year 2001, but I suspect we will be overwhelmed at the outset of the year 2000.) This site features the full text of the papal statement. Understanding Pope John Paul II's ideas on the millennium helps one understand not only the Church's sense of the event but this Pontiff's notion of the very mission of the Church.

As the Third Millennium Draws Near
http://www.crossnet.se/akks/misc.005.htm

The Pope, of course, has not been the only Catholic prelate to speak about the millennium. This second site features a 1994 address by Milwaukee Archbishop Rembert Weakland warning Catholics not to become part of the hysteria that he feels will develop around the year 2000. Weakland counseled Catholics to instead use the year 2000 as a reminder of God's providence and the need to live fully each day as baptized people should, namely, seeking to be God's instruments in building a kingdom of love and goodness.

Weakland Speech

http://www.execpc.com/~chaw/Weakland.html

Increasingly, I am finding important Catholic speeches on the Web. The problem is they appear here and there, without much order. One talk I found especially noteworthy was delivered September 20, 1995, by Milwaukee Archbishop Rembert Weakland. The speech was entitled, "Changing Health Care Delivery: A Changed Catholic Mission." The Catholic Church is the nation's leading source of private health care. Meanwhile, Catholic hospitals, stretching from coast to coast, face growing financial pressures and new ethical considerations. Weakland's speech, delivered to the Catholic Hospital Association of Wisconsin, spells out some of his ideas about the future of Catholic health care.

Vatican II Council Documents

http://wsnet.com:80/~alapadre/catv2doc.html

The Second Vatican Council, or Vatican II as it is frequently referred to, remains the most important church development in the twentieth century. The meeting of the world's bishops in Rome, from 1962 to 1965, ushered in church renewal as never before in Roman Catholic history. Since the council, Catholics have become divided between those who embrace the council renewal and feel it has yet to be completed and those who feel it has been abused and has harmed traditional Church teachings. The documents themselves, the result of compromise between conservative and progressive bishops during the council, can be read to support both sides of the theological debate. All agree that they are critical to interpreting modern Catholicism. This Web site introduces the visitor to the various documents.

Catechism of the Catholic Church

http://www.christusrex.org/www1/CDHN/ccc.html

This site presents the official Catechism of the Catholic Church. As the site explains, the catechism is the result of extensive collaboration; it was prepared over six years of intense work. In 1986, Pope John Paul II entrusted a commission of 12 cardinals and bishops, chaired by Cardinal Joseph Ratzinger, with the task of preparing a draft of the catechism. An editorial committee of seven diocesan bishops, experts in theology and catechesis, assisted the commission in its work. The commission, charged with giving directives and with overseeing the course of the work, followed the stages in editing nine subsequent drafts. The editorial committee, for its part, assumed responsibility for writing the text.

The site explains that a catechism "should faithfully and systematically present the teaching of Sacred Scripture, the living Tradition in the Church and the authentic Magisterium, as well as the spiritual heritage of the Fathers, Doctors and saints of the Church." It should take into account the doctrinal statements, which through the centuries the Holy Spirit has intimated to his Church. It should also help to illumine with the light of faith the new situations and problems that had not yet emerged in the past.

The Catechism of the Catholic Church is divided into four parts: the Creed, the Sacred Liturgy, the Christian way of life, and finally, Christian prayer. The four parts are related one to another: The Christian mystery is the object of faith (first part); it is celebrated and communicated in liturgical actions (second part); it is present to enlighten and sustain the children of God in their actions (third part); it is the basis for our prayer (fourth part).

While the catechism aims to reach the widest audience, its greatest shortcoming is the language used. It uses exclusive terms, contrary to the wishes of the U.S. bishops, who preferred to use inclusive language. For example, when the Catechism states that "all men are created in the image of God," it really means that all men and women are created in the image of God, and so forth.

Ten Commandments
http://webzone1.co.uk/www/jcrawley/decalog.htm#TEN

This site provides an example of information available from the online version of the Catholic Catechism. It aims at helping religious educators and the general Catholic audience brush up on their faith. References in the new Catechism are numbered; the Ten Commandments, a cornerstone of Judeo-Christian faith, for example, is presented as it appears in scripture. Its place in past and current Catholic church teaching is then considered. The text begins:

> 2052 "Teacher, what good deed must I do, to have eternal life?" To the young man who asked this question, Jesus answers first by invoking the necessity to recognize God as the "One there is who is good," as the supreme Good and the source of all good. Then Jesus tells him: "If you would enter life, keep the commandments." (Mt 19:16–17).

Catholic Encyclopedia
http://www.knight.org/advent/cathen/cathen.htm

This site may be the most reliable source of information about the Catholic church on the Web, but with a hitch. The information goes to the year 1913. So it is good for history, but forget the twentieth century.

The *Catholic Encyclopedia* is a 15-volume encyclopedia covering a broad range of topics, secular and religious, from a Catholic perspective. The version being used was published in 1913. (Individual volumes may bear dates ranging from 1907 to 1914, but it's all the same version.) Why the 1913 set? What's wrong with later editions? Later editions, such as the 1974 version, are under copyright protection. The 1913 Encyclopedia is in the public domain.

Slowly the 1913 edition is entering cyberspace as volunteers take on the monumental task of typing articles from the work to put them on the encyclopedia's Web pages. Through letter searches, the visitor can determine if the subject matter he or she is interested in is on the Web site.

To assist volunteers, several indexes of articles are listed on the site. An "A" designation means the article is already online; a "B" means someone is currently working on the article; a "C" designation means it's already scanned and awaiting a proofreader.

Catholic Apologetics

http://cs.sau.edu/%7Ecmiller/religion.html

This site appears to be the most thorough Catholic apologetics site on the Web. It cites a New Testament passage from Scripture to support its mission to defend, explain, and proclaim the faith: "Always be prepared to give an answer to everyone who asks you to give the reason for the hope that you have. But do this with gentleness and respect" (1 Peter 3:15).

Beginning with "the basics," the site deals with "general apologetic information, basic apologetics, God, Jesus, the Trinity, and Creationism/Evolution." From there it gets into "the Bible" and questions of canons, translations, interpretations, and the Catholic belief in a church of Scripture and tradition. Sections on Protestantism and cults appear before Catholicism is presented under the categories of General Catholic, Papacy, Church Authority, Mary and Other Saints, Purgatory, Baptism, Eucharist, Confession, Anointing of the Sick, Holy Matrimony, Holy Orders, Sacraments/Holy Objects, the End of Time, and Miscellaneous Beliefs. Each category presents the official church teaching, though in truth, many Catholics would differ somewhat if they had to explain their beliefs. I'd like a half dozen Catholics to explain, for example, how they view the state of purgatory as an ingredient of Catholic belief. Expressions of faith would undoubtedly vary.

Papacy is given special attention, with presentations under the headings of Infallibility, Peter and the Papacy, Was Peter in Rome, the Primacy of the Pope in the Church, and Who is the Rock. Consider this site a starting point for Catholic belief, but understand that within the Catholic community, heated debates continue over issues this site presents as undisputed elements of faith.

Catholic Doctrinal Concordance

http://www2.best.com/~ipage/concorda.htm

This site is a collection of basic Catholic doctrines with Scriptural references to show how Catholic beliefs are supported by the Word of God. This page contains detailed explanations of Catholic teachings. The site considers Catholic teachings through the following topics: God, Trinity, Jesus's Death and Resurrection, God's Creatures, Angels, Mary, God's Remedies, Grace and Sacraments, God's Gifts, Faith, Hope, and Charity, The Last Things, Death, Purgatory, Heaven, Hell, and additional topics disputed between Protestants and Catholics. Each topic receives numerous Scriptural citations from the Old and New Testaments. The electronic concordance does not have to be used solely as a defense of faith. The references cited are also useful for research and the writings of homilies or for discussion groups.

Catholic Answers

http://www.catholic.com/~answers/

Over the years, Catholic Answers has produced many tracts on different subjects, and it is still producing more. On this site, Catholic Answers makes these tracts available, as well as some that are not yet in general release.

Catholic Answers is the largest Catholic apologetics and evangelization organization in North America. It is run by lay people devoting full-time efforts to promoting the Catholic faith through books, booklets, tracts, *This Rock* magazine, tapes, and television and radio appearances. Some of its staff have always been Catholics, some have returned to the Catholic faith after having lapsed, and some are converts from other faiths. The staff apologists answer questions about the faith and give parish seminars.

Catholic Answers states that it believes the Catholic church was established by Jesus Christ and teaches the fullness of Christian truth. It believes all Catholics, not just the clergy and those in the religious life, are called to evangelize. It wants to spread the Catholic faith "by helping good Catholics become better Catholics, by bringing former Catholics `home,' and by resolving misconceptions non-Catholics may have about the Church and what it teaches."

Catholic Answers relies on tax-deductible donations from the laity for the majority of its support. Even though the work has the approval of many bishops in the United States and other countries, it does not ask dioceses for direct assistance. The balance of its support comes mainly through the sale of Catholic literature and tapes and from magazine subscriptions.

The site lists the tracts by topic. More than 100 tracts are available here. The site also provides information on Catholic Answers and its publications and offers contact information.

Catholic Issues and Facts

http://www.catholic.net/RCC/Periodicals/Issues/Welcome.html

Catholic Issues and Facts addresses topics that frequently trouble both Catholics and non-Catholics. Its tone, however, is often defensive. The authors of this site promise that as it expands it will offer a growing number of position papers that deal with widely misunderstood issues in Catholic history, like the Galileo affair, Pope Pius XII and the Jewish

Holocaust, and the Church's position on the scientific theory of evolution.

The stated purpose of the site is "to clarify and to state the case as concisely as possible." This site also intends to address issues that separate Protestants and Catholics, such as the Protestant belief in sola scripture ("scripture only"). And it will feature topics that trouble Christians, including many Catholics, such as natural family planning. From the looks of the site the day I cruised through it, it has a strong conservative bent. Furthermore, the Questions and Answers I pulled down dealt with abortion and were provided by Dr. and Mrs. J. C. Willke, two of the nation's leading advocates of the natural family planning birth control process.

Catholic Resources for Medical Ethics

http://www.usc.edu/hsc/info/newman/resources/ethics.html

Of all the hot issues of the day, medical ethics is at the top of many lists. Technology is changing so fast it is causing sweeping changes in the way medicine is practiced. With each step forward, the power of physicians over life and death seems to become more pronounced. If a heart transplant, for example, can save a life— but at the cost of tens of thousands of dollars—is it to be for only the wealthy who can afford such operations? If unborn children with severe birth defects can be detected at early stages of pregnancy, should the mother have the right to learn this information? Is such information a right, a privilege, or a scourge? If an elderly mother can be kept alive only through tube feeding should this be a required practice? If so, what about a ventilator? Blood transfusions?

For every answer given, five more questions can be raised. And these, in the minds of many ethicists, are the easy topics. More difficult problems arise when the discussion turns to genetics and genetic research. What about gene transplants to save lives? What about gene transplants from animals to humans? When scientists begin to work with genes, they are working with the basic building codes of life. Does this work smack of moral arrogance? What are the guidelines for such work?

This site provides the Catholic principles and teachings on these complex issues through a variety of sources, including medical ethics journals and Catholic statements on these subjects. The site presents the major statements from the Holy See and Catholic bishops on these issues. It also includes an address given by Pope John Paul II in 1983 on the dangers of genetic manipulation.

Sphaira—A symbol of Unity
http://incolor.inetnebr.com/mdavis/

Consider this site a safe ground for controlled debate over issues of faith. The site begins with the following premise: Among Christian denominations today, there exists a significant variance between one church's dogma and the next church's dogma. This variance has been the cause of real divisions as well as many bitter feelings, and it cripples the effect of the Christian message in the world today. In spite of these divisions, it is the Catholic belief that all Christians are members of the same family by virtue of their baptism, and that this baptism incorporates each member of the human family into the divine family of Jesus Christ. Unity among the members of this family and the incorporation of every member of the human family into this unity is necessarily a fundamental goal of the Christian endeavor, and in particular of the Catholic church.

Sphaira presents itself on this site as a new company, seeking to contribute to that unity by facilitating understanding. Love and understanding go hand in hand, and the mission of Sphaira is to build the community of Christ by developing understanding among the members of His body. Its method is to present a Catholic position on various issues important to ecumenical dialogue and then to field questions and criticisms with regard to these positions. All responses are included within these pages for others to view and receive email replies from Sphaira (these replies are attached to the bottom of each response). Those that successfully counter the position, or a part of it, will be used to revise it so that it more closely resembles the truth (this is similar to a controlled debate in which all discussion is limited to a particular topic).

The name *Sphaira* was taken from the Greek word for sphere, because in classical philosophy the sphere was the symbol of perfection. At the end of time, the Christian church will be made perfect, with no divisions, and with the individual mind of every member perfectly united to the mind of Christ, His Holy Father, and in the Holy Spirit.

Gallagher's Apologetics

http://net2.netacc.net/~mafg/

This Catholic Apologetics site is brought to you courtesy of the Gallagher family, which includes Michael and Maureen, Kristin, Sean, Julie, Sarah, Joseph, Angela, and Brendan—all from Fairport, New York.

The visitor quickly gets the feeling that this enterprise is an act of love—for their church. Catholic Apologetics, the family tells the visitor, is "for Catholics and other Christians." They quote the late Bishop Fulton J. Sheen who once said that "not 100 in the United States hate the Roman Catholic Church, but millions hate what they mistakenly think the Roman Catholic Church is." The Gallaghers feel they can help clarify some misconceptions.

Before getting into the work at hand, the site offers a definition of "apologetics" from the *Catholic Encyclopedia*: "the theological discipline concerned with the defense of or proofs for the Faith. Apologetics attempts a cogent (convincing) explanation of the Faith both to eliminate hostility against it and to elicit understanding and even acceptance in the listener."

The work of apologetics itself is supported by scripture quoted by the Gallaghers. "Always be ready to give an explanation to anyone who asks you for a reason for your hope, but do it with gentleness and reverence, keeping your conscience clear, so that, when you are maligned, those who defame your good conduct in Christ may themselves be put to shame" (1 Peter 3:15-16).

The site is designed to take steps toward accomplishing the objective. "It attempts to present the Catholic perspective on several key issues of faith that are generally misunderstood and therefore tend to be a cause of disunity among Catholics and non-Catholic Christians." The visitor can access the information directly or download software facilitating the effort.

Information about Catholicism
http://web.bu.edu/NEWMAN/classes.html

This site is a general information site about Catholicism run by a Catholic priest in Boston, Massachusetts. It provides a casual contact point for someone interested in learning more about the religion. Some information is provided in the site. Other information is available by emailing Father Chuck Cunniff.

The site answers a number of questions, the first being what is involved in becoming a Catholic. He answers as follows: "Becoming a member of the Roman Catholic Church is a personal decision which involves time, study and prayer. It is a process of spiritual and personal formation and the decision is not to be made lightly. ... For someone who has never been baptized, the Rite of Christian Initiation for Adults is the focal point of the decision process. It is tailored to the person. For some a year is enough time, for others it may take longer. Traditionally, adults are Baptized, Confirmed and receive Eucharist at the Easter Vigil on Holy Saturday night. To reach that point, classes with basic information about the Catholic Church as well as some type of spiritual formation and involvement in the ongoing life and mission of the Church is necessary."

Someone who is baptized in another Christian tradition is not rebaptized. They renew their Baptismal Promises, make a Profession of Faith in the Roman Catholic Church, are confirmed, and receive Eucharist in the Roman Catholic Church. This usually takes place on Easter Sunday or during the Easter season, although exceptions can be made. Prior to their Profession it is expected that they, like the non-baptized person, will participate in information classes (to help them make a wise decision) and in the ongoing life and mission of the local church as lived out in the parish of which they are a part.

Other questions are also dealt with. Information is provided on the sacraments of confirmation, reconciliation, and marriage. Catholic annulments—easily misunderstood—are explained.

People of God
http://www.silcom.com/~origin/ws/theme031

One of the fundamental concepts of Judeo-Christian thought is belief in the idea of being "a chosen people," being called, having a special covenant with God. This Web site explores this theological notion, comparing the way various religions in some way share this belief. Web sites, it seems, not only represent organizations or movements, but also ideas. Some Web sites are used to focus debate; others to preach a religious idea. This one appears aimed at exploring common foundations in religious belief.

This site explains its purpose in the following words: "Any good society, whether a church or a polity, is united with the Absolute and guided by the truth. Many religions, therefore, regard themselves as the unique people of God, bound corporately in a special, covenanted relationship with the Lord. Indeed, not one but several religions— Judaism, Islam, Christianity, Shinto, and Sikhism, among them—have understood themselves to be 'chosen' by God and uniquely qualified to establish a godly society. ...A people that recognizes itself to be the focus of God's special concern, or that devotes itself to the exemplary life called for by the truth, also recognizes that it is responsible to manifest the highest standards of faith and behavior. If it does so, it will be the recipient of great blessings."

The site then goes on to explore specific similarities, beginning with the exploration of sacred texts. Consider this an introduction to a course on comparative religions.

Pope John Center
http://www.pjcenter.org/pjc/pjclink.htm

The Pope John Center is an institute that prizes itself on being "faithful to the Magisterial teachings of the Catholic Church." The Center, established in 1972, engages in research and education in biomedical ethics and publishes ethics studies in health care.

This site features the work of the Center, including:

- Publications in biomedical ethics including the monthly commentary *Ethics & Medics*
- More than 30 books, dozens of audio cassettes, and research task forces on biomedical ethics issues with interdisciplinary groups of scholars and experts from around the world
- Education programs for health care professionals, educators, ethics committees, clergy, and bishops and a consultation service to members of the Pope John Center by experienced ethicists on every topic in the field of biomedical ethics
- Internships and guided independent study programs for professionals and students interested in the ethics of health care, through the Harvard Divinity School

Professional resources of the Pope John Center include:

- Professional staff of directors and associates in research, education, publications, and development
- Consultants who are noted specialists in medicine, philosophy, theology, law, and the natural and social sciences

The site also provides links to other biomedical ethics sites.

Responsum ad Dubium

http://www.knight.org/advent/docs/df95os.htm

The text on this site will go down in history as among the most controversial church utterances by a Roman Catholic pontiff in the twentieth century. For this reason it deserves a Web site of its own.

It was on October 28, 1995, in a *Responsum ad Dubium*, or "a response to a doubt" that the Vatican Congregation for the Doctrine of the Faith declared, on behalf of Pope John Paul II, that it is to be considered "infallible" church teaching that the church can never ordain women as priests. While intended to end the discussion on whether women can become priests, it had the opposite effect, propelling the discussion into theological and episcopal ranks. Rather than laying the question to rest, the declaration led to other questions, including how and when the pope speaks infallibly.

This site allows the visitor to consider and download for personal reference the precise words of this *Responsum ad Dubium*.

Catholic Ecumenical Councils— All the Decrees

http://abbey.apana.org.au/councils/~index.htm

This site explains the nature and history of the most important Catholic church gatherings during its history, ecumenical councils. It also features all the decrees that were issued during those meetings. This site is important for the historical significance and for a better understanding of the way Catholic teachings have developed over the years.

Councils are legally convened assemblies of ecclesiastical dignitaries and theological experts for the purpose of discussing and regulating matters of church doctrine and discipline. The terms *council* and *synod* are synonymous, although in the oldest Christian literature the ordinary meetings for worship are also called synods, and diocesan synods are not properly called councils because they are only convened for deliberation.

Ecumenical councils are those to which the bishops, and others entitled to vote, are convoked from the whole world (*oikoumene*) under the presidency of the pope or his legates, and the decrees of which, having received papal confirmation, bind all Christians. A council, ecumenical in its convocation, may fail to secure the approbation of the whole Church or of the pope, and thus does not rank in authority with ecumenical councils.

This site deals chiefly with the theological and canonical questions concerning councils that are ecumenical in this strict sense. Special attention is given to the history of each important synod under the head of the city or See where it was held. In order, however, to supply the site visitor with a basis for the discussion of principles that follows, a list of the 21 ecumenical councils is offered, with a brief statement of the purpose of each.

Education

Catholicism has always been marked by a commitment to scholarship and learning; this partnership is as old as Christianity itself. The most frequent title for Jesus in the New Testament is "teacher." Christianity inherited the Jewish appreciation for scholarship. The early Christian Apologists (120–220) used their classical education to present Christian faith to the learned. They posed Christianity as the true and ultimate philosophy. Centuries later, monastic scholarship flourished; the Church's schools and universities of the late Middle Ages spawned the next era, the Renaissance, revived the classical learning of Greece and Rome, and championed a humanism centered on the dignity and value of the individual person. These traditions continue in modern times.

This chapter features Catholic educational Web sites in a variety of forms, lists, ideas, groups, organizations, universities, colleges, and high schools. I've selected only a few of the many possible education-related sites to show the ways Catholic education is being enhanced by the World Wide Web. For each one chosen, dozens were not. The sites in this chapter are not necessarily the most glamorous; others, arguably, are of equal interest. This list offers a sense of the many approaches Catholic educators have taken to enhance Catholic scholarship by means of the Internet.

Top 50 Catholic Universities

http://wsnet.com:80/~alapadre/cathuniv.html

Alapadre lists categorize Catholic topics by subject; they are self-explanatory. This list appears on Alapadre as the "top 50 Catholic universities." One click and the visitor can find one of the top U.S. Catholic colleges or universities. I did not find the criteria for the list selection and will leave it to others to decide if they agree with the choices. I admit to being a list buff. Show me a Catholic list of any sort and I will feel the urge to explore it. I may save it, thinking that one day I may need it. Obviously, a list of the top 50 Catholic universities will be of use to many, starting with high school students (or their parents) pondering the choice of Catholic college or university. This list is alphabetical. No ranking is involved. Enjoy.

Catholic Primary and Secondary Schools on the Net

http://www.microserve.net/~fabian/files/school.html

The World Wide Web, with its lists—and lists of lists—is great for directory lovers. Virtually any group or organization belongs to some list and can be found on the Web. If it is not on a list, it takes only sending an email to the appropriate Webmaster. The lists grow daily. This Web site lists Catholic primary and secondary schools on the Net. International in scope, it is a long way from being complete, but the ambitious undertaking deserves credit. It is maintained by Marty Kirwan and finds a home through Scott Fabian. The site states that school home pages are listed first, then email-only addresses. Schools are listed alphabetically by country (then by state\province, if necessary) and then by name. City names have been provided to distinguish similarly named schools.

To get your school on this list with no cost, a Web address is offered for future contact. The first countries to be categorized are Australia, Austria, Canada, Estonia, Greece, Hong Kong, Hungary, Japan, Russia, South Africa, the United Kingdom, and the United States. The United States is broken down by state.

Faith and Science

http://www.cco.caltech.edu/~newman/sci-faith.html

The Roman Catholic church has been too slow to warm up to science. The Church's condemnation of Galileo is the most notable example, but there have been others. Many church leaders today, for example, continue to be suspicious of the social sciences. Insights gained through the social sciences, for example, have challenged some precepts of Catholic moral theology, especially in the area of human sexuality. Pope John Paul II, while open to the natural sciences as no other pope in modern history, deplores the use of the social sciences in the development of moral theology, which, he says, is absolute and not subject to circumstance or social conditions.

In any case, this Web site represents a positive step forward in the Catholic church's interest in science. The story of science is, after all, God's story. The insights gained from science, in the minds of the faithful, only seem to enhance the wondrous beauty of creation, providing new glimpses of the Creator's divine plan.

Speaking to scientists in 1985, Pope John Paul II said:

Through the natural sciences and cosmology in particular, we have become much more aware of our true physical position within the universe, within physical reality—in space and in time. We are struck very forcibly by our smallness and apparent insignificance, and even more by our vulnerability in such a vast and seemingly hostile environment. Yet this universe of ours, this galaxy in which our sun is situated and this planet on which we live, is our home. ... What we discover through our study of nature and of the universe in all its immensity and rich variety serves on the one hand to emphasize our fragile condition and our littleness, and on the other hand to manifest clearly our greatness and superiority in the midst of all creation—the profoundly exalted position we enjoy in being able to search, to imagine and to discover so much.

This Web site offers various Catholic papers and speeches on science, including one especially notable paper by the late French theologian, Jacque Maritain, "God and Science." The site also links with a page called The Jesuits and the Sciences.

Catholic University of America
http://www.cua.edu/

This is the home page of the Catholic University of America, located in Washington, D.C. CUA has one of the most active Web pages of any U.S. Catholic college or university. The CUA Web page provides links to research and special academic resources made available by the Catholic University of America, and these are considerable. The site also puts the visitor in touch with the Catholic University of America's library, offering telephone numbers, hours of operation, schedule information, circulation services, inter-library loans, references, and a "how to" contact leading to the director of library operations. Contact numbers for other CUA libraries are also provided, as are library telephone numbers and office hours. And so there can be no excuses for not returning late books, the site has a section entitled Library Regulations.

Catholic Perspectives on University Life
http://www.cco.caltech.edu/~newman/uni-life/

This page aims to provide resources of particular interest to Catholics involved in higher education. It introduces the visitor to, among other educational resources, John Henry Newman's "Idea of the University," which is actually a famous series of lectures delivered by Newman in 1852 and 1854. Newman was a Catholic convert, and he delivered his speeches on the occasion of the founding of the Catholic University of Dublin. Catholic students not familiar with Newman's "Idea of the University," are missing some fine writings that speak to the purpose of an education.

What is a university? Newman writes that it is "the place to which a thousand schools make contributions; in which the intellect may safely range and speculate, sure to find its equal in some antagonist activity, and its judge in the tribunal of truth. It is a place where inquiry is pushed forward, discoveries verified and perfected, and rashness rendered innocuous, and error exposed, by the collision of mind with mind, and knowledge with knowledge. ... It is a seat of wisdom, a light of the world, a minister of the faith, an Alma Mater of the rising generation."

Newman's writings have had a profound impact on the development of Catholic colleges and universities in the United States. It is fitting that there is a Web page dedicated to Newman and his writings.

Newman Centers
http://www.cco.caltech.edu/~newman/OtherNC.html

Closely related to the previous site, this one highlights Newman Centers, places at most colleges and universities that provide worshipping communities for Catholics interested in developing faith lives. These centers also provide space for Catholics to meet other Catholics and to form faith bonds. Many Catholics become so attracted to Newman Center liturgies and communities while away at college that it becomes difficult for them to find similar intimacy in their local parishes after graduation.

Parents, uncertain about what kind of Catholic atmosphere exists in a prospective college or university, find contacting the Catholic Newman Center chaplain can be helpful. Sometimes, however, it is not clear how to reach the chaplain. As the list of Newman Centers fills out, making contact with them is easier.

This site is currently compiling a list of Newman Centers by region within the United States while developing lists of foreign centers by nation. This list is being maintained by the Newman Center at Caltech, where Web developers continue to seek useful additions to their enterprise. The number of Newman Centers on the Web is also growing.

Marquette University

http://www.mu.edu/

Marquette University's Web site provides an excellent introductory look at this Jesuit school, located in downtown Milwaukee, Wisconsin, which has grown relatively well over the past three decades; Marquette University has grown well with it. This site captures some of the vitality of this growth. "Striving for excellence defines Marquette, its dedicated faculty, its talented students and alumni from all parts of the world..." Most university Web sites are maintained by public relations or communications departments; it is their purpose to "sell" the school as they recruit potential students. That said, the information in every Web site is useful to someone. On this site, there is plenty of information available to many.

This site offers information about students and alumni, faculty and staff. Alumni are asked to register their email and Web addresses. Under Academics, information is available in the following categories: Graduate Schools, Summer Sessions, Academics, Department of History, College of Engineering, College of Business Administration, College of Communication, Biomathematics, and others. There is a Fun @ Marquette heading that provides an online campus tour, random images, sights and sounds, facts, and even weather information. Information is also available about Marquette athletics and from the university's newspaper and other publications. Finally, the visitor can check out student affairs, student organizations, and other general university information under research programs, as well as the Haggerty Museum of Art.

University of St. Michael's College

http://www.utoronto.ca/stmikes/index.htm#TOP

This is one of my favorite sites. Its theological resources are impressive and easy to find. Anyone interested in Catholic theology will find this site of interest. There is much more than theology here, however. The site provides links to all sorts of other Catholic Web sites, where information can be found on virtually any aspect of the Church. Pro-life to marriage encounter, bishops' statements to information on religious education, church documents to Latin liturgical texts, diocesan home pages to links to religious orders, this site provides all the necessary links.

One of the recent interesting Web developments has been the way lists under various headings have developed. To make some sense out of the Web, enterprising Webmasters—frequently young students or faculty—have taken on the work of compiling lists of sites. Soon after these appear they end up as part of other lists. Now we have lists of lists of lists.

Aside from the Catholic information, this site invites the visitor to learn more about what is going on at St. Michael's College. "Please take time to browse the University of St. Michael's College, Faculty of Theology Bulletin to learn more about our Faculty and our Degree programs." There is a clickable map of the campus and color images. St. Michael's Faculty of Theology, with its fine reputation for scholarship, is a welcome addition to the Web.

Welcome to Saint Louis University

http://www.slu.edu/

Most universities in the past two years have developed—or are developing—Web sites to recruit new students. It is a buyer's market as institutions of higher education compete for students. Home pages are one more means of getting out the information; the Saint Louis University Web site is no exception in this effort. St. Louis University is an exceptional institution, not least of all because of its place in American history as the first university founded west of the Mississippi.

Saint Louis University, a private university under Catholic and Jesuit auspices, traces its history to the founding of the Saint Louis Academy by Bishop Louis William DuBourg, Bishop of Louisiana, in 1818. At Bishop DuBourg's request, the Society of Jesus took over the direction of the school in 1829. This small Jesuit college received its charter as Saint Louis University in 1832, becoming the first university established west of the Mississippi River. The university, settled at its current site since 1888, enrolls more than 11,500 full-time and part-time students, including 1,000 foreign students from 76 countries. Some 80,000 alumni are engaged in professional pursuits throughout the world.

This site offers information about the university under the following headings: General Information, Colleges and Schools, University Services, News and Publications, Alumni News, Libraries, Health Care, and Athletics.

Alliance for Catholic Education
http://www.nd.edu:80/~ace/index.html

This Web site builds on the altruism of young Catholics who want to serve the needy as well as the desire of young college graduates to get experience in the field of education before determining what course to follow in their professional careers.

The Alliance for Catholic Education (ACE) sees as its aim the development of a corps of highly motivated and committed young educators to meet the needs of the country's most under-served elementary and secondary schools. Begun in 1994 by Fr. Timothy R. Scully, C.S.C., and Sean D. McGraw, ACE currently has 110 recent graduates from the University of Notre Dame and Saint Mary's College, as well as a number of other select colleges and universities. These graduates teach in 70 parochial schools throughout the urban and rural southern United States.

To carry out its core teaching mission, ACE recruits graduates from a variety of undergraduate disciplines, representing diverse backgrounds, and provides an intensive two-year service experience encompassing professional development, community life, and spiritual growth. On completion of summer training, ACE teachers travel to their respective communities to serve as full-time teachers during the school year. They work in needy parochial schools in the south and southeast. In addition to the support of mentor-teachers in the parochial schools where they teach, all ACE teachers are brought together twice a year in retreats to deepen and enhance their commitment to becoming professional educators.

University of Notre Dame Archives
http://archives1.archives.nd.edu/

This is more than a university archive; it is an archives guide. The nice thing about this Web site, which has tons of information gathered by the university over many years, is that it has a search engine to allow the visitor to find out if particular information is in the archives. Working for the National Catholic Reporter Publishing Company, whose papers are kept by Notre Dame University, I was able to locate NCR letters and documents in minutes by going to the letter *n* for National Catholic Reporter.

Notre Dame, of course, is one of the pre-eminent Catholic institutions of higher learning in the world. Having its archives available online is an important research tool. The ND archive guide provides instructions for use, collection codes, search inventories, and a calendar for abstracts of individual documents. Also on this Notre Dame site is an index of school press releases, lists of students (1850–1910, for researchers), as well as a list of early teachers at the university—and much more Notre Dame information.

Catholic Research Forum

http://www.execpc.com/~mcieslak/crf/index.html

The expressed mission of the Catholic Research Forum is to share the results of applied empirical research about the Catholic Church. The forum is composed of researchers and planners, most of whom are employed by Catholic archdioceses and dioceses and are members of the Conference for Pastoral Planning and Council Development. The work of the forum is outlined in four goals: share diocesan research with church researchers and policy-makers, promote practical research through sound methodology, gather a base of information that can be analyzed by the forum, and encourage analysis of information and disseminate the results.

To meet the pastoral needs of Catholics in the twenty-first century, a sound understanding of the church's demographics and racial and ethnic make-up is essential. The work of the Catholic Research Forum will be a vital tool for getting a better handle on the church of the future. The problem sometimes is that church leaders are slow to respond to the findings of the researchers. Nevertheless, the forum's work needs to grow. This Web site can broaden the forum's audience, seeing to it that meticulously gathered empirical information gets into the hands of planners throughout the church. The Web provides the exciting prospect of having the work of academicians break out of their journals.

Yale Divinity School Library

http://www.library.yale.edu/div/overview.htm

This site is not strictly Catholic, but it is useful to Catholic students and educators, especially those interested in the fields of theology and religion. It begins with an overview of the Divinity School Library's electronic resources, with information on accessing catalogs and bibliographies, indexes to periodical and essay literature, editions of relevant works, Internet client software, and further information.

One of the new developments in education is the growing availability of online research. The Yale Web site is a good example.

One of the many features available on this page is the American Theological Library Association's Religion Database. It provides electronic access by author, title, subject, and keyword to articles published in periodicals and journals, essays and articles published in multiauthor monographs, and book reviews in the fields of religion and theology.

Université Catholique de Louvain
http://www.ucl.ac.be/intro-en.htmls

The Université Catholique de Louvain was established December 9, 1425, by a papal bull issued by Pope Martin V. The university was abolished in 1797 as a result of French occupation and forced to remain closed until 1817, when it reopened as a state university. Following the foundation of the Kingdom of Belgium in 1830, the "Free" Catholic University was reestablished, first in Malines in 1834, and the following year in Louvain. The university split along language lines as a result of political turmoil in the late 1960s. A law recognizing separate Flemish-speaking and French-speaking universities was passed in 1970. The former remained in Louvain while the latter moved to a new location on the outskirts of Ottignies. This new campus became the town of Louvain-la-Neuve. Within the Catholic church the word *Louvain* has become synonymous with scholarship. The school has a reputation for progressive-minded theology. This is notable at a time when progressive thinking is under attack in the church from the Vatican and other church forces.

This Web site, available in both English and French, offers information on study programs, research projects, faculties, libraries, and other administrative nuggets. For anyone wanting to contact the institution, mailing and email addresses are offered. Many American students have studied and are continuing to pursue their academic credentials at Louvain.

International Institute of Catechetical and Pastoral Studies

http://www.luc.edu/or/sj/lumen/index.html

The International Institute of Catechetical and Pastoral Studies, or the Lumen Vitae Institute, based in Brussels, Belgium, is run by the Jesuit Fathers. This usually means the theology will be moderate to progressive within the Catholic context. Since its inception in 1957, the institute admits students from more than 30 countries. Through the international membership of staff and students, the Lumen Vitae Institute provides opportunities for sharing pastoral and catechetical experiences in diverse contexts. The institute, affiliated with the highly reputable Theology Faculty of the Catholic University of Louvain (UCL), at Louvain-la-Neuve, offers "Higher Studies and Post-Graduate Programs."

For many years, U.S. Catholic theology students have been among the international students who have studied at the Lumen Vitae Institute. This Web site offers an overview of the classes and programs offered at the institute. The site lists courses under several headings including Multidisciplinary Training for Priests, Lay People, and Men and Women Religious. It cites courses in theological reflection, practical theology, and developmental studies. The site says the institute is attempting to meet the challenges of today's world by linking faith and justice, through the inculturation of the faith, interreligious dialogue and evangelization in a secularized society.

Finally, the site offers information on the diplomas and certificates available through the completion of studies at the institute. Note, however, that although this Web site is available in Spanish, English, or French, institute seminars are conducted in French.

St. Ambrose University Library

http://www.sau.edu/cwis/libhome/mainindx.htm

The mission of the St. Ambrose University Library is to support the curriculum and research of faculty members. St Ambrose sees its responsibility as "not only to provide a collection of appropriate materials, but also to provide access to those materials, through purchase and cataloging of reference sources, through instruction in proper library use, and through cooperation with other libraries."

I liked to read on this site the disclaimer that the World Wide Web "has a lot to offer, but not all sources are equally valuable or reliable." I'll add an "Amen" to that.

Here, then, are some points to consider in evaluating a home page. These come from the St. Ambrose library Webmaster: What is the purpose of the Web page and what does it contain? How complete and accurate are the information and links provided? What is the relative value of the Web site in comparison to the range of information resources available on this topic? What other resources (print and nonprint) are available in this area? What are the date(s) of coverage of the site and site-specific documents? How comprehensive is this site? What are the link selection criteria if any? Are the links relevant and appropriate for the site? Is the site inward-focused, pointing outward, or both? Is there an appropriate balance between inward-pointing links ("inlinks") and outward-pointing links ("outlinks")? Are the links comprehensive or do they just provide a sampler? What do the links offer that is not easily available in other sources? Who is the author or producer? What is the authority or expertise of the individual or group that created this site? How knowledgeable is the individual or group on the subject matter of the site? And is the site sponsored or cosponsored by an individual or group that has created other Web sites?

College of St. Benedict & St. John's University

http://www.csbsju.edu/

The College of Saint Benedict and Saint John's University are two liberal arts colleges located four miles apart in central Minnesota. Saint Benedict's is a college for women and Saint John's a college for men. The students of these two colleges share in a common education, as well as coeducational social, cultural, and spiritual programs. Saint Benedict's and Saint John's have a common core curriculum, identical major requirements, and a common academic calendar. Most departments are joint; those that are unique to one college allow full enrollment to students of the other college. There is one admission office, a single registrar's office, a combined library system, joint academic computing services, and a myriad of joint student activities and clubs. The two campuses are linked by free bus service throughout the day and late into the night.

This site details the size and shape of these colleges, which together enroll 3,600 students from 43 states and 20 foreign countries and trust territories. Saint Benedict's enrolls 1,800 women; Saint John's enrolls 1,800 men. The combined faculties include approximately 260 professors, among them Benedictines and lay professors with diverse religious and cultural backgrounds. Many faculty members, both lay and Benedictine, live on or near the campuses and participate in campus life.

The liberal arts education provided by the College of Saint Benedict and Saint John's University is rooted in Catholic and Christian tradition and guided by the Benedictine principles of the colleges' founders stressing the cultivation of the love of God, neighbor, and self. Recognition of individual worth without regard for wealth or social standing is explicit in the Rule of Benedict. In harmony with this principle, Saint Benedict's and Saint John's say they seek to exemplify an authentically Christian concern for human rights and to make education broadly available to students on the sole criterion of ability to benefit from enrollment in the colleges.

The site introduces the visitor to the two schools. Information can be accessed under the following headings: News & Events, Library Resources, Admission, Alumnae & Alumni, and Internet Resources. Telephone numbers, mailing addresses, and email contacts are provided.

The Scriptorium

http://www.scriptorium.org/scriptorium

Traditionally, the scriptorium was the place in a monastery where books were copied—where scribes, illuminators, and skilled artisans toiled together to produce texts, to pursue learning as a holy quest, and to preserve for the next generation the wisdom of the past. The union of manual labor and contemplation fulfilled the monastic vocational ideal. The preparation and study of biblical and ecclesiastical texts played an especially significant role in monastic education. At the same time, the monastic library became a rich resource for the secular lover of learning. It is on this historic precedent that The Scriptorium: Center for Christian Antiquities has been established. Serving students and faculty members who share common interests in Christian history, the Scriptorium has designed programs to encourage relevant discussion and the development of the highest quality of biblical scholarship.

The Scriptorium is located on the shores of Lake Michigan in Grand Haven, Michigan, approximately 30 miles west of Grand Rapids. Members of the Scriptorium faculty are specialists in the areas of ancient languages, antiquities, and textual research. In publications and teaching methods, the faculty seeks to bring a fresh approach to, as well as a continuation of, the historical discipline of Christian scholarship. This Web page might fit under the "fresh approach" clause of its mission statement. The site offers information about the Scriptorium, hours open to the public, admission fees, and exhibition and tour notes.

A Guide to Christian Literature on the Internet

file://iclnet93.iclnet.org/pub/resources/christian-books.html

This Web site contains links to accessible literature related to classical Christianity, a term coined by C.S. Lewis, according to an introduction to the page, to describe a theology that affirms the importance of a transforming faith in Christ as God and Savior. The literature accessible through this site is of interest to both Catholics and Protestants, who, while differing on aspects of faith, share much of the same belief and history. Links continue to be updated on this site. Contents are divided into the following headings: Bibles, Books (by title), Articles (by title), Sermons, Bible Studies/Devotionals, News Sources/Newsletters, Periodicals, Creeds/Confessions, Miscellaneous Texts, and Publishers/Bookstores.

The diversity of Christian resources becomes readily apparent on these pages. Want to read the Bible in Swahili? Dabble in St. John of the Cross's "Dark Night of the Soul"? Read a speech by Mother Teresa? Take another look at G. K. Chesterton's "Orthodoxy"? Study the development of Christian Creeds through the centuries? It is all possible on this rich site.

Ethics Home

http://www.depaul.edu/ethics/

The Institute for Business & Professional Ethics was established in 1985 by a joint effort of the Colleges of Liberal Arts and Sciences and Commerce at DePaul University. Its mission: to foster ethical behavior. The primary focus: teaching and training individuals to think before they act. "Not to design or impose rules, regulations and controls.

Instead, we will concentrate on stirring an individual's conscience by stimulating moral imagination; by encouraging ongoing ethical debate; and by insisting upon individual responsibility."

The institute claims to be one of the first ethics-related resources to pioneer a hypertext-linked ethics network on the Internet. An example of the institute's work during the academic year (1994–1995) was a series of workshops in DePaul's College of Commerce seeking to encourage Commerce faculty to integrate ethics teaching in their courses. The institute is funded through DePaul University's Colleges of Commerce and Liberal Arts & Sciences, membership fees, and individual or corporate donations. Besides information on the institute, this site connects visitors with ethic resources on the Web.

Catholic Education Network

http://www.catholic.org/cen/default.html

This site states that Catholic educators, in particular, have a special responsibility to feed the church of God with the truth of Christ. Catholic educators have several reasons for their existence: to help form our young Catholic minds, to provide reliable information about what is going on in the Church. "As educators for our Catholic youth, we have both the opportunity and the responsibility to present with clarity and in an attractive manner the teachings of the Holy Bible, the Holy Father and of the bishops," the site states. It is with this purpose that Catholic Online presents on this home page the Catholic Education Network (CEN).

Here is a Web site that blends these goals with electronic technology, offering among other things, a U.S. Catholic school search database. The Catholic Education Network claims to have the complete list of U.S. Catholic schools with addresses and telephone numbers. More than 10,000 U.S. Catholic schools are on the list. (I did not count them, but I have no reason to doubt the claim.) This Web site also offers to place any Catholic school on a Web server. "Special rates" are available.

Other features of the Catholic Education Network include a Conference Web, a Web Classroom, and an Administrative Center, offering "the best Catholic and educational links." Books, videos, and software are also available, as are Catholic Network Seminars information.

Jacque Maritain Center
http://www.nd.edu/Departments/Maritain/ndjmc.htm

The founding of the Jacques Maritain Center in 1957 consolidated this French Catholic philosopher's association with the University of Notre Dame. For some years, Maritain had been coming to Notre Dame to lecture and stay for short periods of time. Holy Cross Father Theodore M. Hesburgh, the president of the university, friend and admirer of Maritain, wanted to make the relationship permanent. The center was founded to ensure that the thought and spirit of Jacques Maritain would remain at Notre Dame.

Jacques Maritain was born in 1882 to a French Protestant family. A year later, Raïssa Oumansouff was born into a Jewish family in Russia. The two met in Paris as university students, where both were chiefly interested in science and philosophy. Raïssa and Jacques married in 1904. Their love for each other did not prevent them from making a pact to commit suicide if they had not, within a year, discovered the meaning of life and existence. The lectures of Henri Bergson, but more importantly the influence of Léon Bloy, helped them find the answers they sought. They converted to Catholicism, entering the Church with Raïssa's sister Vera, in 1906.

Jacques Maritain is a paradigmatic Catholic philosopher, providing a model of the way in which religious belief and various cultural, intellectual, and political concerns can be interwoven. Maritain responded with enthusiasm to the Church's recommendation of St. Thomas Aquinas to the faithful as their master in theology and philosophy. His writings exhibit how his mind was permeated by Aquinas's thought.

The center exists to contribute to the continuing influence of the spirit of Jacques Maritain at Notre Dame and houses a special collection featuring the works of Jacques and Raïssa Maritain in their original editions; a fair collection of translations, which includes all English translations of works that originally appeared in French; books to which Maritain contributed a chapter or a preface; and a backup collection, consisting of the works of people associated with the Maritains, as well as books devoted to the thought of Maritain.

Saint John's School of Theology and Seminary

http://www.physics.csbsju.edu/sot/MinistryLink/

Theological education at Saint John's takes shape in an environment fashioned and sustained by the 1,500-year-old Benedictine tradition. Within the Catholic context, this means much attention is given to good liturgy and worship; it means that prayer and work thread themselves through all school activities. Saint John's is located on a 2,400-acre tract of woods and lakes. "This setting, apart from the work of city, town, and farm," the site states, "provides room for developing sensitivity to the needs of the world, especially of its poor and oppressed people. Time apart for study, contemplation and reflection nurtures committed love for a world under the guidance of a faithful, compassionate God. Theological education at Saint John's," the site continues, "works from tradition and community to mission and service. The shared value of reverence for the Christian tradition is the gateway for a journey of faith which links the students of Saint John's with the early Christian community of Antioch as well as the poor of Sao Paulo, Brazil."

This site offers an overview of the school of theology and seminary, a course catalog, calendar of events, and admissions information. The page also offers a link to MinistryLink, an employment opportunities classified for church ministry positions.

Catholic Schools, Colleges, and Academic Departments

http://www.cs.cmu.edu/Web/People/spok/catholic/schools.html

This Web page, courtesy of Scott Fabian, lists Catholic schools at all levels throughout the world. It also lists academic departments at these schools, in most cases providing links to the schools. Countries are listed alphabetically. Clearly, this is an exciting Web site, but it still offers lots of room for growth. In the end, the shape and dynamics of this site will depend, it seems, on the imaginations of the educators whose links appear here. In many cases, only two or three school names appear under a foreign country. But this appears to be changing weekly.

Some 50 U.S. schools of higher learning are listed. These include:

- Allentown College of Saint Frances de Sales (Pennsylvania)
- Alverno College (Wisconsin)
- Assumption College (Massachusetts)
- Barry University (Florida)
- Benedictine College (Kansas)
- Boston College (Massachusetts)
- Canisius College (New York)
- Catholic University of America (District of Columbia)
- Christendom College (Virginia)
- Christian Brothers University (Tennessee)

- Clarke College (Iowa)
- College of St Benedict & St John's University (Minnesota)
- College of the Holy Cross (Massachusetts)
- College of St. Scholastica (Minnesota)
- Creighton University (Nebraska)
- DePaul University (Illinois)
- Duquesne University (Pennsylvania)
- Emmanuel College (Massachusetts)
- Fairfield University (Connecticut)
- Fontbonne College (Missouri)
- Fordham University (New York)
- Franciscan University of Steubenville (Ohio)
- Gannon University (Pennsylvania)
- Georgetown University (District of Columbia)
- Gonzaga University (Washington)
- Incarnate Word College (Texas)
- John Carroll University (Ohio)
- Lasalle University (Pennsylvania)
- Le Moyne College (New York)
- Lewis University (Illinois)
- Loyola College (Maryland)
- Loyola Marymount University (California)
- Loyola University Chicago (Illinois)
- Manhattan College (New York)
- Marquette University (Wisconsin)
- Marymount University (Virginia)
- Mercyhurst College (Pennsylvania)
- Molloy College (New York)
- Notre Dame University (Indiana)

- Pontifical Catholic University of Puerto Rico (Puerto Rico)
- Providence College (Rhode Island)
- Quincy University (Illinois)
- Rockhurst College (Missouri)
- St. Ambrose University (Iowa)
- St. Anselm College (New Hampshire)
- St. Bonaventure University (New York)
- St. Edward's University (Texas)
- St. John's University (New York)
- St. John's University of Collegeville (Minnesota)
- St. Joseph College (Connecticut)
- St. Joseph College (Indiana)
- St. Joseph's College (Maine)
- St. Joseph University (Pennsylvania)
- St. Louis University (Missouri)
- St. Mary-of-the-Woods College (Indiana)
- St. Mary's College (California)
- St. Mary's College (Indiana)
- St. Mary's University (Minnesota)
- St. Michael's College (Vermont)
- St. Thomas University (Florida)
- St. Vincent College (Pennsylvania)
- St. Xavier University, Chicago (Illinois)
- Santa Clara University (California)
- Seattle University (Washington)
- Seton Hall University (New Jersey)
- Spring Hill College (Alabama)

- Stonehill College (Massachusetts)
- Thomas More College (Kentucky)
- University of Dallas (Texas)
- University of Dayton (Ohio)

This gives a general sense of who is out there.

Boston College
http://infoeagle.bc.edu/

No one needs to convince Boston College, the Jesuit-run school, to take advantage of the electronic communications revolution. The school has built a network of computers, with one installed in every student's room.

Founded by the Society of Jesus in 1863, Boston College operates a 115-acre main campus, in a suburban setting just six miles from downtown Boston. Its towering gothic buildings surrounded by campus green spaces provide a tranquil atmosphere for its 8,500 undergraduate and 4,300 graduate and professional students. BC boasts an international student body that comes from all 50 states and 90 countries. There is much to learn about Boston College on this site—information about faculty, summer sessions, advanced degrees, facilities, athletics, and libraries. Boston College confers more than 3,500 degrees annually through its 11 schools and colleges. Bachelor's degrees are offered in 50 fields of study through the College of Arts and Sciences. The site addresses its "connectivity to the Internet and electronic mail." The Boston College Web visitor is invited to explore Boston College through various links. Also on the site is information about undergraduate degree programs, student life, cost and financial aid, and the application process.

DePaul University

http://www.depaul.edu/

DePaul University derives its title and fundamental mission from Saint Vincent de Paul, the founder of the Congregation of the Mission, a religious community whose members, Vincentians, established and continue to sponsor DePaul.

Since its founding by the Vincentian Fathers in 1898, DePaul University's hallmark has been its foundation of Catholic and Vincentian values. The Vincentians endowed the university "to foster in higher education a deep respect for the God-given dignity of all persons, especially the materially, culturally and spiritually deprived; and to instill in educated persons a dedication to the service of others." DePaul serves more than 17,000 students in day, evening, and weekend programs at five locations in the Chicago metropolitan area. Eight colleges and schools offer a range of academic and professional programs on site or via distance learning.

DePaul states as its central purposes its dedication to teaching, research, and public service. When admitting students, the university says it focuses on intellectual potential and academic achievement. It also says it seeks diversity in students' special talents, qualities, interests, and socioeconomic background. This site highlights the background, purposes, and programs at DePaul.

Fordham University

http://www.fordham.edu/

Founded in 1841, Fordham is New York's City's Jesuit University, attracting more than 14,000 students annually to its 10 undergraduate, graduate, and professional schools. Fordham's Jesuit tradition "encourages students to develop both intellectually and ethically, emphasizing that learning encompasses all aspects of life." With residential campuses at Lincoln Center in Manhattan and Rose Hill in the north Bronx, as well as academic centers in Tarrytown and Armonk,

New York, the university offers Bachelor's, Master's and doctoral programs.

This Web page offers the basic information about Fordham, including admissions, campus life, maps, financial aid, and alumni school bulletins. One interesting aspect of the Fordham Web page is its links to other home pages created by Fordham students. "Cognizant of the educational importance of hands-on experience with the Internet, Fordham University encourages members of the Fordham Community to experiment with creating and maintaining personal World Wide Web pages," the site says. "Links from this page are to the personal home pages of Fordham students, staff and faculty." Of course, the university is quick to offer a disclaimer—as it must—that these (student and faculty) pages "do not in any way constitute official Fordham publications."

Once again, the visitor finds the tug of war between support for freedom of speech and the instinct to censor offensive material. The Internet is causing headaches for censorship advocates. Fordham appears to be staking out ground in the middle. On the one hand, it is offering links to the home pages to all students and faculty; on the other, it is taking "offensive" material off the Web when it is encountered.

Jesuit Secondary Education

http://www.math.luc.edu/~vande/sj/sj_high.html

This Web site contains a list of Jesuit high schools. As the Jesuits will tell you, "the apostolate of secondary education has been very important to the Society of Jesus almost since its founding." For many years the Jesuit order in the United States recruited from its high schools. That is, some of the brightest Jesuit high school graduates went to Jesuit seminaries. This has changed somewhat. In the late 1960s and early 1970s, many priests began to leave the religious life. Jesuit high schools, meanwhile, that were drawing a dozen or more novices into their order, mostly from Jesuit high schools, found their numbers dropping dramatically. Today, the Society of Jesus in the United States is finding the same replacement problems that other religious orders are finding—the older Jesuits are dying off faster than young, new Jesuits are being found to replenish the ranks.

This Web site contains not only the names and addresses of U.S. Jesuit high schools, but others around the world. The names of U.S. schools are broken down by state. Jesuit schools in other countries are also on these pages, with requests for the names and addresses of still more schools to fill out the lists. Finally, it should be noted that the page is maintained by Jesuit Father Richard VandeVelde of the Department of Mathematics at Loyola University of Chicago. Like many other home pages, this one appears to be the personal hobby—and/or passion—of a Web junkie.

Georgetown University

http://www.georgetown.edu/

Founded by the Jesuits in 1789, Georgetown University is the oldest Catholic institution of higher learning in the United States. Located just minutes away from the activities that go on in the nation's capitol, Washington, D.C., Georgetown has emerged as one of the most attractive Catholic universities. The Georgetown Web page provides standard information about the university: admissions, schools (Georgetown College, Graduate School of Arts and Sciences, School of Business, Edmund A. Walsh School of Foreign Service, Law Center, School of Medicine, School of Nursing, Graduate Public Policy Program, School for Summer and Continuing Education), faculty, publications, student life, alumni, athletics, etc. It also offers a special fact sheet to answer the most frequently asked questions about Georgetown, such as "What's a Hoya?"

The Georgetown Web site, rich and active, is updated frequently and solicits suggestions for visitors. Not only does the site provide abundant information about the university in an easy-to-read format, it offers its own and other guides to the World Wide Web. Additionally, it provides Web authoring tools, directories of Net and Web resources, a Web virtual library, and a Web consortium of home pages. Visiting the Georgetown Web site, then, is akin to stopping off at a local AAA before going on a trip. The difference may be the excitement of discovery along the way. On the Web, as much as one might want to go directly to some location, the temptation is to take a side trip along the way. The Web's abundance will likely distract the most determined travelers.

Georgetown Preparatory School
http://www.gprep.pvt.k12.md.us/s

The Web explosion has meant that hundreds of Catholic high schools now have sites. They are on the Web for the same reasons as most other Catholic educational institutions: to get their message out to the public. That said, Georgetown Preparatory School is unlike other Catholic high schools. It makes the claim of being the nation's oldest Jesuit high school. Founded in 1789 by America's first Catholic bishop, Georgetown Prep is the only Jesuit boarding school in the United States. Although it shares roots with Georgetown University and at one time was located on the same campus in downtown Washington, D.C., Georgetown Prep is now a separate and independent institution. Since 1919, Georgetown Prep's campus has been located on 92 acres of rolling hills and woodland in North Bethesda, Maryland. There are currently some 430 students at Georgetown Prep, just under 100 of whom are resident students who come to Prep from throughout the United States and around the world.

The day I looked at it, the Georgetown Prep Web site noted that it was "undergoing major changes." So what's new? Besides basic information on the school and its history, the site headlines Jesuit philosophy, its publications, people, and technology. With bright students getting on the Web, a high school home page is just another playground. Stay tuned here.

Marquette University High School

http://muhs.edu/

First a disclaimer. While I like this Web site I feel I must say up front this is my alma mater. I graduated from MUHS in 1962. I am pleased to see the old school is still breaking new ground, not that it is unique among high schools on the Web, but its pages appear to have special spunk. They are informative and fun, perhaps showing that an interesting home page should be appealing in more ways than one. Certainly high school home pages ought to reflect the fun high school students have when they are not cracking books.

A few words on Marquette High: It is a four-year, Jesuit-run, college preparatory school located in Milwaukee, Wisconsin. This is the way the MUHS Web site speaks of the traditional approach to Jesuit education: "This tradition emphasizes a comprehensive study of the liberal arts and a commitment to social awareness. The Jesuit tradition also stresses a conception of personal growth and habits of self-discipline, which are all fostered in an atmosphere that is pointedly Christian by work and practice."

The Marquette Web site offers information about the school, its history, when students can take the school's entrance exam, faculty and teacher–student ratio (1:15). Some 907 students from 150 primary schools in five countries were enrolled at Marquette last year. Non-Catholic enrollment ran at 19%. The site also has information on alumni, the school's calendar, news events, school athletics, and, of course, Jesuit vocations.

Creighton University

http://bluejay.creighton.edu/

Located in Omaha, Nebraska, Creighton is a Catholic university operated by the Jesuits. It has an enrollment of approximately 6,300. Creighton enrolls students in the following schools: the Colleges of Arts and Sciences and Business Administration, the Graduate School, University College and schools of Nursing, Medicine, Law, Pharmacy and Allied Health Professions, Dentistry, and Summer Sessions.

Much like other university home pages, the Creighton University home page provides basic information about admissions, college and schools, libraries, student life, athletics, etc. The Creighton home page, however, also acts like a big tent to students, faculty, and others associated with the institution who want to express themselves, as part of Creighton's family, on the Web. Participation is invited, and the result is a lively mix of Web life. The approach highlights the basically democratic nature of the Web. Creighton understands this and uses it to its advantage.

The university's Web guidelines, the Creighton site notes, are intended to provide a framework for providing university information in an appropriate, consistent, and user-friendly manner while allowing flexibility for university departments and personnel who publish information that is linked to the university's home page.

Who are the intended audiences of the Creighton home page? Looking at university home pages, I found myself sometimes asking the same question. Creighton spells it out: "Creighton University's Home Page Committee has identified several audiences that the University Web pages are intended to serve. These audiences in priority order are: 1. Prospective Students 2. Current Students 3. Alumni 4. Parents of Current and Prospective Students 5. Creighton University Faculty and Staff 6. Professional Educators/ Academic Communities 7. Friends of Creighton.

The bottom line, it appears, is building for the future.

Religion and Philosophy Resources on the Internet

http://web.bu.edu/STH/Library/contents.html

I found this presentation of Religion and Philosophy on the Internet impressive. It was created by Sara A. Memmott, former Religion and Philosophy Bibliographer at the Mugar

Library of Boston University. She knows her subject matter. The stated purpose of this guide is to provide a selected listing of local and worldwide Internet sources for religion and philosophy. The author then briefly comments on each item to provide guidance. The visitor is requested to view this list as a "starting point" of interesting and important general resources rather than an attempt to list everything available.

St Bernard Prep School
http://iquest.com/~deesqrd/saint/SBP.html

This site is another example of how a preparatory school can use the Web to recruit students. As the popularity of the Internet grows, these sites will become increasingly effective in achieving their stated purpose. Because many on the Web are both academically oriented and relatively affluent, preparatory schools will find the Web a good recruiting environment.

St. Bernard Preparatory School is a co-ed, grade 9–12 college prep school operated by the Benedectine monks of the Saint Bernard Abbey. It is located in the mountain lakes region of northern Alabama, about an hour's drive north of Birmingham. The stated purpose of St. Bernard Preparatory School is to help students become intellectually alert, socially responsible, physically healthy, and spiritually awake. This site provides information on the school, including the higher-than-average student test scores. This is an attractive site. Other schools may find themselves imitating the simple straightforward presentation of this site.

Math for a Change
http://www.luc.edu/or/sj/misc/mathchange.html

Two mathematics teachers, one from each of the Jesuit high schools in the Chicago area, have authored a text that supplements mathematics courses by giving real-world examples. These examples deal with socially relevant issues like AIDS, teenage pregnancy, world population, inflation, and women on welfare. This text has also resulted in another text with student-generated examples.

Math for a Change is written for teachers of mathematics at the secondary school level to assist them in making their students more aware of world injustices and to make their teaching more interesting and effective. The book describes 41 situations of injustice that need mathematics in order to be fully understood. They tell of poor children in Peru who never get a chance to play and of kids in our own country who play around with what should be taken seriously. The authors of Math for a Change are Kevin Mistrik of Loyola Academy in Wilmette, Illinois, and Robert Thul, S.J. of St. Ignatius College Prep in Chicago, Illinois. The site offers information about this special teaching text and the costs of purchase.

CHAPTER 8

Communications

This chapter is all about sharing. The word *communication* stems from the Latin word *communicatus*, meaning shared, or to hold in common. Communication, then, is the interchange or sharing of thoughts. It is derived from the same root word as Communion, which is the sharing of the Body and Blood of Jesus. The ideas of sharing, of common responsibility, of common education, of finding God in community—all these are very Catholic ideas. The notion of the Communion of saints, the idea that the living and dead are one in the Body of Christ, is central to Catholic belief. This chapter, then, is a most Catholic chapter. It is about how Catholics teach and help each other in the faith, how they pass it from generation to generation.

There is a particularly "communal" aspect to every site that appears in this chapter. These sites, of course, appear in a broader context of communication and communion that is developing on the World Wide Web among Catholics as they encounter each other, often for the first time beyond traditional limitations of geographical distance and national boundaries. For a church that proclaims a universal message— calling the faithful to holiness, compassion, justice, and mercy—the Web is providing a revolutionary setting in which faith sharing is taking place. As Catholicism enters its third millennium, the technological communication upheaval is affording Catholics bold new opportunities to celebrate the Spirit in interconnected Christian communities. It is an exciting time for this communal religion.

Pope John Paul II on Communications

http://listserv.american.edu/catholic/church/papal/jp.ii/
computer-culture.html

The Vatican, normally viewed as holding fast to old ways, has quickly and comfortably embraced the Internet; as this book shows, it has several Web sites and is among the more active on the Catholic institutions on the Internet.

Few underestimate Pope John Paul II's ability to communicate his message of holiness and sanctification to the world. He has seen himself primarily as a missionary to the world, having taken more than 75 trips abroad during his pontificate. He wants to reach out to the world's peoples. To this end, he has not only traveled but published books, including prayer books. He was also quick to understand the possibilities for communication made possible by emerging electronic technologies. As this site indicates, the Pontiff has embraced the computer age.

Speaking May 27, 1989, World Communications Day, the Pope shared his thoughts about new technologies, focusing on how they could be put to use on behalf of the mission of the Church. This site features the text of Pope John Paul's World Communications Day talk—complete, of course, with hypertext links.

Consortium Ethics Program: Temple University

http://astro.temple.edu/~dialogue/

The site includes information about the Center for Global Ethics and deals with an effort to forge a global ethic to build mutual understanding and world peace. Or, in the words of the site's author, "build ecumenical bridges to prepare for the next millennium as a period of mutual understanding, respect, and enrichment." As part of this effort, two Catholic scholars, Father Hans Kung, a noted European theologian, and Leonard Swidler, a professor at Temple University, address the global ethic effort.

It was in 1992 that the Council for a Parliament of the World's Religions in Chicago commissioned Kung to draft a "Declaration of the Religions for a Global Ethic." Kung has worked on the project since. The idea is to write an ethical declaration of religions that could later be followed by a general world declaration. These declarations would include binding values, irrevocable standards, and interior fundamental attitudes that the world's leaders could agree on and live by.

SisterSite

http://www.maxwell.syr.edu/maxpages/faculty/msthomps/sisters.htm

SisterSite proposes to serve as a clearinghouse for information on women's religious congregations, the history of religious life, and the contemporary concerns of women in church and society. While its content and focus is primarily Catholic, it also hopes to serve the needs of those in other religious traditions.

SisterSite is an outgrowth of sister-l, an Internet discussion group founded in 1994 that currently has almost 900 subscribers. Initially started for the purpose of addressing the "history and contemporary concerns of Catholic women religious," sister-l has expanded to welcome an eclectic range of both topics and subscribers, including married and single (as well as vowed and ordained) women and men from many Christian (and other) denominations. SisterSite reflects this diversity, as well as an ongoing openness to new directions.

SisterSite states a twofold mission. The first is to serve as a central clearinghouse for links to relevant Web sites, including a large list of home pages for congregations of nuns and sisters, those for individual sisters and other participants in sister-l, some of their ministries (including colleges, hospitals, and other institutions), and efforts under the sponsorship of congregations. Additionally, there will be links to sites that contribute to broader insight and action on behalf of women's concerns, social justice, and ministry. Other "linklists" will connect SisterSite users to sites focusing on publishing and scholarship relevant to these purposes in fields such as theology, women's studies, and history.

Second, SisterSite plans to provide a place where new scholarship and creative efforts relating to religious life can be made widely available and a forum where such efforts can be fostered and advanced. Writers are invited to submit drafts of work-in-progress so that others may read and comment on them; unpublished conference papers and talks will also be presented. This is also a place to announce new books and relevant periodical articles or reviews, as well as upcoming conferences and workshops of interest to sisters and religious women.

ParokiNet

http://www.parokinet.org/

This site contains information about ParokiNet, an international mailing list for the purposes of discussing issues related to Christian faith, particularly from Catholic perspectives. Membership comes from all over the world including the United States, the U.K., Canada, Indonesia, Australia, New Zealand, Japan, the Netherlands, France, Thailand, the Philippines, Italy, Switzerland, and Germany. In early 1996, several hundred members were listed.

ParokiNet was formed in November 1991 at the initiative of an Indonesian priest and several Indonesian Catholic students in United States. Membership is open to persons from anywhere of any religion who wish to participate in the discussion and fill out a registration form.

According to the site, the scope of discussions is quite broad. Any topic that would be of interest to several members is welcome. This is an unmoderated mailing list. The site provides basic information on the function of the list and information about participating clergy and religious.

This site is an interesting example of how the Internet is bringing Catholics of different nationalities together around topics of similar interest. Consider, for a moment, what it would be like to be a Catholic in Muslim-dominated Indonesia. Being able to communicate inexpensively with other Catholics, also largely isolated on the thousands of islands that make up Indonesia, would be a great boon.

Topics discussed include: Abortion, Euthanasia, Interreligious Marriage, Christmas, Easter, Purgatory, Sacrament of Reconciliation, the Sacraments, How to Read and Understand the Bible, Adultery, Women Priests, Personal Sharing on Scriptures and in Poetry, Genetic Engineering, the Book of Genesis, Celibacy, and Humor.

UNDA International

http://www.catholic.org/orgs/unda-int/

Founded in 1928, *Unda* (the Latin word for *wave*) is the international Catholic Association for Radio and Television. This is its official site. UNDA International, legally registered in Switzerland with its General Secretariat in Belgium, represents 139 national and 26 international Catholic associations of various international organizations.

"UNDA," the site states, "coordinates a network engaged in broadcasting and provides them with a forum for professional collaboration. It also networks with comparable Catholic and non-Catholic organizations. UNDA enjoys consultative status with UNESCO, ECOSOC (United Nations Committee on Economic, Social and Cultural Rights), and with the Council of Europe."

The site features information about UNDA, its membership, aims, objectives, regional and international activities, publications, and address. Also on the site is information about UNDA's next World General Assembly, to be held in Montreal, Canada, in 1998.

1996 Catholic Media Directory

http://www.nd.edu/~theo/RCD/Directory5.html

This site provides a wealth of information about Catholic communications throughout the world, including print, broadcast, and electronic services. The site, the work of Kern Trembath of the Theology Department at Notre Dame University, was created as an aid to diocesan and church communications. The site warns, however, that it is a partial file and that the full file is available in the April 1996 PJ Kennedy Official Catholic Directory.

Our Sunday Visitor

http://128.235.249.100/RCC/Periodicals/OSV/indexosv.html

Crisis Online

http://www.catholic.net/RCC/Periodicals/Crisis/index.html

Cross Fire Magazine

http://pages.map.com/~david/crossfire.html#Table of Contents

Our Sunday Visitor is one of several national Catholic weeklies. It is considered middle-of-the-road to conservative and is noted for its colorful feature articles. This site allows the visitor to sample some of these articles and to order the publication. A toll-free number is provided on the site.

This site allows the visitor to get free issues of *Crisis Magazine*, a Catholic monthly noted for its analysis of Church matters. The viewpoint of the publication is generally conservative, with articles covering both church matters and those in the wider society.

Cross Fire Youth Ministry Magazine, a little more than one year old, is an online publication aimed at youth. It states that it is committed to the spread of the Gospel, with an emphasis on the concerns and needs of young people and those dedicated to ministry of youth. In the Gospel of Matthew, Jesus challenges us all to "go, then, to all peoples everywhere and make them my disciples." Through the technology of the Internet, *Cross Fire* states that it intends to respond to this call with an attempt to communicate greater awareness of issues affecting today's youth. The publication is looking for submissions and provides information both about writing for and reading this new effort.

EWTN

http://www.ewtn.com/

This is the site of Eternal Word Television Network (EWTN), a superconservative broadcasting network run by the colorful and always provocative Mother Angelica. Her order, the Poor Clare Nuns of Perpetual Adoration, moved to Birmingham, Alabama, the site of her network, after Mother Angelica established Our Lady of the Angels Monastery in the suburb of Irondale in 1962. In 1973, she began to write various books on the spiritual life, which the nuns printed and distributed all over the world. When she was given the opportunity to make video tape programs for television, Mother Angelica realized the impact television could have in spreading the faith. She then founded EWTN and built a television studio behind the monastery.

EWTN began airing programs on August 15, 1981, via satellite to cable companies and home satellite dishes. In 1992, Mother Angelica founded WEWN to broadcast Catholic programs worldwide via short-wave radio, in an effort, according to the site, "to help fulfill the prophecy of Revelation 14:6" ("Then I saw another Angel, flying high overhead, sent to announce the Good News of Eternity to all who live on the earth, every nation, race, language, and tribe.") In 1996, EWTN was added to the Dish Network-SM, which beams programs via satellite to small, 18-inch dishes that can be mounted on roofs. Access to WEWN's radio programs will be made available to AM/FM radio stations worldwide via satellite. EWTN also acquired the Catholic Resource Network, formerly known as CRNET, out of which has come EWTN On-line Services. Like her or not, Mother Angelica has become a highly successful broadcasting tycoon—something no U.S. bishop has managed to do.

This site provides information about the network, its programming schedule, even a list of guests lined up for Mother Angelica Live. The site encourages interaction with the network and offers daily Catholic news briefs, regular Vatican reports, and worldwide news features.

American Catholic Online
http://www2.americancatholic.org/americancatholic/

American Catholic Online is a service of St. Anthony Messenger Press and Franciscan Communications in Cincinnati, Ohio, one of America's oldest and finest publishers of popular, inspirational, and educational Roman Catholic spirituality resources. On this site the visitor will find information on Catholicism and Christianity. The site also provides information about subscribing to *St. Anthony Messenger*, the Catholic monthly magazine with more than 300,000 subscribers. The site allows the visitor to browse recent issues for articles to get a flavor of the publication. It also features books, audiocassettes, and videos for sale.

St. Bede's Publications
http://www.stbedes.org/

Saint Bede's Publications, a religious publishing company staffed by Benedictine nuns, specializes in works on monastic spirituality and theology. Recent publications, according to the site, include:

- *The Undivided Heart*, by Michael Casey, OCSO
- *To Love Fasting*, by Adalbert de Vogüé, OSB

- *The Catholics of Harvard Square*, edited by Jeffrey Wills
- *Catching the Spirit*, by Maureen McCarthy
- *In Praise of Benedict*, by Basil Cardinal Hume, O.S.B.

The site features the increasingly popular Gregorian chant and a complete title list, by book title and by author.

The American Catholic

http://www.vfr.com/tac/

This is the site of the *American Catholic*, an independent Catholic newspaper. "The *American Catholic* is a paper," the site states, "that can talk about anything that concerns American Catholics from women's issues to preaching, to rearing children and dealing with people with AIDS, to life in the parish, and diocesan funding, to what our bishops are up to and whether or not it really is connected to the faith life of the people in a particular diocese."

The *American Catholic* made its debut in June 1993. It was born not too long after the leading editors and editorial writers on the official weekly newspaper of the Archdiocese of Hartford resigned, saying policies of Archbishop Daniel A. Cronin had seriously compromised their journalistic integrity. It was born after a group of concerned Catholics published an ad in the *Hartford Courant* under the heading "Catholics for Free Press." The ad was sponsored by more than 200 Connecticut signers who stated "We, the under-signed, support a Catholic Press that is free, open, and truthful. We further support all those who have sacrificed a great deal for this vision."

The *American Catholic* publishes monthly whenever possible. It has featured:

- Texts of speeches by Joan Chittister, Charles Curran, and Matthew Fox from the national Call To Action conference

- In-depth interviews with Auxiliary Bishop Francis Murphy of Baltimore and historian John Boswell
- Inspirational pieces by theologians and prominent religious writers including Bishop Kenneth Untener of Saginaw, Michigan

The site provides subscription information to this Farmington, Connecticut, publication.

Catholic Network of Volunteer Service

http://www.catholic.net/rcc/Cnvs/cnvshome.html

Catholic Network of Volunteer Service (CNVS), challenged by the message of the Gospel, aims to promote and assist member programs serving in the United States and through-out the world. It states that it is a resource for people who feel called to volunteer service, are in service, or have returned from service. It advocates an increased role for women and men to use their gifts in service to the Church and the world. It publishes a directory, *RESPONSE*, of full-time service programs hosted by Catholic and Protestant organizations.

This site offers information about volunteering possi-bilities as well as about receiving *RESPONSE* by snail mail. The site shows many opportunities for service, from one- to five-year placements to two weeks to three months. The site also has a search engine that allows volunteers to search by type of work: domestic or international, short term or summer. A listing by age group is also available.

Catholic News Service

http://www.catholicnews.com/

This site provides information about Catholic News Service, which performs its mission, according to the site, by report-ing news that affects Catholics in their everyday lives. The role of the news service was defined from the beginning:

"The aim (of the service) is to present a continuous word and photographic picture of current Catholic events and thought everywhere, and moreover, a record of such other events and thought as are of interest to Catholics as such," stated an informational brochure of the 1930s.

Catholic News Service is the primary news service source of national and world news that appears in the U.S. Catholic diocesan press and a leading source of news for print and broadcast media throughout the world. CNS speeds news daily to clients on a satellite-delivered network that blankets the United States. The network also extends to Canada via satellite and to Australia and across Europe via bulletin boards and email, with the service provided to many other areas around the world via airmail. Almost every English-language Catholic newspaper in the world uses CNS. About 180 U.S. Catholic newspapers and broadcasters and more than 70 other news organizations in nearly 40 countries that rely on CNS touch the lives of more than 8 million people throughout the world. Vatican Radio, which broadcasts news around the globe in more than 30 languages, is among the users of the daily news report.

The site features information about Catholic News Service publications as well as information about subscribing to them.

U.S. Catholic

http://www.claret.org/~uscath/

U.S. Catholic, the site states, "is a forum for lay Catholics, covering issues of concern to Catholics in their everyday lives." Recent issues have included reports and reader surveys on the death penalty, welfare reform, and America's culture of violence.

U.S. Catholic, a Claretian publication, celebrates Catholic tradition yet embraces the spirit of Vatican II reform and rejuvenation. Each issue is a source for contemporary theological and spiritual discussions and includes an interview or investigative report of a social or religious issue. This site states that it is particularly interested in the opinions of its reading audience.

The site offers examples of articles that appear in *U.S. Catholic* as well as subscription information.

Cistercian Publications
http://www.ultranet.com/~trappist/

Cistercians are men and women who follow Saint Benedict's Rule for Monks and the Constitutions of Cîteaux. Settling in 1098 in a remote burgundian marsh (in Latin, a *cisterna*), the first Cistercians determined to live simply and to balance in their lives common prayer, personal reflection, and manual labor. For guidance they read the Bible, the writings of the Church Fathers, and the documents of centuries of Christian monasticism. The literature they created resonates their love of God and their reasoned analysis of the intensely personal experience of growth through self-knowledge to self-acceptance to the perception of God.

"Cistercian Publications," this site states, "brings the insights of these twelfth-century writers into English in its Cistercian Fathers Series." A companion Cistercian Studies Series augments these texts with translations of ancient, medieval, and modern monastic literature and works of scholarship and spirituality touching the claustral tradition. Translators work from the finest available critical scholarship and strive to strike a balance between fidelity to the original and contemporary ways of expression.

This site provides information about new and forthcoming books, the bestsellers list and ordering information.

National Catholic Reporter
http://www.natcath.com

The *National Catholic Reporter* is a lay-edited Catholic newsweekly that features up-to-date information and analysis about the Church and the wider world. Its lively features, columns, opinion pieces, and editorials engage the reader, who is invited to respond on the paper's equally lively letters pages.

NCR was founded in 1964 during the Second Vatican Council to spread the spirit and openness of the historic gathering throughout the Church. It is progressive in politics and favors Church renewal but maintains a deep spirituality that directs Christian energies toward responses to the Beatitudes and the Church's social teachings. The Web site also features back issues and invites the visitor to interact with the editors. Subscription information is also available. Daily updates on the Web site make it one of the few places on the Catholic Web where browsers can stay in touch with worldwide Catholic events. The site links with other NCR Publishing Company products, including *Celebration*, a popular monthly liturgical planner, and *Credence Cassettes*, excellent as a source of inspirational talks, meditation, and church music. This is a first-rate Web site. (Oh, yes, to maintain even a sliver of integrity, I feel obliged to disclose that I have been *NCR* editor for the past 16 years.)

Sheed & Ward

www.natcath.com/sheedward

This site features Sheed & Ward, one of the most distinguished names in Catholic publishing, which relates the history of the company, selections of its products, and information about ordering them.

Sheed & Ward, founded in London in 1928 by Frank Sheed and his wife Maisie Ward, has a long and distinguished history in Catholic publishing in this century. Since moving to the United States in the mid-1930s, Sheed & Ward has been known for publishing some of the foremost religious writers and theologians that the Catholic Church in America has produced. Sheed & Ward was instrumental in making such theologians as Hans Kung and Edward Schillebeeckx, among other prominent European theologians, known to American Catholic audiences.

Since 1985, Sheed & Ward has been a division of the National Catholic Reporter Publishing Company, carrying on the tradition of publishing some of the finest Catholic and ecumenical religious writers. Sheed & Ward publishes more than 30 new titles every year in the areas of Spirituality, Pastoral Ministry, Theology, Medical Ethics, and Moral Theology. Sheed & Ward has a commitment to publishing practical resources for the working, ministering Church; resources for small intentional faith communities, especially now working in partnership with RENEW International; stewardship programs for parish and diocesan use; catechetical materials for families and classrooms; and Sheed & Ward Electronic Publications, including SermonPrep software and the new Bitlogic format for computerized books.

Sheed & Ward's offerings on the Internet include introductions to some of their latest titles, sample articles, and useful information from ongoing projects, as well as reviews of some of their more helpful and interesting bestsellers.

Catholic Press Association
http://www.catholicpress.org/index.htm

This is the site for the Catholic Press Association of the United States, the trade and professional association of Catholic newspapers, magazines, and general publishers in North America. The CPA was established in 1911. It serves a professional Catholic press of nearly 2,000 persons who work at more than 600 publications, with a wide variety of services, meetings, publications, and special projects such as research, general promotion, and representation of Catholic press interests in postal, tax, legal, and special-interest concerns. The association headquarters are in Ronkonkoma, New York.

This site provides information about the various publications in the association and provides links to those publications with Web sites. The site also explains the purpose and services provided by the association.

Catholic Digest

http://www.CatholicDigest.org/

Notre Dame Magazine

http://www.nd.edu:80/~ndmag/

Catholic Digest publishes mostly reprints from other Catholic publications. It patterns itself after the better-know Reader's Digest. *Notre Dame Magazine* is one of the best Catholic college and university magazines. It presents interesting and often lively feature articles about Catholic life in and outside of the university. It is a quarterly publication of the University of Notre Dame. The site allows the visitor to order sample copies, to subscribe, change an address, or contact the staff regarding article suggestions. The site also offers writer's guidelines.

Sojourners Magazine

http://www.sojourners.com/sojourners/magazine.html

Sojourners states that it is more than a magazine. It represents a grassroots network for personal, community, and political transformation. Rooted in the ground of the prophetic biblical tradition, *Sojourners* brings together diverse people for reflection and action. It states that it offers old truths and new visions for changing times. *Sojourners* describes itself as a progressive Christian voice with an alternative vision for both the Church and society: "beyond both the religious right and the secular left, beyond empty piety and rootless activism, beyond individualistic and ideological religion, beyond old dogmas and new age, beyond the false choices and social walls that divide."

Sojourners includes Evangelicals, Catholics, Pentecostals, and Protestants; liberals and conservatives; blacks, whites,

Latinos, and Asians; women and men; young and old. It states that it is a group of Christians who want to follow Jesus, but who also sojourn with others in different faith traditions and all those who are on spiritual journeys. The site offers current and back issues and information on subscriptions.

Company Online

http://www.luc.edu/or/sj/Company/index.html

Company is a quarterly, nonprofit magazine of the Society of Jesus (Jesuits) in the United States. It contains stories and features of Jesuits and lay people who work with them in a variety of ministries in the United States and abroad.

Why "Company?" "*Company* is also an important Jesuit word," the site states. St. Ignatius strongly wanted his group to be known as the Company of Jesus, recalling both his own military background and the military metaphor for following Christ in the struggle of good against evil. And while the Jesuit order was called *Societas* in Latin (thus society in English), the equivalent of company was retained in many European vernaculars. A company is not a casual association, but a group of persons joined in common work or purpose or achievement. The root of *company* refers to persons who share bread—a powerful ancient symbol of life; companions are persons whose lives intertwine, whose lives depend on one another.

Company states that it hopes to tell this story and to join people together; it hopes to "inspire and unify all who are part of Jesuit work; and it hopes finally to do its part in building God's kingdom and in bringing others to share the Lord's gift to us, the bread of his own life."

Company Online provides news of Jesuit institutions and summaries of the 34th General Congregation, the world gathering of Jesuits in Rome. Also online are books of interest and feature stories as well as Jesuit resources worldwide—and a map of the provinces of Jesuits in the United States.

Salt of the Earth

http://www.claret.org/~salt/

This is the Web site of *Salt of the Earth*, a bimonthly review of social-justice issues and practical ways men and women across the United States are seeking social change.

"Each issue," the site states, "offers a toolbox of resources, strategies, and information that can help parish- and community-based organizers and volunteers fulfill the social mission of the church in their parish community through their direct service or advocacy work." The site states that *Salt of the Earth* is one way to introduce the long tradition of Catholic social teaching and the social mission of the church to the local parish community. Each issue includes an interview or investigative report of an issue of importance to the parish community. Recent issues have included reports on the welfare and immigration reform debates, violence among young people, and how America is caring for its children. The site features articles, back issues, and information about subscriptions. *Salt of the Earth* is published by the Claretian Missionaries.

The Georgia Bulletin

http://www.archatl.com/bulletin.htm

The Georgia Bulletin is the official newspaper of the Archdiocese of Atlanta. Five or six articles from each issue appear on this site, as does information of events in and around the archdiocese. The day I looked at the site I found information on an upcoming talk entitled "Social Issues and Public Morality: What Is the Catholic Role?" Also listed was a talk entitled "Alternatives to Euthanasia." And I learned that the St. Theresa Conference of St. Vincent de Paul Society was to hold a community yard sale. Web sites are linking Catholics in new and interesting ways.

Southern Catholic Review

http://www.interpath.com/~mdoyle/regnews/regnews.html

This site is remarkable. It bands together ten diocesan newspapers that span Appalachia, one of the most economically deprived regions of the nation. The region, according to some definitions, ranges from the northeastern part of the United States through Georgia. This way, a number of Catholics are linked by region and by common interest. This region of the country is not heavily Catholic. However, Catholic social agencies have operated here for decades trying to work with the local needy for social and economic reform. This site pools the resources and feature stories and information common to the ten publications and publishes them. In cyberspace, the distances and rough terrain of the mountains disappear, drawing Catholics together. Hopefully, this site will serve as an example for other Catholic organizations that might find their efforts improved by working together on the Web.

Passionist Communications' Home Page

http://www.serve.com/mass/

Passionist Communications, one of the apostolates of the Passionist Fathers of America, is the producer of the television program, *The Sunday Mass*, which can be seen every week. This site provides the schedule for the mass in local communities around the nation. Participating in the mass on television is enhanced by the official *Television Prayer Guide*, the site maintains. A 128-page book with the responsorial readings and Gospels for a particular Sunday, it also includes a brief *Homily*, or thought of the day. In the center of the book is the Order of the Mass to help one follow the mass. The book is issued twice a year, in December and May. The site provides information on obtaining a copy of the book.

Catholic Family Perspectives Weekly

http://www.vivanet.com/~jwagner/cfpw.htm

It is the intent of this weekly electronic magazine site to provide a forum for the presentation of Catholic perspectives on issues that affect families generally or the Catholic family in particular. Each issue includes several short articles written by either the editors or others. Submissions for possible inclusion in future issues of *Catholic Family Perspectives Weekly* are accepted, and an email address is given. The site also links to other Web sites of interest to Catholic families. It is the work of John F. Wagner Jr. and Helen Ann Wagner who live in Rochester, New York. They are the parents of six children, ages 4 to 14.

Oregon Catholic Press

http://www.ocp.org/

Oregon Catholic Press is a publisher of a wide variety of music and worship materials. "Its worship programs, including missals and hymnals," the site states, "are used in over one-half of all U.S. Catholic churches." The music composers, liturgists, editors, customer service representatives, and production workers at OCP comprise a wide range of talents and skills. The distinguishing characteristics of the Oregon Catholic Press workforce, according to the site, are the commitment of the members to service and production of the highest-quality products possible.

OCP is a nonprofit religious corporation, meaning that nobody "owns" the company or benefits personally from any of its profits. Because of its nonprofit status, any profits OCP makes are used to further the goals of the organization, which are religious and educational. Oregon Catholic Press is the successor of the Catholic Truth Society, an organization created in the 1920s by a handful of Oregon priests to combat anti-Catholic bigotry. Society officials published informational pamphlets about the church, organized lectures, and arranged radio broadcasts. The society also prepared articles for newspapers, including the *Catholic Sentinel,* the statewide diocesan newspaper founded in 1870 and acquired by the society in 1928.

In 1934, the society responded to a need to help Catholic parishioners better understand Sunday liturgy, which was in Latin at the time. The Society began publishing a small monthly publication called *My Sunday Missal,* which contained each Sunday's readings and prayers in English, as well as a selection of familiar hymns. After the Second Vatican Council, changes in the Church's liturgy restored congregational participation in the mass, resulting in a major increase in the demand for participation aids. To keep pace with these changes in the liturgy, *My Sunday Missal* was revised; the format was enlarged; the 12 monthly issues became nine seasonal issues; and an expanded music section was included. With this revision it was renamed *Today's Missal.*

In the 1980s, to better reflect its mission, the society changed its name to Oregon Catholic Press, or OCP. Today, Oregon Catholic Press is the largest missal publisher in the country. Its liturgical music is distributed and used in liturgies throughout the world.

Catholic Video Club

http://www.inetbiz.com:80/cvc/

Creative Communication Center

http://www.connect.net/ccca/

Videos have become one of the most popular means of religious education in the U.S. Church. Throughout parishes from coast to coast, religious education is being assisted by increasingly professional-quality videos. These sites make the wares available to both individuals and parishes.

The Catholic Video Club states that it has been serving the Catholic community since 1987, providing family and religious video programming. The site catalog contains listings, descriptions, and pictures of more than 800 videos "suitable for the family, schools, churches, and retail bookstores." The club states that it makes available complete video libraries on special purchase terms to churches and schools. These libraries may be used for lending or renting as a fund-raiser.

The Creative Communication Center is another video production company selling Catholic videos. Its site states that it is committed to the production of high-quality Catholic videos for the family. These videos include a number of productions on the lives of the saints and documentaries on the life of Pope John Paul II. The site provides information on the videos, along with order information, including mail and email addresses and telephone and fax numbers.

Catholic Joke

ftp://ns.southern.edu/people/clleeds/text/vatican.html

This site is different—it features a joke. I couldn't resist finding a place for it somewhere in this book. A couple of years back, this was the most widely distributed spoof on the Internet. The author is unknown. Originally, this work was made to look as if it were a wire service story. Most people recognized it as a joke, but apparently some were fooled.

It began, "In a joint press conference in St. Peter's Square this morning, MICROSOFT Corp. and the Vatican announced that the Redmond software giant will acquire the Roman Catholic Church in exchange for an unspecified number of shares of MICROSOFT common stock. ..."

Mother of All

http://www.ghawk.com/~wspotter/

Want to make your computer monitor more Catholic looking? This site accomplishes that by allowing the visitor to download the Mother of All screen saver.

The Mother of All home page is dedicated to the Blessed Virgin Mother. This screen saver contains many images of the Blessed Virgin Mary. It comes in two versions, and both are several megabytes in size. The full-blown version has more than 60 images and retails for $20.00. The light version contains 50 images and retails for $15.00. A portion of the proceeds benefit local charities in the Archdiocese of Baltimore.

St. Bede's Publications

http://www.stbedes.org/

Saint Bede's Publications is a religious publishing company staffed by the Benedictine nuns. It specializes in works on monastic spirituality and theology. This site introduces the visitor to Saint Bede, then goes on to list some of the house's new publications. These include books on Christian suffering, Christian mystery, and monastic formation. It also lists upcoming and recent publications, including a book by Benedictine Cardinal Basil Hume of England. A search engine is provided so the visitor can check books by title or author. Manuscript submission guidelines are also provided. Finally, the site offers links to other Catholic publishing houses. (The list of Catholic publishers on the Web is growing by the month.)

CHAPTER 9

Information

A computer magazine not long ago spoke of the "Information rush" on the Internet. For information junkies it *has* been a rush! Furthermore, Webmasters have been rushing to outdo each other in posting information on Web sites, including Catholic Web sites. Everyone, it seems, has something to say and information to share. The problem, of course, can be the development of a terminal case of information overload. (On the other hand, any good Catholic knows temperance is a cardinal virtue.) So the answer, it seems, is to know how to go after useful information, or at least mostly useful information.

In just a year or two, an enormous amount of information has become available on the World Wide Web. What follows in this chapter, then, are sites that open doorways to interesting Catholic information. These sites, of course, lead to others, so watch out! Don't become intemperate. And, oh, yes, I could not resist beginning this chapter with a list of all the Popes of Roman Catholic Church history. After all, no Catholic information banquet would be complete without one.

List of Popes

http://www.knight.org/advent/Popes/ppindx.htm

List of Cardinals

http://www.avenue.com/v/rccardn.html

The first site features a list of Roman Catholic popes. The visitor will find 265 names on this list. However, not all Catholic lists carry that number. At times, two or more popes have contested leadership of the Church, and this leaves room on many Catholic lists for some discrepancy. The Church has been blessed with some great popes; the truth is it has had more than its share of scoundrels, too. This list, in any case, takes the visitor through 20 centuries of history—and is impressive in anyone's book.

The list of current cardinals gives detailed information (name, nationality, age, and date of birth) of each. It also lists the year each became a cardinal and tells current and past ecclesiastical positions. "Cardinal" is a purely honorary title because the only thing a cardinal can do that a bishop cannot do is vote for a pope in a conclave. Canon law, meanwhile, states that there can be no more than 120 active cardinals, and only cardinals under the age of 80 can vote. Those over 80 keep the title but have no extra ecclesial clout.

Tad Book's List

http://davinci.marc.gatech.edu/catholic/web/

This Web site is the work of Theodore Book, a student in computer science at Georgia Tech in Atlanta. He has a bright future in computers. Among the Catholic sites on this directory are some that link the visitor to Catholic authors. Also on this list are some links to European Catholic sites. It is helpful—but not required—for visitors to this site to read Spanish and German. The directory begins with Art and Architecture, Bibles and Books, and moves through to Saints and Spiritual Resources to Student Organizations.

Catholic Files

http://listserv.american.edu/catholic/

The Web sites on this directory were compiled piecemeal by a group called the Free Catholic Mailing List, which has existed as an electronic mailing list (catholic@american.edu) and on Usenet (or Net News) as bit.listserv.catholic. The two are mirror images of each other. This is another of the growing number of directories available to Catholics wanting to find more links and lists. Maintained by Ed Sayre, it has one of the better lists of religious orders. This site appears to be updated regularly.

Documents of the Roman Catholic Church

http://listserv.american.edu/catholic/church/church.html

This site features Catholic documents, pure and simple. It is a thorough source of information of Church documents, including those from the Council of Trent (moved the Church to the right) and the Second Vatican Council (moved the Church to the left). Also listed here are major encyclicals, Vatican statements, U.S. bishop statements, and excerpts from the new Catechism. This site provides an overview of important Catholic documents. I was especially pleased to find many of the writings of Pope John XXIII on this site. They don't show up on some of the more conservative Catholic Web sites.

Ecclesia Web Service

http://www.usbusiness.com/

A parish youth minister from St. Luke's Parish in Stroudsburg, Pennsylvania, Scott Fabian, a modern Catholic missionary/ pioneer on the Internet, organized this site in early 1995 as a free resource and conferencing area for other parish youth ministers in the United States and beyond. Fabian's Web service is devoted to providing quality Web sites to Catholic organizations and promoting Catholic research and networking on the Internet. Many of the directories on the Web are labors of love of individuals or small groups who want to help others make sense of the Web. Ecclesia appears to fall into this category. It sponsors several Web sites, including the Catholic Internet Directory. When the history of the Catholic Internet is written, Fabian deserves a special place. One sentence might read: "He was there early and he was always generous."

Mission Net's Catholic Resource Mall

http://www.missionnet.com/~mission/cathlc/home.html

This is a general Catholic information site. There are scores of links on this site, each with information about some aspect of the Catholic Church. These links include Bible Study, Books, Literature, and Audio and Video Tapes. They also include Catholic newspapers and magazines. Under Catholic Information, many Catholic links are cited. Other categories of sites here include Convents, Monasteries, Religious Orders, Devotional Prayers, Diocesan and Parish Connections, and Family and Marriage sites. For those interested in Mary, the Saints, Spiritual Conferences, and Apparitions, there are also plenty of sites listed. The weakness of this site index is that it lacks order. Most information junkies, however, will find it interesting. Mission Net is located in Metamora, Illinois. Many of the links on this site have a Midwestern tie.

1997 World Youth Day Unofficial Site

http://www.stjean.com/wyd/wyd.html

This is one of the growing number of sites dedicated to a particular event, in this case World Youth Day 1997, which is to be held in August in Paris, France. The way this site—and others like it—works is that before the event they contain information about signing up, accommodations, programs, transportation, and lodging. As the event gets closer, schedules and program updates are added. During the event, frequent news information is added and then followed by summary articles and other wrap-up information. The site then stays online indefinitely as a kind of historical reference. (The Pope's 1995 U.S. visit spawned several sites like this.)

As for this site, the information listed one year before Paris was still sketchy. Visitors were simply asked to contact "your diocesan youth ministry office." Other contacts in France and at the Vatican were also offered. Form-driven mail was available to get information. The Vatican's Pontifical Council for the Laity, which sponsors the event, was also offering information about a twice-a-year magazine entitled *Youth-Church-Hope*, which contains much information about World Youth Days. The site also featured words from Pope John Paul II and links to other Catholic French sites of interest, including two of my favorites, Information about Some Monasteries in France and Information about Taizé, an ecumenical order that inspires the young from around the world. (On a personal note, I would encourage any visitors to World Youth Day 1997 to spend several days at Taizé; it is a real spiritual lift.)

CICI Super Search Page
http://www.catholic.net/RCC/homepage/Searchpage.html

This site, by the Catholic Information Center on Internet, is an all-purpose Catholic Web site search engine. This means that simply by following the instructions on the site the visitor can find all sorts of information from Catholic Web sites. It's a working Catholic Internet directory. If the visitor is unfamiliar with Web searches, help is available on the site by activating a search without an entry. If you want to search the bible for a specific passage, this site makes it possible. It also links to standard Web search engines. It is an excellent information page.

MinistryLink

http://www.physics.csbsju.edu/sot/MinistryLink/

This site is one of the most useful ministry sites on the Web. It essentially works as a Catholic ministries classified. This site is an online database of employment opportunities in the Church sponsored by Saint John's School of Theology and Seminary. MinistryLink consists of brief descriptions of the following categories: Work Needed, Positions Available, and Volunteer Organizations, all to tweak the imagination. For information to be submitted for inclusion in a database, snail mail and email addresses are offered. There is nothing complex about this site; in fact, its simplicity makes it work. And when I looked at it, no costs were involved. Some databases work by trying to get folks hooked on the service only to charge for it later. To this point, MinistryLink appears to be, well, a voluntary ministry—and only that.

Amazing Facts

http://www.nj.com/popelow/bio.html

While this site does not quite meet the "Ripley's Believe it or Not" standard, it does provide some interesting information about the man who heads the Roman Catholic Church, His Holiness Pope John Paul II. It appears this information was gathered when the Pope came to New Jersey in the fall of 1995. I don't want to steal the thunder from this site by revealing all that is here. However, allow me to share with you the fact that John Paul II is the first non-Italian pope in 455 years and the youngest elected pope of this century. You get the drift.

Librarian's Guide

http://www.sau.edu/CWIS/Internet/Wild/Majors/Religion/
Catholic/catindex.htm

This site is intended to help the faculty at St. Ambrose University in Davenport, Iowa, but it is a blessing to all Catholic researchers who visit it. Marylaine Block, who apparently put this index together, deserves an award for some fine pioneering in the area of electronic libraries.

Consider this site a grand reference room where Catholics can come and find information about Catholic matters by searching the Internet. The nice thing is that the site visitor can do this from his or her desk in the den of a home rather than having to travel to Davenport. No doubt, this is not the final word. Ms. Block, on the site, pleads for more ideas and information from faculty. What I like about the site is its apparent openness and eagerness to serve researchers in any way possible. In this light, the site carries on an almost sacred tradition begun ages ago in monastic libraries, where sacred documents were kept for careful research. I would keep an eye on this site.

United States Catholic Bishops Search

http://www.catholic.org/bishops/data/index.html

U.S. Catholic School Database Search

http://www.catholic.org/cen/data/bwdbw1.htm

We are all familiar with political campaigns for various issues from welfare reform to deficit reductions. At the end of each political pitch, the targeted person is encouraged to contact one's local senator or congressperson. Telephone numbers and mailing addresses are provided. The result: We know how to contact our political representatives.

But who knows how to contact one's ecclesial leaders? The Bishops Search site is the answer. It names all the U.S. bishops, states their positions, and the Sees they head or work in. It further provides fax and telephone numbers and email addresses. There is no longer any reason to be out of touch with the shepherds of the church. This is a useful site created by Catholic Online, the California-based Internet organization that has a strong presence on the World Wide Web.

By the way, want to contact your old Catholic high school but have forgotten the address? The second site—U.S. Catholic School Database Search—is a useful database for U.S. Catholic schools. The inquiry can begin with a simple word search, even partial words, and lead to old friends not seen or heard from since graduation.

On-Line Catholic Related Companies

http://www.cs.cmu.edu/people/spok/catholic/companies.html

The several dozen companies on this site make up a kind of electronic Catholic shopping mall. These are Web pages for commercial establishments that may be of interest to Catholics or that make a special effort to market to a Catholic clientele. Catholic businesses that want to be on this list can contact it by email, providing a URL and a brief description of their business.

Pope John Paul II Commemorative Coin

http://www.cyberearth.com/popecoin/

This site is not for everyone. It is dedicated to the selling of 24-karat gold-plated and pure silver-plated commemorative coins of Pope John Paul II. The coins, the visitor is told, come in protective plastic capsules. Special prices are offered to churches that sell the coins as part of a fund-raising effort.

PART III

Catholic Activism

Part III of this book gathers together Web sites of individuals and organizations who fall into the very large and (by necessity) loosely defined category of "activists." In Chapter 10, we look at those whose agendas include peace, justice, and preservation of the environment. Chapter 11 holds more closely to specifically Catholic issues, with sites related to Church renewal, especially as it has developed since Vatican II. Chapter 12 focuses on perhaps the most hotly contested field of conflict and activism in modern Catholicism—pro-life movements, including of course those that address abortion and euthanasia as well. Chapter 13 has as its topic ministry sites that serve Catholics, or that Catholics run as services. And Chapter 14 describes those sites concerned with evangelization—spreading the Good News.

CHAPTER 10

Peace, Justice, and the Environment

The call to Christian service is as old as the Sermon on the Mount. Compassion is at the heart of the Gospel. Christians know they are called to love others as they love themselves. A tall order!

Meanwhile, Catholic social teachings, a collection of statements by popes, bishops, and theologians over the past hundred years, is helping Catholics rediscover the importance of service and love. These teachings are changing the way Catholics look at their roles in the world. They are learning anew that they must become involved in efforts to build a more compassionate, more just, and more peaceful world.

The Web sites in this chapter are aimed at giving Catholics more effective tools to achieve these ends. While many of these sites have been designed and run by Catholics, many others are simply sites that Catholic activists have found useful in their justice- and peace-building efforts. The approximately five dozen sites listed here can be considered foundational—they address basic social issues. At the same time, they lead to hundreds of other useful and informative sites. Spending time among these Web sites, I came to the realization that the Church is entering a new and dynamic phase of global networking. It is a phase made possible through relatively inexpensive and effective communications on the Web. The potential begins to leap out from the pages of this book—and, as you will likely find, from Web sites listed in this chapter.

Progressive Directory
http://www.igc.apc.org/igc/igc.html

The U.S. bishops have written: "The quest for justice arises from loving gratitude for the saving acts of God and manifests itself in the wholehearted love of God and neighbor." ("Economic Justice for All," 1986). Pope Paul VI had this to say: "If you want peace, work for justice." Whether out of self-interest or for the well-being of the larger community, the justice quest is essential and must be on the Christian, and Catholic, agenda.

But how to get involved? How does one learn the "issues" beyond newspaper headlines and CNN news? It requires getting connected and knowing where to go for information. It means learning the organizations and developing political skills. This is where the Progressive Directory comes in and becomes a useful tool. This is the activist's gateway to resources worldwide.

The work of the Institute for Global Communications, this directory features five networks, each with an enormous amount of information on progressive organizations, from bulletin boards and discussion groups to issues analysis and organization profiles. The five networks are PeaceNet, EcoNet, ConflictNet, LaborNet, and WomensNet.

The institute aims, it states, "to expand and inspire movements for environmental sustainability, human and workers' rights, nonviolent conflict resolution, social and economic justice, and women's equality by providing and developing accessible computer-networking tools." IGC is the U.S. member and a founding member of the Association for Progressive Communications, a nonprofit organization. Journalists and others who need to stay informed on a host of social and economic issues keep returning to this Web site. This rich information quickly opens avenues for further exploration.

Virtual Library on International Development

http://www.synapse.net/~acdi03/indexg/welcome.htm

The stated purpose of this Web page is "to support sustainable development in developing countries, in order to reduce poverty and to contribute to a more secure, equitable and prosperous world." That sounds heady, but fear not. This is a great site. It is colorful, interactive, fun-filled, and informative! There is so much information here, assembled from so many sources, that the only problem a visitor has is remembering the initial purpose of the visit. You can get lost here and end up overdosing on statistics, databases, reports, and news about Third World countries, nonprofit organizations, governments, or the latest (up-to-the-second) world population report.

This site is the work of Canada's Official Development Assistance (ODA) Office. The people there know their data, issues, and resources, and they know how to place them on the Web. I would encourage Web travelers to visit this site. One of the things I like about it is that it comes out of Canada. It lacks the normal U.S.-centric point of view. Of course, that does not keep the site from gathering information from the CIA and U.S. Census Bureau. The ODA appears eager to gather Third World data from any seemingly reliable source it can get its hands on.

This site features country profiles, an urgent action center, a "global information and early warning system," answers to frequently asked questions, emergency information notes, and *contemporary conflicts*. General information sources also include statistics from the *World Factbook 1995*, various CIA publications, and country commercial guides, to name a few. Don't miss this site. You will want to bookmark it for sure.

Diocese of Cleveland Social Action Offices

http://www.catholic-action.org/

It is said that the best-kept secret in the Catholic Church is its social teachings. What a delight to find a site that summarizes them. The hope is that the principles and ideas on this site will stimulate interest and lead to further exploration.

And what are Catholic social teachings? The site describes them as follows:

> A collection of teachings on key themes that have evolved in response to the challenges of the day that are designed to reflect the Church's social mission. This tradition calls all members of the Church, rich and poor alike, to work to eliminate the occurrence and effect of poverty, to speak out against injustice, and to shape a more caring society and a more peaceful world.

The fundamental principles of Catholic social teaching are these: All men and women are made in the image of God and have a preeminent place in the social order; human dignity can be recognized and protected only in community; a preferential love should be shown to poor people, whose needs and rights are given special attention in God's eyes. *Poor* is understood to refer to the economically disadvantaged who, as a consequence of their status, suffer oppression and powerlessness.

The work for social justice is, first and foremost, a work of faith, a profoundly religious task. It is Jesus who calls the church to this mission, not any political or ideological agenda. Some of the key themes addressed in Catholic social teachings include: economic concerns, the role of workers and owners, the rights to private property and its limitations; employment and unemployment; economic rights and initiative, debt, and development; poverty and wealth; urban and rural concerns; the common good, political responsibility, and solidarity.

Also on this site are major papal encyclicals, which are major statements popes have made on important world issues; these are part of Catholic social teachings. Meanwhile, the U.S. bishops have also spoken out on many social problems; these, too, are on this site. I highly recommend this site. It is sound, succinct, and informative. The Cleveland diocese social action offices have done the world a favor.

Parish Social Justice Tool Box

http://www.mtn.org/justice/psj.htm

This site is the work of the Archdiocese of St. Paul and Minneapolis. Here the visitor will find a variety of resources to help parishes and individual Catholics learn and do more in the arena of social justice. The site features 95 Social Concerns Resources No Parish Should Be Without and Principles from Catholic Social Teaching, Charity and Justice—examine the distinction. In a very nice move, the site lists liturgical music related to justice and peace themes, allowing liturgists to better construct justice and peace liturgies. Also here is a newsletter for parish social justice leaders. The site explains the work of the archdiocesan social justice office; it relates the office's aims, including legislative priorities and upcoming events. It connects with other Catholic justice organizations and features a quote of the week. Lots of ideas are here for Catholics working at the diocesan level in justice and peace ministries.

Food First

http://netspace.org/hungerweb/FoodFirst/index.htm

Global Network on Food Security

http://www.ncf.carleton.ca/ip/social.services/global-food/

The Food First Institute is a proven leader in the area of hunger education. The purpose of the Institute for Food and Development Policy, or Food First as it is often called, is "to eliminate the injustices that cause hunger." It sees the current globalization of food system as a threat to this effort. Food First sees its grand strategy as working to change consciousness, awakening people to the possibility of social change and their own power to bring it about.

The Institute for Food and Development Policy is an alternative "peoples" think tank with a mission to move people to take action to end the injustices that cause hunger, poverty, and environmental degradation. It attempts to do this through research, analysis, education, and advocacy about both the underlying causes of these problems and new ways to address them. Founded by Frances Moore Lappé and Joseph Collins 20 years ago, following the success of the book *Diet for a Small Planet*, the institute has an internationally recognized record of leadership on issues of food, hunger, and the environment.

Food First says it can help shed hunger eradication pessimism by showing successful cases and making the argument that the planet has the potential to amass a winning antihunger coalition. "If we can score successes in consciousness-raising, mobilization and change in the battle against the globalization of the food system, then it will be an easier next step to take on the issues of the global loss of our jobs and livelihoods," the site states. The site features, among other things, current projects, news and announcements, Food First links, publications, and information on how to become a member or intern.

The Ottawa, Canada–based Global Network on Food Security is a coalition of dozens of international antihunger organizations. The network's aim is to promote community action linked to global discussion on food security. The site offers news on hunger-related topics, background papers, upcoming global events, and information about its history. This is an excellent site for tuning into hunger issues from other than U.S. perspectives.

CatholicMobile:Hunger
http://www.mcgill.pvt.k12.al.us/jerryd/cm/poverty.htm

"We all share responsibility for the fact that populations are undernourished."

—*Pope John XXIII, 3 May 1960*

Many times over the years, I have found myself dividing the world into two groups: those who eat and those who do not.

It remains an outrage that in a world of plenty, so many go to bed hungry. Worse, millions are starving to death. The thought boggles my mind. What makes it so depressing is that the human family has the intelligence, wealth, and capability to ensure that everyone eats. What the human family lacks is the will to make it happen.

This site is all about hunger. It belongs on the Web list of every person daring to call himself or herself a religious believer. We cannot walk away from the issue of hunger. It defines who we are—or have allowed ourselves to become. And hunger is not always overseas, as documents on this site point out. It is too frequently down the block, in the neighborhood, or nearby.

There are many links on this site worth highlighting. Among these, I recommend Hunger-Related Data, Hunger in America, Hunger and Public Action, How America Fights Hunger, Ethics Updates: Literature on World Hunger, an article by Joe McConnell on wasted food and hunger, and Skip-A-Meal, a program from the Religious Studies Department of Santa Clara University. Also listed are many hunger-related organizations, including steps required to join them or volunteer.

Bread for the World

http://www.bread.org/

Bread for the World is a nationwide Christian movement that seeks justice for the world's hungry people by lobbying our nation's decision makers. Its 44,000 members write, call, and visit their members of Congress to win specific legislative changes that help hungry people and place the issue of hunger high on the nation's policy agenda.

The site features information on Bread for the World, one of the most respected lobbying groups in America. The day I looked at the site it featured this year's campaign "to make hunger among children in the United States a significant issue in this year's congressional elections." The site states that it is asking all candidates running for Congress for a commitment that, if elected, they will vote for legislation and support federal programs that will help overcome childhood hunger in this country.

The site also features the Action of the Month update, an initiative one can take toward ending childhood hunger. Bread for the World resources, including books, papers, brochures, and other materials, are also featured here. This important antihunger organization must be in the lexicon of every Catholic activist. It certainly should be bookmarked to stay abreast of lobbying initiatives against hunger.

Literature on World Hunger

http://pwa.acusd.edu/~hinman/world_hunger.html

HungerWeb

http://www.brown.edu/Departments/World_Hunger_Program/

So where does one go to become informed on the critical problem of world hunger? The reading list on this first Web page is not a bad start. This list has been assembled with great sensitivity to the issues at hand. The site is divided into four parts. The first gives some helpful links to Internet resources dealing with world hunger. The second provides a short survey of some of the more important philosophical works on world hunger. It is based on the bibliographical essay in *Contemporary Moral Issues: Diversity and Consensus*, edited by Lawrence M. Hinman (© Prentice-Hall, 1996). The third part contains short summaries of recent articles on world hunger. The author of each summary is indicated at their end. The fourth is devoted to discussion topics and term paper topics on this issue.

HungerWeb is a project of the Alan Shawn Feinstein World Hunger Program at the Watson Institute of International Studies at Brown University. Its aim is to help prevent and eradicate hunger by facilitating the free exchange of ideas and information regarding the causes of, and solutions to, hunger. This site contains both primary information, made available by the World Hunger Program and its partners, and links to other sites where information of relevance to hunger can be found.

The HungerWeb has been organized along four categories, responding to four types of interest in hunger—researchers, advocates, educators, and field workers:

- For researchers, there are research institutions, research results, and bibliographies on hunger-related research worldwide, including a compilation of hunger-related data.

- For advocates, there are advocacy organizations and materials, upcoming legislation, and fund-raising ideas.

- For educators, there are education and training syllabi, training materials and ideas for hunger education in primary and secondary schools, and undergraduate courses.

- For field workers, there are operational agencies, situation updates, reference materials, and other resources useful to those engaged in hunger prevention and mitigation in the field.

CAFOD

http://www.cafod.org.uk/cafod/fact-sh.html

CAFOD is the Catholic relief agency of the Catholic Church of England and Wales. It works in Third World nations, financing long-term development programs, such as health, education, food production, and irrigation, and it responds to emergencies overseas.

This is what its chairman, Bishop John Crowley, wrote when he recently appealed for help:

The gap between the world's richest and the world's poorest people is increasing rather than closing. Today the poorest 20 per cent of the world's population have only a 1 per cent share of world trade. The rapid pace of technological change has meant that economic growth is no longer bringing a proportionate increase in employment. Poverty and the lack of work opportunities are forcing increasing numbers to migrate at the same time as countries are tightening immigration and asylum laws. The debts of the poorest countries continue to mount, strangling any hope of economic recovery.

More than ever, the Church today must be seen to be a Church of the poor.

"In a world like ours, marked by so many conflicts and intolerable economic inequalities," wrote Pope John Paul II in his apostolic letter looking forward to the millennium, "a commitment to justice and peace ... is a necessary condition for the preparation and celebration of the Jubilee." The work of CAFOD is a powerful expression of that commitment.

This site offers information on matters that pertain to development in the Third World, including arms sales, child labor, debt, education, famine, health, land mines, racism, refugees' poverty, water, and the place of women. The work of CAFOD is worthy of support. Few North American Catholics would ever hear of its good work were it not for the World Wide Web.

Pax Christi

http://listserv.american.edu/catholic/other/paxchristi/
paxchristi.html

Pax Christi USA

http://www.utia.cas.cz/user_data/hench/px/px-intl-eng.html

These sites introduce the visitor to the international and U.S. Catholic peace organizations, Pax Christi International and Pax Christi USA. Much of the information on the former site comes from Janet Gianopoulos, who understands Pax Christi's work. The visitor learns that *Pax Christi* (Peace of

Christ) was started in 1945 as an organization of Catholics in Europe who wanted to promote reconciliation at the end of the second World War, that Pax Christi USA was founded during the Vietnam war and currently has about 12,000 members, including about 100 bishops.

Pax Christi USA priorities are listed as: spirituality of non-violence and peacemaking, disarmament, demilitarization and reconciliation with justice, economic and interracial justice in the United States, human rights, and global restoration. Pax Christi's vision grows out of Catholic faith and teachings. Members commit themselves to inform others, to affirm the ideal of nonviolent conflict resolution, and to address issues of violence, war, and oppressive structures.

Phrases Pax Christi embraces in a special way are from Jesus:

- Blessed are the peacemakers.
- Love your enemies.
- Whatever you do to these littlest of my sisters and brothers, you do to me.

The vow of nonviolence commits one to nonviolence by:

- Striving for peace with self and seeking to be a peacemaker in daily life.
- Accepting suffering rather than inflicting it.
- Refusing to retaliate in the face of provocation and violence.
- Persevering in nonviolence of tongue and heart.
- Living conscientiously and simply.
- Actively resisting evil and working nonviolently to abolish war and the causes of war.

Pax Christi USA believes that peacemaking starts on an individual level. That's why it invites people to take the vow and to apply it in their lives. Hopefully, this site will lead many to become familiar with Pax Christi USA, its ideas, and the vow of nonviolence.

Nonviolence Web

http://www.netaxs.com/~nvweb/

The Nonviolence Web, according to this Web site, is the fulfillment of a dream to bring the nonviolence community together on the Internet. On this site the visitor is a mouse click away from some favorite peace organizations, where upcoming dates, campaigns, membership information, and documents can be found. Another click links the visitor with all sorts of nonviolence Web sites throughout the world.

The Nonviolence Web is an umbrella site that tries to help the nonviolence community, even providing free typesetting and display on the Web to regional, national, and international groups working for social change through nonviolent action. "Too good to be true?" the site asks. Find out how to get your material online on the Nonviolence Web. The site says it is a completely free service for member organizations. The site is supported, it says, through grant money and volunteer labor.

There are dozens of peace organizations listed here, and quick access is possible; dozens more links take the visitor into documents, peace networks, publications, and campaigns on behalf of nonviolence. Under Organizations, the visitor finds a list with explanations, mission statements, and contacts.

Peace Tax Fund

http://www.nonviolence.org/~nvweb/peacetax/

> "The rights of conscience we could not submit to the state. We are answerable for them to our God."
>
> —*Thomas Jefferson*

This site supports a Peace Tax Fund and is the work of the National Campaign for a Peace Tax Fund, a nonprofit advocacy organization based in Washington, D.C. The campaign works solely to pass legislation that would provide a way for citizens to participate in the tax system without violating beliefs about conscience and war. It begins with a question: Is there a way to permit sincere conscientious objectors to pay their full tax obligation without violating deeply held religious or ethical beliefs? "The U.S. Peace Tax Fund Bill," the site answers, "is a proposal designed to make such accommodation and to insure that legal penalties are not imposed because of those beliefs."

The Peace Tax Fund Bill would amend the Internal Revenue Code to permit taxpayers conscientiously opposed to participating in war to have their income, estate, or gift tax payments spent for nonmilitary purposes only. The Bill excuses no taxpayers from paying their full tax liability. The percentage of an individual's taxes equaling the current military portion of the federal budget would go into a special trust fund, called the Peace Tax Fund. Money in this fund would be allocated to governmental programs such as: the Special Supplemental Food Program for Women, Infants and Children (WIC), Head Start, the U.S. Institute of Peace, and the Peace Corps.

Although conscientious objectors to war have not been forced to serve in active combat for more than 50 years, they are still required to support the military through taxation. Today, citizens who are conscientious objectors risk fines and jail sentences if they withhold taxes that support war. Some will impoverish themselves and their families rather than be legally bound to pay such taxes and thus violate their deeply held beliefs. These are people deeply driven by values borne of conscience.

Fellowship of Reconciliation

http://www.nonviolence.org/~nvweb/for/

The Fellowship of Reconciliation (FOR) is an interfaith and international movement with branches and groups in more than 40 countries and on every continent. It is composed of women and men "who recognize the essential unity of all creation and have joined together to explore the power of love and truth for resolving human conflict." The site explains that while it has always been vigorous in its opposition to war, the fellowship has insisted equally that this effort must be based on a commitment to achieving a just and peaceful world community, with full dignity and freedom for every human being.

The site states, "In working out these objectives the FOR seeks the company of people of faith who will respond to conflict nonviolently, seeking reconciliation through compassionate action." In the development of its program, the FOR states that it depends on persons who seek to apply the following principles to every area of life:

- Identify with those of every nation, race, gender, sexual orientation, and religion who are the victims of injustice and exploitation and who seek to develop resources of active nonviolence to transform such circumstances

- Refuse to participate in any war or to sanction military preparations; work to abolish war and promote good will among races, nations, and classes

- Strive to build a social order that will use the resources of human ingenuity and wisdom for the benefit of all, an order in which no individual or group will be exploited or oppressed for the profit or pleasure of others

- Advocate fair and compassionate methods of dealing with offenders against society; serve as advocates for victims of crime and their families who suffer loss and emotional anguish

- Endeavor to show respect for personality and reverence for all creation; seek to avoid bitterness and contention in dealing with controversy and to maintain the spirit of self-giving love while engaged in the effort to achieve these purposes

War Resisters League

http://www.nonviolence.org/~nvweb/wrl/

The War Resisters League affirms that all war is a crime against humanity. The site states that the league, therefore, is determined not to support any kind of war, international or civil, and to strive nonviolently for the removal of all causes of war.

Across the political spectrum—left, right, and center—everyone says they want peace. Too often, they also want a gun, an army, or a bomb to ensure they get the "right kind of peace," the site states. The War Resisters League claims it is unique because it believes, "There is no way to peace—peace is the way." It rejects the use of violence for national defense or revolutionary change. Deeply influenced by the teachings of the Indian leader Mohandas Gandhi, as well as Thoreau, Tolstoy, King, Deming, and others, the War Resisters League believes in using peaceful means to create a society that is democratic and free of economic, racial, and sexual oppression. The methods it uses range from education to demonstrations and from lobbying to direct nonviolent action.

"The nonviolence of the War Resisters League," the site states, "may seem radical simply because it is different." It goes on to say: "We know that all social change involves pain, suffering, and often tragedy. The pacifist does not deny conflict exists, but we believe nonviolence achieves social change with the least injustice and suffering because we focus on the evil of institutions rather than seeing individuals as evil."

This site features the league's philosophy and politics, program, history, and the statement of purpose of the league. It also connects with other peace resources.

Land Mines: The Human Cost

http://www.crossnet.org/temp/landmine.html

It is said a picture is worth a thousand words. This site, sponsored by the Red Cross, contains a dozen photographs graphically depicting the human impact of land mines. An international campaign is currently attempting to ban these antipersonnel weapons. The problem is they are readily planted in shallow ground, but then often forgotten by combatants. Years later, it is the innocent who stumble upon them, losing limbs and lives. These photos make one think.

Arms Transfers Working Group
http://www.fas.org/pub/gen/fas/atwg/

The Arms Transfers Working Group (ATWG) is an alliance of primarily Washington, D.C.–based national arms control, disarmament, development, economic conversion, human rights, and religious organizations concerned about the spread of conventional weaponry around the world. Formed in the aftermath of the 1991 Gulf War—and motivated by the humanitarian, economic, and security implications of arms trafficking—this forum serves as a clearinghouse of information and a point of contact for strategizing and coordinating activities among the diverse member-groups.

The stated goals of the Working Group, according to the site, are passage of the Code of Conduct on Arms Transfers Act and enactment of a global ban on land mines. In addition, the alliance works to oppose various U.S. government subsidies for arms exporting. ATWG works to affect U.S. arms export policy through Congress and the executive branch. Its grass roots work focuses on outreach, education, and activation.

The site features information about the working group and its members. It also offers news, features, and resources helpful to those interested in curbing militarism. Much useful information is here, not only for members of the working group, but to anyone interested in dipping into the pressing arms issues that face the nation and the wider human community.

European Network Against Arms Trade

http://www2.dk-online.dk/users/amk/enaat.htm

This site introduces the visitor to the European Network Against Arms Trade. While the United States is today the largest arms exporter in the world, the nations of Europe are doing their share to keep the arms trade going. It is a lucrative trade. This site is one way for North American peace activists to stay in touch with their counterparts in Europe. The site states that at the top of the European arms trade are the following items: British fighter jets, Dutch military electronics, German submarines, French missiles, Czech tanks, and Spanish munitions. The European Network Against Arms Trade has set itself the task of monitoring European military cooperation and exchanging information, which is then put to use in education, political action, and public relations. Information about the arms industry and about co-production and arms planning on a national or European level are available from the network. This site provides information on the network, including contact information for all the European members—a list that reads like a "Who's Who" of the European peace movement.

NGO Committee on Disarmament

http://www.igc.apc.org/disarm/

This is the home page for the NGO Committee on Disarmament, the principal service organization for non-governmental organizations involved with disarmament in the context of the United Nations. It aims to maintain open channels for communication between citizens' groups, governments, and U.N.-related bodies. This site aims to bring together issues, networks, and activist campaigns; it also has valuable peace-related links.

A.J. Muste Memorial Institute

http://www.nonviolence.org/~nvweb/ajmuste/

The A.J. Muste Memorial Institute was organized to keep alive the spirit of the man whose name it bears, functioning in his area of primary concern—the exploration of the link between nonviolence and social change. Muste (1885–1967) was a Dutch-born American radical who over the course of his political career moved from fairly conventional Christianity through Marxism/Leninism and finally to Christian pacifism and social activism. A publicly supported charitable educational foundation that promotes the principles and practice of nonviolent social change, the A.J. Muste Memorial Institute is dedicated to peace and disarmament, social and economic justice, racial and sexual equality, and the labor movement. This site explains the history and mission of the institute and features its publications and programs.

NISBCO

http://www.netaxs.com/~nvweb/nisbco/

There are two traditions in the Catholic Church concerning war. The "just war" tradition states that Christians can morally participate in wars if certain criteria are met; the "nonviolent" tradition states that Christians cannot morally participate in wars. The just war theory is traced back to Augustine; the nonviolent tradition is traced back to Jesus and his command "love your enemies." In either tradition, circumstances arise that require the young to examine their consciences to determine if they can morally participate in a war. This site should be helpful in such cases.

The National Interreligious Service Board for Conscientious Objectors (NISBCO), formed in 1940 as the National Service Board for Religious Objectors, states that it is committed to helping and supporting all who conscientiously question participation in war. NISBCO is a nonprofit service agency sponsored by a broad association of religious bodies who join to protect, defend, and extend the rights of conscientious objectors.

NISBCO states that some of the ways its supports conscientious objectors are by:

- Providing information on how to document one's convictions as a conscientious objector

- Providing help and support for conscientious objectors in the armed forces who seek discharge or transfer to noncombat status

- Providing draft counselor training

- Providing nondirective advice and referral for those who conscientiously object to the payment of war taxes

- Advocating for conscientious objector rights before the Selective Service System, the White House, the Courts, Congress, and international bodies

- Alerting concerned persons to changes that take place or are under consideration regarding military conscription and coercive national service proposals

- Acting as a national resource center for documents relating to the draft and conscientious objection

- Educating citizens through articles, speaking engagements, and publications

Catholic Committee of Appalachia

http://www.interpath.net/~mdoyle/aplchnot.html

Founded in 1968, the Catholic Committee of Appalachia (CCA) abides in these mountains to bring to life the challenges set forth in the Appalachian Bishops' pastoral. Through annual meetings, newsletters, and workshops, the Committee supports clergy, religious, lay church workers, and local organizations who work to address the causes of poverty in Appalachia. This site draws attention to the committee and its important work on behalf of the poor. Wrote the Appalachian bishops:

Action on behalf of justice and participation in the transformation of the world fully appear to us as the Church's mission for the redemption of the human race and its liberation from every oppressive situation. ... Supporting the ministries of Appalachian church workers is not enough. We think it is important to also be involved in issues of justice and dignity in accordance with Catholic social teachings. These issues include education, health care, labor, and the environment. Presently, we are encouraging the management and the union of a meat-packing plant to peacefully resolve a 16-month old strike. We are also involved in a task force that unites diverse groups such as coal industry representatives, mining enforcement officials, and local residents to cooperatively develop uses of reclaimed land that best serves the needs of the community.

The site also provides contact information, addresses, and telephone numbers for anyone who wishes to provide assistance to the committee.

Uniya—Jesuit Social Justice Center

http://www.vicnet.net.au/~cardoner/uniya.html

Uniya, or the Jesuit Social Justice Center, is an Australia-based, Jesuit-run organization involved with refugees; asylum seekers; aboriginal issues; social, economic, and mental health policies; and East Timorese issues. The organization seeks to respond to situations of structural injustice through ties with marginalized people. It does this, according to this Web site, in the following ways:

- Research and practical support to the poor
- Influencing public opinion and promoting effective action
- Seeking law and policy reform
- Encouraging Christian participation in government and society training in social justice issues
- Providing technical advice and assistance to marginalized groups

The site lists a number of projects these Jesuits are currently involved in. They place at the top of their list their Aboriginal Issues Desk; next in line is their East Timor Desk. East Timor is part of an island on the Indonesian archipelago invaded by the Indonesian army more than two decades ago. This is a largely Catholic island that once belonged to Portugal. For years, reports have revealed Indonesian human rights abuses by occupation forces. Indonesia sees East Timor as its territory. The latest Nobel Peace Prize winners, Bishop Carlos Filipe Ximenes Belo and Jose Ramos Horta, are from East Tinior. Jesuits in many parts of the world have focused on refugee problems. The Jesuits of Australia do this, but they also supply important information on the Aborigines and East Timorese.

The site lists Jesuit publications dealing with human rights issues and provides order forms for general information and related books. The site also has an index of useful online articles regarding these issues. Finally, the site provides names and contact numbers, addresses, and email addresses for further information.

Father Bucko's Mighty Home Page
http://maple.lemoyne.edu/~bucko/index.html

Jesuit Resources on the World Wide Web
http://maple.lemoyne.edu/~bucko/jesuit.html

The Jesuit Centre for Social Faith and Justice
http://maple.lemoyne.edu/~bucko/jcfj.html

Promotio Justitiae
http://web.lemoyne.edu/~bucko/sj_pj_64.html

Father Raymond A. Bucko is a Jesuit missionary and social-justice pioneer on the Internet and is responsible for a number of interesting and informative Web sites. The first listed above is his home page, which opens with a warm "Welcome to Fr. Bucko's Mighty Home Page."

(The visitor must check out the page to understand its title.) Located at Le Moyne College, in Syracuse, New York, Bucko attempts to raise the consciousness of Web surfers to contemporary moral issues, especially those with social and economic components. And he has fun doing it.

On his home page, Bucko introduces himself and his wide-ranging interests. These, of course, include World Wide Web publishing and computer-assisted instruction. Bucko explains that his major Internet project is developing a Jesuit Resource home page with Fr. Richard Vande Velde, S.J., at Loyola University in Chicago, Illinois.

These Bucko sites reveal the priest's passion for social justice and his deep commitment to spreading the spirituality and mission of the Society of Jesus. The Jesuit Centre for Social Faith and Justice was initially established in September 1979 by the Upper Canada Province of the Society of Jesus. The Jesuit Centre is one more expression of the Society of Jesus' commitment to the service of faith, of which the promotion of justice in the world today is seen as an integral dimension.

The Jesuit Centre for Social Faith and Justice is an interfaith, interdisciplinary team of women and men working to promote social, economic, and political change in Canada and Central America. The Centre engages in overseas development work, social analysis and research, public education, and policy advocacy and action on issues of justice as they affect Canada, refugees, and Central America. This Jesuit Center is located in Toronto, Ontario.

Promotio Justitiae features a number of important Catholic talks and speeches on the subject of social justice, including one in which Pope John Paul II reemphasizes the Church's "preferential option for the poor."

Jesuits of Mexico

http://www.uia.mx/crt/ap.html

Speaking of social justice and the Jesuits, this site contains a listing of Social Apostolates coordinated by the Jesuits of

Mexico. It speaks once more to the Order's impressive worldwide presence in the social apostolate. This site is in Spanish.

Science and Culture

http://www.luc.edu/or/sj/misc/scicult.html

Want to read an intellectual treatise on why the Western world is so screwed up today? Want to trace the worldwide environmental problem to its intellectual roots? What to get a sense of human complicity in the destruction of the world's ecosystems? Then this article, written by Jesuit Father Chris Moss, is for you. Don't scoff. Understanding how we got into the current ecological mess may be a starting point for extracting us from it. And if the visitor to this site does not agree—or has a reflection to add—the author's email and physical addresses are listed.

Catholic Documents by Subject

http://www.catholic.net/RCC/Indices/subs/by-subject.html

This site contains Church documents likely to be helpful to Catholic activists. The documents are listed by subject. The Web visitor only needs to check his or her area of interest to find what Church leaders have said. This is good to bone up on official Church teachings. Some of the topics listed include: Abortion and Human Life Issues, America, Asia, Bible and Scriptural Studies, Bishops, The Church, Communication, Eastern Churches, Education and Evangelization, Errors and Heresy, The Eucharist, Europe, Lay People, Liturgy, Marriage and Family Issues, Mary, Moral Teachings, Other Religions and Traditions, Priests, Sexuality, Social Justice, and Women. The documents listed are generally Vatican penned and not the work of U.S. bishops. Each subject contains at least a half dozen important documents aimed at getting the word out on official Church teachings.

Public Policy Matters at the Dioceses of Fargo and Bismarck, North Dakota

http://rrnet.com/~sedaqah/ndcc4.html

This site is the work of some bright and informed Catholics in North Dakota, a sparsely populated region of the United States. The Catholics here keep up on the moral implications of public policy matters—locally, regionally, and nationally—through this Web site.

The day I visited the site, interest was keen on President Clinton's veto of the partial birth abortion ban. Most Catholics viewed the veto as bad morality and bad policy. The site dealt with the morality of the partial birth abortion issue.

Also on the agenda in North Dakota were the Omnibus Private Property Rights Act Action Item, the Kassebaum-Kennedy Insurance Reform bill, a comparison of proposed federal welfare reforms (along with the U.S. bishops' position on welfare reform), information on a series of congressional bills, and health care policy links. Going through the site, I was struck not only by the enormous amount of information on policy matters available to Web users, but also by the neat and clean way it is being assessed and presented on a number of Catholic sites, including this one.

This site also invites the visitor to become further informed by reading the *Legislative Action Network Perspective*, the newsletter of the North Dakota Catholic Conference.

The site also links to other Catholic social justice sites, including the Office of Social Justice—Archdiocese of St. Paul and Minneapolis and Wisconsin Catholic Conference, two exceptional sites in this field. The site also maintains its local flavor by offering links to North Dakota state government sites that deal with social-justice issues, including health, welfare, and other human services. Finally, it links to a list of more than 75 other North Dakota Internet sites.

Wisconsin Catholic Conference

http://www.execpc.com/~chaw/WisconsinCatholicConf.html

The Wisconsin Catholic Conference (WCC) was founded in 1969 by the bishops of Wisconsin. The stated purpose of the conference is to fulfill the vision of Vatican Council II, which called upon the Church to be more involved in the world. With the message of the Gospel and the social teachings of the Church as its foundation, the WCC offers a specifically Catholic contribution to state and federal public policy debates.

The bishops of Wisconsin comprise the board of directors of the Wisconsin Catholic Conference, which meets three times a year to review issues and set the conference's legislative agenda. The Madison-based conference offers a statewide response to issues common to its five dioceses. It achieves this, the site states, by:

- Serving as an advocate on matters related to the interests and values of the Church

- Providing legislators and other decision makers with studied positions on social and moral issues

- Offering a forum for diocesan personnel to meet, exchange information, deliberate, and recommend policies or actions to the bishops.

- Formulating and publishing Catholic opinions and positions on legislation and public policy

This site also provides information on conference newsletters, issues, policy proposals, and moral principles that guide the conference as it approaches these policy matters. The site invites wider Catholic participation by subscribing to the conference's *Capitol Report* newsletter and becoming part of the conference's legislative network. The *Capitol Report* comes out every other month, alerting readers to key issues. One goal of the *Report* is to inform

Catholics about "legislative training sessions" so they can become more involved in helping shape public policy.

Social Justice Ministry

http://rrnet.com/~sedaqah/_sjm2.htm

The stated mission of the Archdiocese of St. Paul and Minneapolis Social Justice Ministry is to serve the parish as its primary resource and catalyst for the work of social justice by developing an understanding of the basic principles of Catholic social teaching. Its work is rooted in Scriptural values and in the principles of Catholic social teaching, which it refers to as the Church's "best-kept secret." The principles of Catholic social teaching, according to the site, are these:

1. **The Dignity of the Human Person.** As Catholics, we believe we are made in the image of God (Genesis 1:27). We believe the person is sacred, the clearest reflection of God among us. Human dignity comes from God, not from nationality, race, sex, economic status, or any human accomplishment.

2. **The Call to Live in Community—Concern for the Common Good.** The human person is not only sacred, but also social. We realize our dignity and achieve our rights in relationship with others. … No community is more central than the family— the basic cell of society.

3. **Rights and Responsibilities of the Human Person.** Pope John XXIII declared, "… every [person] has the right to life, to bodily integrity, and to the means which are necessary and suitable for the proper development of life. These means are primarily food, clothing, shelter, rest, medical care, and finally the necessary social services."

4. **The Dignity of Work.** Workers have basic rights to decent work and just wages, to form and join unions, and so forth. The economy exists for the human person, not the other way around.

5. **Option of the Poor and Vulnerable.** Justice will never be fully attained unless people see the poor person, who is asking for help to survive, not as an annoyance or a burden, but as an opportunity for showing kindness and a chance for greater enrichment.

6. **Solidarity.** Solidarity implies acceptance and recognition of the fact that we, as a human family, are interdependent. Solidarity calls us to stand united with the poor and powerless as our own brothers and sisters.

This site is the work of one of the best archdiocesan social justice offices in the country. Visiting this site is an educational experience.

Abolition Now!!!
http://www.abolition-now.com/

> An execution is not simply death. It is just as different from the privation of life as a concentration camp is from prison. It adds to death a rule, a public premeditation known to the future victim, an organization which is itself a source of moral sufferings more terrible than death. Capital punishment is the most premeditated of murders, to which no criminal's deed, however calculated can be compared. For there to be an equivalency, the death penalty would have to punish a criminal who had warned his victim of the date at which he would inflict a horrible death on him and who, from that moment onward, had confined him at his mercy for months. Such a monster is not encountered in private life.
>
> *—Albert Camus*

Abolition Now!!! started in December 1995 and within a few months became the most visited anti–capital punishment site on the Web. It is understandable this should be the case. This is a one-stop "everything you need to know" anti–death penalty site. It is also an umbrella site for a host of antideathly groups. Plenty of information and plenty of links are here. Importantly, this site also provides up-to-date execution alerts.

The site features, among other things, arguments against capital punishment, death penalty facts and figures, worldwide capital punishment information, wrongful executions in the twentieth century, current inmates on death row, executions since 1991 and yearly breakdowns, thoughts from death row inmates and information on various anti–death penalty campaigns.

The site also provides information by state: which states have the death penalty, which states do not, and how the death penalty is applied in various states. Some states execute children, for example. Catholic social teaching opposes capital punishment. While I did not find any specific links to Catholic sites on these pages, virtually every site listed would be useful to Catholic activists who work in the areas of prison reform and anti–capital punishment efforts.

CatholicMobile:The Death Penalty
http://www.mcgill.pvt.k12.al.us/jerryd/cm/death.htm

"Abolition of the death penalty is most consonant with the example of Jesus, who both taught and practiced the forgiveness of injustice."

—*U.S. Bishops on Capital Punishment*

It was in 1980 that the U.S. Catholic Bishops' Statement on Capital Punishment eloquently addressed the issue. This site is really a directory of sites that deal with the issue of capital punishment. At the top of the list is the bishops' statement. It is followed by other individual statements by bishops on this issue. The site also includes a speech by Sister Helen Prejean after whom the book and movie *Dead Man Walking* was made.

There are many other statements and arguments opposing the death penalty on this site. For example, the visitor finds the 1991 statement of the Evangelical Lutheran Church in America on the death penalty.

Also here are summaries of recent articles on punishment and the death penalty as well as discussion topics and term paper topics on punishment and the death penalty. The visitor will also find U.S. Supreme Court decisions on capital punishment, including the full texts. Also here are the U.N. member states and their positions on the death penalty for crimes committed by persons younger than 18 years of age. Many other resources are here, including links to other anti–death penalty sites. This is another first-rate resource site by CatholicMobile.

Poverty and Welfare

http://pwa.acusd.edu/~hinman/poverty.html#internet resources

One of the most unsettling findings for anyone who examines current economic trends from a moral perspective is that the gap between rich and poor is widening in many parts of the world. This is happening not only in the so-called Third World, where the poorest of the poor live; it is also happening in the United States, where wealth is becoming increasingly concentrated in the top 5 percent of income earners while the bottom 40 percent find themselves falling further behind.

While these issues pose critical policy questions for public leaders, they also pose moral questions to all who believe it is important to live ethical lives. Catholic social teaching demands Catholics consider the morality of public policy. It is in public policy—not only in private acts—that nations respond (or fail to respond) to growing inequities.

This site is divided into four parts. The first gives some helpful links to Internet resources dealing with world hunger. The second provides a short survey of some of the more important philosophical works on poverty and welfare; it is based on the bibliographical essay, *Contemporary Moral Issues: Diversity and Consensus*, edited by Lawrence

M. Hinman (© 1996, Prentice-Hall). The third contains short summaries of recent articles on poverty and welfare. The fourth is devoted to discussion topics and term paper topics on this issue.

CatholicMobile:Poverty

http://www.mcgill.pvt.k12.al.us/jerryd/cm/poverty.htm

> "The needs of the poor take priority over the desires of the rich."
>
> *—Pope John Paul II, Toronto, Canada, 1984*

This is a good introduction to Catholic social teachings on poverty. It begins with a section on poverty from the U.S. bishops' 1986 Pastoral Letter "Economic Justice for All." That letter represented a three-year effort by the bishops to discern the principles of Catholic teachings on economics as well as some applications of those principles given the U.S. economic system. Also here is a piece from the Alabama bishops on poverty written in 1990, an essay on poverty and Christianity, a Dorothy Day essay entitled "The Mystery of the Poor," and other essays entitled "Poverty in a World of Plenty" and "Fifty Facts about Poverty."

The site also links to the Institute for Research on Poverty, gives data on poverty by race and age, U.S. census information on poverty, and many other resources. Organizations working with the poor are also listed on this site, as are "localized efforts" to alleviate poverty. Another first-rate Web page.

Environmental Ethics

http://pwa.acusd.edu/~hinman/environmental_ethics.html

Catholics have been among those slow to realize you cannot forever trash the planet without paying the consequences. We have been polluting the oceans, depleting top soils, junking hazardous wastes, opening ozone holes in the atmosphere, and throwing millions of tons of carbons into the air. Planet Earth is hurting; some say it is dying. If it goes, so do its inhabitants. That's why environmental ethics is important, and perhaps the most overlooked moral question facing humanity.

All Christians and non-Christians need to be engaged in some serious examination of conscience here. This Web site could help. It is divided into four parts. The first offers a guide to selected Internet resources dealing with environmental ethics and issues. The second provides a short survey of some of the more important philosophical works on environmental ethics. It is based on the bibliographical essay in *Contemporary Moral Issues: Diversity and Consensus*, edited by Lawrence M. Hinman (© 1996, Prentice-Hall). The third part contains short summaries of recent articles on environmental ethics. The author of each summary is indicated at its end. The fourth is devoted to discussion topics and term paper topics on this issue.

This site also connects to other environmental Web sites, including one called The Best Single Starting Point on the Web for Environmental Ethics by the Center for Environmental Philosophy at the University of North Texas. The page is as rich as it is important.

Euthanasia

http://pwa.acusd.edu/~hinman/euthanasia.html

Cardinal Joseph Bernardin of Chicago first popularized the conception-to-death "Pro-life ethic." He spoke of it as the "Seamless Garment." The Catholic Church speaks of protecting life from conception to death.

Euthanasia, or mercy killing, is an issue contemporary Western society finds itself increasingly wrestling with. It seems that among the most divisive issues that face humanity today are moral questions that arise at the beginning or end of the life journey. Both abortion and euthanasia seem to elicit widely different moral responses.

The Catholic Church teaches that all life must be respected. It teaches that mercy killing is wrong. As for how life should be preserved, the Church differentiates between "ordinary" and "extraordinary" means. "Ordinary" means, like water and food, need to be provided; "extraordinary" means, like tube feeding and oxygen tents, might not have to be provided. Under such circumstances, other considerations, like the availability of technology and cost, might enter into the discussion. What is never allowed, according to Catholic teaching, is direct intervention to intentionally end life.

This site is aimed at trying to understand the moral considerations that surround the euthanasia question. The site is divided into four parts. The first offers some useful Internet links relating to euthanasia. The second provides a short survey of some of the more important philosophical work on euthanasia. It is based on the bibliographical essay in *Contemporary Moral Issues: Diversity and Consensus*, edited by Lawrence M. Hinman (© 1996, Prentice-Hall). The third contains short summaries of recent articles on euthanasia; the author of each summary is indicated at its end. The fourth part is devoted to discussion topics and term paper topics on this issue. While this site is not intended to present a specifically Catholic view on euthanasia, much of the literature on the site includes Catholic and other Christian perspectives.

Compassionate HealthCare Network

http://www.awinc.com/partners/bc/commpass/lifenet/chninfo.htm

The Compassionate HealthCare Network (CHN) was formed in 1992 and consists of both professional and lay people who care about the crisis medicine and health care is experiencing. CHN states that it opposes euthanasia by actively defending the inherent value of all human life. CHN's work is international and comprises a network of people that provides speakers, workshops, and research data pertaining to euthanasia, assisted suicide, palliative care, advance directives (living wills), and videos.

The site also features the West Virginia–based Citizens United Resisting Euthanasia. Founded in 1981, this is a nationwide network of concerned citizens of diverse professional, political, and religious backgrounds bound together in a common cause: uncompromising opposition to euthanasia. To this end, it states that it practices compassion, unity, research, and education. The site provides information about the organization, including addresses and telephone numbers.

There is plenty of good information on this site about living wills and other advance directives. These are often not easy questions. Considering them, backed by good dispassionate information, could prove helpful. This site also has information from the international anti-euthanasia movement and briefs of pertinent court decisions. The issues this site deals with will not go away; they will only get more pressing as they become more complex. This site helps establish values out of which potentially difficult decisions can be weighed.

Reproductive Technologies
http://pwa.acusd.edu/~hinman/reproductive_technologies.html

Bioethics has burst forth as a critically important field of study. The issues are complex, made especially so by the ever-increasing speed of technological advance. But should everything that can be done be done? What is ethical? This site contains many perspectives on bioethics, including the Vatican's position and reasoning on these issues (*The Congregation for the Doctrine of the Faith, Instruction on Respect for Human Life in Its Origin and on the Dignity of Procreation: Replies to Certain Questions of the Day* (Boston, MA: St. Paul Editions, 1987).

This site is divided into two parts. The first provides a short survey of some of the more important philosophical works on reproductive technologies. It is based on the bibliographical essay in *Contemporary Moral Issues: Diversity and Consensus*, edited by Lawrence M. Hinman (© 1996, Prentice-Hall). The second part contains short summaries of recent articles on reproductive technologies.

The author of each summary is indicated at its end. The visitor is invited to suggest articles for this section.

There are a number of excellent anthologies available on this site. Additionally, special attention is paid to the issue of genetic screening by sex, a practice that seems as common as it is controversial, especially in some Third World nations. Attention is drawn to resources in regard to questions of genetic engineering.

Race and Ethnicity

http://pwa.acusd.edu/~hinman/race.html

One of the most basic Christian beliefs is that all people are sons and daughters of God—made in God's image. No distinctions here for race, color of skin, even creed. Yet the human family remains divided and talks about there being four or five distinct races. Geneticists, however, say all human beings share almost entirely the same gene pool. Could it be that there is only one race—the human race?

Any discussion of race, ethnicity, and multiculturalism is bound to surface some pretty barebones values while revealing differences in perspective and opinion. This site can serve to get some important ideas on the table. It contains a great deal of information about the literature of race and ethnicity.

It is broken into several areas. The first offers selected Internet resources on race, ethnicity, and multiculturalism. The second provides a short survey of some of the more important philosophical works on race and ethnicity. It is based on the bibliographical essay in *Contemporary Moral Issues: Diversity and Consensus*, edited by Lawrence M. Hinman (© 1996, Prentice-Hall). The third contains short summaries of recent articles on race and ethnicity. The fourth is devoted to discussion topics and term paper topics on this issue.

This site also contains a helpful list of links to human rights and civil rights organizations, an extensive bibliography, and links on race and multiculturalism from the English Department at Carnegie Mellon University. It also contains an affirmative action issue of *Internet Herald* from the University of California at Berkeley and a survey of selected philosophical literature on race and ethnicity.

Gender and Sexism

http://pwa.acusd.edu/~hinman/gender.html

The Vatican and U.S. bishops have both explicitly stated that sexism is a sin and should not be tolerated, but many Catholics (and others) accuse their hierarchy of being sexist. These critics go on to say that the very structure of Catholicism is sexist, that is, it is prejudiced against women. This is because the Catholic Church officially states that women can never be priests and priests are the authority figures in the Church. Many women, therefore, see themselves as second-class Catholics. No issue is more current or more difficult for the Church to handle today than the issue of women. Should women be allowed to become priests? Pope John Paul II in 1995 said the Church does not have the authority—and never will—to ordain women. He called for an end of the discussion—but it has not ended.

This site includes the official Catholic position on women and their roles in the Church, including the Apostolic Papal Letter to Women in preparation for the Beijing Conference, June 29, 1995, and *Mulieris dignitatem* (On the Dignity and Vocation of Women). This resides alongside other papers and books that take the official Catholic issue to task.

This site is divided into four parts. The first gives some helpful links to Internet resources dealing with gender and ethics. The second provides a short survey of some of the more important philosophical works on gender. It is based on the bibliographical essay in *Contemporary Moral Issues: Diversity and Consensus*, edited by Lawrence M. Hinman (© 1996, Prentice-Hall). The third part contains short summaries of recent articles on gender. The fourth is devoted to discussion topics and term paper topics on this issue.

Animal Rights

http://pwa.acusd.edu/~hinman/animal.html

If one believes that life is sacred (as Christians believe it is), then all life forms have value and are worthy of respect and protection. This, animal rights activists believe, is especially true when it comes to higher life forms, including animals. The animal rights movement has spread through North America and Europe in the past 20 years, as millions have begun to see the connectedness of life and have begun to show greater sensitivity to all life forms. It is in this context that many Catholics, with others, are speaking out on behalf of the protection of a variety of species beyond the human family.

This site is divided into four parts. The first gives some helpful links to Internet resources dealing with animal rights. The second provides a short survey of some of the more important philosophical works on animal rights. It is based on the bibliographical essay in *Contemporary Moral Issues: Diversity and Consensus,* edited by Lawrence M. Hinman (© 1996, Prentice-Hall). The third contains short summaries of recent articles on animal rights, and the fourth is devoted to discussion topics and term paper topics on this issue.

This site also includes selected Internet resources on animal rights and recent Supreme Court decisions on animal rights. There are a number of excellent anthologies here as well, all dealing with issues regarding the status of animals.

CatholicMobile: Justice and Peace

http://www.mcgill.pvt.k12.al.us/jerryd/cm/jp.htm

This site provides an excellent overview of justice and peace writings sorted by topic. I can think of scores of ways this site could come in handy for researchers, scholars, journalists, activists, and others who might want to brush up on the subjects of choice.

To give an example of what this site looks like, take the general category of Catholic Social Teaching. There the following subtopics have sites linked to scores of documents and other resources: Poverty; Hunger; Homelessness; Racial Justice; Women, Men, & Justice; Peace; and Human Rights. This is a most informative site.

Seamless Garment Network (Canada)
http://www.interchange.ubc.ca/pfeeley/sgn.html

The Seamless Garment Network (Canada) is a network of member organizations and individuals who support the consistent life ethic. "We are committed to the protection of life, which is threatened in today's world by war and the arms race, abortion, poverty, racism, capital punishment, and euthanasia," the site states. "We believe that these issues are linked under a `consistent life ethic'. We challenge those working on all or some of these issues to maintain a cooperative spirit of peace, reconciliation, and respect in protecting the unprotected."

The consistent life ethic movement is just that: a movement, not an organization. The SGN works on raising the consciousness of the community to affirm reverence for human life. The network publishes ads; continues to ask peace, justice, and life organizations to join as members; continues to ask people who are advocates for human life, peace, and justice to sign the mission statement; and tries to do other things as well to place its message before the community.

The Seamless Garment Network states that it exists to provide leadership, resources, and information to enable people and organizations who affirm the consistent ethic of reverence for life to find each other, communicate, and work together. The site makes suggestions about how people can work with the network; it offers membership information and lists members and member organizations.

Chiapas Information

http://lanic.utexas.edu/la/Mexico/chiapas.html

Some 90 percent of Mexico's 90 million people are nominally Catholic. Mexico is also one of the poorer nations in the Western hemisphere. Where there is Mexican wealth, it is concentrated. Millions of Mexicans, however, live in poverty without land or much hope of education or employment. Traditionally, the Catholic Church's attitude toward poverty has been to teach resignation and accept suffering, to associate it with the redemptive suffering of Jesus on the cross. This has changed in recent decades, especially since the Second Vatican Council in the 1960s, when the church began to pay more attention to "social" sin as opposed to solely "personal" sin. The former includes sinful structures that maintain injustices. In other words, the Church began to examine the roots of poverty, teaching that building the reign of God requires working to eliminate poverty and to build just structures as a means of finding lasting peace.

Since the 1970s, many Catholics in North America have paid more attention to the poverty in Central and South American nations, asking what U.S. actions and policies might be playing into this impoverishment. Do U.S. economic ties, for example, play a part? In this light, during the past five years, U.S. Catholics have been watching the situation in and around a Mexican town called Chiapas, where a Mexican bishop, living close to the poor of the region, has denounced local injustices. It is there that groups of landless peasants have confronted rich landowners demanding land and jobs.

This Web site provides the visitor with news and information about developments in Chiapas. These are important not only to Mexicans but also to anyone who cares about finding peace in a world in which the rich get richer and the poor get poorer. In this light, the analyses coming out of Chiapas are very important to Catholics who believe the mission of the Church must include continued dedication to eliminating the causes of poverty and injustice.

Brazil Franciscans

http://www.jca.or.jp/hr/brazil.htm

The gap between rich and poor in Brazil is massive, and it continues to grow. The poor of Brazil are impoverished almost beyond belief. Fathers are without work and without land and are unable to feed their families. Catholic bishops and priests have protested these conditions and have worked for more equitable land ownership.

But the situation is still dire. In Brazil today, 1 percent of the population still controls almost 50 percent of the land, while the poorest 40 percent have access to less than 1 percent of the land. In response to land-reform initiatives taken by the Church, unions, the landless movement, and others, the landed elite often employ *jaguncos* (killers) to violently suppress the landless struggle. Not pretty, this— but at least now you can make your personal protest known.

This site represents a promising new use of the Web— in the service of the fight for human rights. The site was created in September 1996 to rally public opinion to free from prison a Brazilian Catholic priest and his land-reform colleagues. They were imprisoned for standing up on behalf of landless people who occupied the estates of wealthy absentee Brazilian landowners.

In the summer of 1996, a Brazilian judge sentenced Franciscan Friar Anastacio Ribeiro, coordinator of the Pastoral Land Commission, and six of his colleagues to 5-year prison terms for organizing the landless poor. Ribeiro's colleagues include: Clodoaldo de Santana Sena, Marinaldo Santos Silva, Elias Rodrigues do Santos, Iris de Fátima da Silva, Rosilda de Fátima Soares da Silva, and Dorival Fernandes. This site tells the history that led up to these arrests and offers important background information. Check out this site and, if word of their release has not yet appeared, follow the instructions to protest these unjust judicial actions.

Economic Policy Institute
http://epinet.org/

Catholic social teaching calls on Catholics to inform themselves about the social, economic, and political issues that affect people's lives. These issues all have moral components. The Church teaches moral principles so that social issues can be examined and judged in the light of morality.

There is no one place where basic information can be found that gets beyond the newspaper stories of the day and informs and educates consciences. Information can be pruned from all sorts of sources. Over the years, I have found the Economic Policy Institute, a nonprofit, nonpartisan think tank that seeks to broaden the public debate, offers fair and insightful information about many social issues facing U.S. citizens. The Economic Policy Institute seeks to broaden the public debate about strategies to achieve a prosperous and fair economy.

EPI was founded in 1986 by a group of economic policy experts, including the economist Barry Bluestone; columnist and editor Robert Kuttner; Ray Marshall, secretary of labor in the Carter administration; Robert Reich, currently secretary of labor; the economist Lester Thurow; and Jeff Faux, who now serves as EPI's president. EPI is supported by grants from foundations, corporations, labor unions, and individuals. What these experts have to say is always informative and usually very useful in weighing the moral issues of the day.

Among other things, this site introduces the visitor to the institute and an Internet feature, Reading Between the Lines, which is updated weekly. Some of the recent articles that have appeared include the following:

- Issue Brief: "The Economic Case for Corporate Responsibility to Workers," April 3, 1996. With the Dow Jones industrial average above 5500 and corporate profits at a 25-year high, corporate America may have fulfilled Wall Street's highest expectations. But higher profits and productivity have failed to deliver higher wages and job security, and business finds itself accused of putting corporate greed ahead of the nation's economic interests.

- "Wide Cast for Safety Net: Over Time, Middle Class as Well as Poor Rely on Entitlement Help," by Howard Chernick. While there are numerous reports that document the importance of entitlement benefits to low-income families, this study examines both short-term and long-term receipt of such income—and finds the middle-class, over time, also receives substantial help from these programs.

Global Corporate Responsibility
http://www.europa.com/~rover/sjopsocl.htm

In September 1995, three religious organizations—from Great Britain, Canada, and the United States—simultaneously announced a set of principles that spelled out a new responsible business philosophy for the global economy. The principles were presented in a document entitled "Principles for Global Corporate Responsibility: Bench Marks for Measuring Business Performance."

This was the first time that religious groups and shareholders developed comprehensive global standards for responsible corporate citizenship. "Global companies are facing a new set of issues that go well beyond their traditional business focus," stated the Rev. David Schilling, director of global corporate accountability programs for the Interfaith Center on Corporate Responsibility. The Principles for Global Corporate Responsibility called on companies to base their corporate policies "on a vision of themselves as one of many stockholders in the global community and to set high standards of conduct in relation to their employees, the environment and the communities where they operate."

The principles were released by the Ecumenical Committee for Corporate Responsibility of the United Kingdom (ECCR), the Task Force on the Churches and Corporate Responsibility of Canada, and the Interfaith Center on Corporate Responsibility in the United States (ICCR), a coalition of 275 Protestant, Roman Catholic, and Jewish institutional investors. The three groups announced the principles in press conferences in New York, London, Toronto, and Montreal. This site introduces the Web visitor to the document and its principles and invites the visitor to learn more about the efforts to build socially responsible corporate behavior.

National Coalition for the Homeless
http://nch.ari.net/

The National Coalition for the Homeless (NCH) is a national advocacy network of homeless persons, activists, service providers, and others committed to a single goal: ending homelessness. The coalition states that it takes it as a first principle of practice that homeless and formerly homeless persons must be actively involved in all levels of the coalition's work. "We are committed to creating the systemic and attitudinal changes necessary to end homelessness. At the same time, we work to meet the urgent needs of persons who either are homeless or are at risk of becoming homeless," the site states.

This site features a What's New area publicizing upcoming events and features, including an Online Library on Homelessness and Poverty, Homeless Voices, Facts about Homelessness, Current Legislative and Policy Issues, and Legislative Alerts. The site also features an Online Directory of State and National Homeless/Housing Advocacy Organizations, a Calendar of Events, Notice of Funding Availabilities for Homeless Programs, and information on how to become a member of the national coalition.

Internet NonProfit Center

http://www.nonprofits.org/

Top Forty Charitable Organizations

http://www.nonprofits.org/lib/dir.html#CCUSA

This site is especially useful in helping anyone fulfill his or her most generous instincts, whether it be volunteering to serve or donating to a worthy cause. And there is never a reason to be out of work when it is possible to volunteer. Volunteering comes with a twist; virtually everyone who serves on voluntary agencies end up saying they receive more than they give.

This site is advertised as providing more information on nonprofits than any other site in the world. The generosity and idealism on which these nonprofits are built is inspiring. It is also a means of living out the work of the Gospel.

The site features: the Gallery of Organizations, including information from government sources and many nonprofits (nonprofits may use this space to put online brochures, annual reports, and home pages); the Library, a repository for publications and data about nonprofit organizations and the nonprofit sector (generally from sources other than the nonprofits themselves); the Parlor, where the visitor may learn something while chatting by the water cooler (see GIVING) or glancing at the bulletin boards (see Volunteer Opportunities); and the Heliport, where the visitor can link to additional resources of special interest to donors and volunteers. (It tries to help people obtain information about nonprofit organizations.)

Just looking at this site restores hope. So many organizations doing so much good for so many—it is inspiring.

Also, for interest and fun, take a look at the Top Forty Charitable Organizations. This includes Catholic Charities USA. The list provides detailed information on how money comes in and goes out of these worthy organizations.

It was St. Paul who wrote: "Faith, hope and charity—and the greatest of these is charity."

FOCUS

http://www.nautilus.org/focusweb/

Economic development is a crucial concern to the human family when a third or more of the world's population goes to bed hungry each night. Many organizations have come into being to focus on development concerns. This site introduces the visitor to one of these organizations. FOCUS is a program of development policy research dedicated to regional and global policy analysis, micro-macro linking, and advocacy work. It has worked with nongovernment organizations in Asia and other regions, beginning in April 1995, from its Bangkok-based office. FOCUS is a nonprofit organization supported by independent organizations and individual donors in both the south and north. It does not seek nor will it accept any direct government funding.

Why FOCUS? Even as the wealthy and some sections of the middle class around the world have progressed economically, the oppressed and poor have over the last 15 years suffered major setbacks. There has also been a significant and steady erosion of a large portion of the population's economic base.

The mainstream paradigms of development are in serious crisis. In the post–Cold War period, most people have little desire to return to the state-assisted protectionist, communist, or socialist regimes. Yet radical "free-market" economic policies and experimentation with structural adjustment lending by the International Monetary Fund (IMF) and the World Bank have crippled the state as an agent of development and protector of the community from the poverty-reducing, equitable, and sustainable alternatives that advance the interests of poor and marginalized peoples.

To articulate, link, and develop greater coherence between local community-based and national, regional, and global paradigms is the niche of FOCUS. Thailand, India, Bangladesh, Laos, and the Philippines are the countries of initial work for the first three-year period—emphasizing economic liberalization and sustainable development alternatives as two broad themes for the program. Conferences, papers, policy briefs, and occasional books will be major products of FOCUS's programs. Beginning in January 1997, FOCUS will publish a quarterly journal tentatively titled, *Southern Perspectives.*

This site describes the purpose and goals of FOCUS and offers contact names; addresses; and telephone, fax, and e-mail numbers.

Transcontinental Peace Letter
http://www.nonviolence.org/~nvweb/tpn/

The *Transcontinental Peace Letter* is an electronic newsletter, published several times a years, aimed at keeping track of large and small European and International peace initiatives. The newsletter is not copyrighted; it can be reproduced as long as there is no intended commercial use. Those who take information from the newsletter are merely asked to cite it. The newsletter is based in Germany; its mail and email addresses are listed, along with telephone numbers and contacts. Much of the information in the newsletter stems from local organizing and the peace initiatives of ordinary people. As examples, consider the following news bits.

"Soldiers of Fortune" Banned in Germany

After a three years' long struggle the "Armaments Information Office" in Baden-Wuerttemberg succeeded in putting one of the most violent mercenaries' magazines on the German "List Magazines Harmful to Young Persons". Thus "Soldiers of Fortune" which praises war actions, describes "optimal killing approaches" and denounces opponents as "inferior people" will no longer be available on newsstands in Germany. The "Armaments Information Office" will check how other war and soldier magazine might be banned from German news-stands and has announced possible corresponding criminal charges. Information: RIB, Postfach 5261, Freiburg, Phone and fax: +49-7665-51868

Polish Environment Periodical

The English "Ecological Bulletin" is edited from the Polish Ecological Club (Upper Silesian Branch) and intends to exchange information between organizations and persons who are interested in ecology, environment protection and sustainable development in Poland. The bulletin includes brief informational reports and information on recent and upcoming events. Contact: Robert Marek, phone and fax +48-32-594315

"School Children support Life"

For three years children from 300 German schools have partici-pated in various projects supporting children and young people in Ex-Yugoslavia. Source: Sueddeutsche Zeitung, March 6, 1995, Page 10

No Conscripts in Nicaragua

Unanimously the Nicaraguan parliament abolished the draft and renamed the army from "Sadinistas' Peoples Army" into "Nicaraguan Armed Forces". Source: Frankfurter Rundschau, November 25, 1994

Catholic Worker Roundtable

http://www.catholicworker.org/roundtable/abrief.htm

This unofficial Catholic Worker site is produced and sponsored by an admirer of the Catholic Worker movement. It states that no funds donated to any Catholic Worker house have been used to produce it, and the views expressed do not represent any official Catholic Worker statement.

By now, many Catholics know the outlines of the Catholic Worker story. The movement began simply enough on May 1, 1933, when a journalist named Dorothy Day and a philosopher named Peter Maurin teamed up to publish and distribute a newspaper called

The Catholic Worker. This radical paper promoted the biblical promise of justice and mercy. Grounded in a firm belief in the God-given dignity of every human, their movement was committed to nonviolence, voluntary poverty, and the works of mercy as a way of life.

It wasn't long before Dorothy and Peter were putting their beliefs into action, opening a "house of hospitality" where the homeless, the hungry, and the forsaken would always be welcome. Over many decades, the movement has protested injustice, war, and violence of all forms. Today there are some 130 Catholic Worker communities in the United States. The Catholic Worker movement is made up of people motivated by the teachings of Jesus, especially as they are summarized in the Sermon on the Mount, and the teachings of the Catholic Church, in the writings of the early Fathers and the social encyclicals of the modern popes, to bring about a "new society within the shell of the old, a society in which it will be easier to be good."

The site contains essays about the movement and information about Catholic Worker communities and allied movements on the Web. The writing here is clear and clean. This site is a very good introduction to the thinking and work of the Catholic Worker movement today.

Center of Concern

http://www.coc.org/coc/

This site introduces the visitor to one of the most knowledgeable and respected Catholic peace and justice organizations in the world, the Washington D.C.–based Center of Concern. The site briefly tells the story of the center and through the story establishes its purpose and vision for a more just and peaceful world.

It was the 1971 Rome Synod of Bishops that framed Justice in the World, the statement that set the justice and peace agenda for the decade. Jesuit Father Bill Ryan, founder and first executive director of the Center of

Concern, attended that synod. He was co-director of the Social Action Department of the Canadian Catholic Conference when, in October 1970, Father Pedro Arrupe, S.J., Superior General of the Society of Jesus (the Jesuits), asked him to go to Washington, D.C., to assist in the establishment of an international center to study issues relating to development, justice, and peace from a Christian perspective. The proposed center, a joint initiative of the United States Catholic Conference (USCC) and the Society of Jesus, was to be established as an independent organization. On May 4, 1971, the Center of Concern was formally announced by Father Arrupe and Bishop Joseph Bernardin, then General Secretary of the USCC (now Cardinal Archbishop of Chicago), at a meeting with United Nations Secretary General U Thant in his New York office.

From the outset, the Center of Concern has defined itself as international in perspective, ecumenical in outlook, and autonomous in structure. The Center's overriding goal is to enable all people to realize the truth that humanity is united in a common destiny and to assist them in exercising their common responsibility to shape that destiny. In its early years, the Center provided strong, ground-breaking leadership in helping thousands to discover the link between faith and justice and in raising new awareness of Third World and women's issues.

During the 1980s, the center shifted away from a primary focus on institutions to participation in social movements—the peace movement, the women's movement, and the labor movement. In the 1990s, the center has pressed for greater cooperation among nongovernmental organizations (NGOs) as an alternative approach in working for global justice.

This site also links with other peace and justice sites and connects to resources of interest to Catholic activists and others.

Faith Based Political Resources

http://internetco.servco.com/~norway/religious.html

The Catholic Church speaks a political message. Its faith-based messages have serious political repercussions. If one has any doubt, it is only necessary to become familiar with the Church's social teachings. Consider, for example, that the Church teaches that women and men, made in the image of God, have a preeminent place in the social order, that human dignity must always be protected, that the community must show a preferential love for the poor, that all people enjoy rights that are political/legal (e.g., vote, free speech, migration) and social/economic (e.g., food, shelter, work, education) and that these rights must be respected and protected by all.

The Church also teaches that love of neighbor is an absolute demand for justice because charity must manifest itself in actions and structures that respect human dignity, protect human rights, and facilitate human development. The Church further teaches that the economy is for all people and that the resources of the earth are to be shared, that labor is to take precedence over both capital and technology in the production process, and that just wages and the right of workers to organize are to be respected.

None of this happens in a political vacuum. For Catholics to live their faith they must be engaged in the social, political, and economic issues of the day. It is in this context that this site comes into play. It is an important connection point between faith and politics on the World Wide Web. Listed here are scores of sites where moral considerations drive political ideas and agendas. The visitor will find articles, references, and organizations aimed at clarifying a faith-based political vision.

COPRED

http://www.igc.apc.org/copred/

The Consortium on Peace Research, Education and Development (COPRED) is a community of educators, activists, and researchers working on alternatives to violence and war. COPRED spreads methods of nonviolent social change among different racial and socio-economic populations.

Founded in 1970 by a small group of teachers and scholars, COPRED has grown to almost 500 institutional and individual members, including K–12 educators, peace activists, conflict-resolution practitioners, university professors, and clergy. COPRED has become the hub for more than 300 university degree programs in the study of peace and nonviolence around the world and works to strengthen public school programs and networks.

This site aims to interest people in the work of COPRED and to encourage people to share in its ideals. COPRED's work is unusual in that it unites activists, researchers, and teachers. It does this by providing bibliographies, syllabi collections, curriculum services, a speakers' bureau, an annual conference, the quarterly academic journal, *Peace & Change*, and a networking newsletter *The Peace Chronicle*. COPRED also publishes a *Global Directory of Peace Studies Programs* at various colleges and universities and works with libraries to establish peace collections.

Zapatista Liberation Page
http://www.peak.org/~justin/ezln/ezln.html

This site is the official Web page of the Zapatista Front of National Liberation. Many Catholic activists in North and South America have been sympathetic with the goals—if not all the means—of this organization. What are those goals? As stated on the Zapatista liberation page, they are to:

- Struggle so that land, housing, work, food, health, education, information, culture, independence, democracy, justice, liberty, and peace are made a reality for all Mexicans
- Be a space of convergence for various thoughts and intentions

- Organize the demands and proposals of common citizens so that they who lead do so by obeying

- Organize the solution to collective problems of society, without the intervention of political parties and the Mexican government

- Struggle against the system of a Party of State

- Struggle for a new constituency and a new Constitution

Wordy and heady, but at issue here are questions of justice that have earned the Zapatistas sympathetic ears.

When you think about it, this site is an extraordinary development, a low-cost information (critics might call it propaganda) channel to the world. It becomes clear that this liberation struggle, like others before it, is for the hearts and minds of the people—and not only of Mexico but of the international community.

At this site, the visitor can learn the history of the struggle; the declarations of the Zapatistas; their demands, interviews with leaders in the movement, news about current negotiations—or lack of negotiations—and what one can do to help. Also in this site are links to further information about the Zapatistas and Mexico.

Anti-Racism Sources
http://www.efn.org/~dennis_w/race.html

CatholicMobile: Racial Justice
http://www.mcgill.pvt.k12.al.us/jerryd/cm/race.htm

Racism is a pernicious sin that is difficult to root out because it is often subtle or denied. It is basic Christian and Catholic teaching, however, that all women and men are made in the image and likeness of God, that all are brothers and sisters in Christ, that all are God's children—none better or worse for skin color. Yet enormous prejudice exists in many, if not most, societies and cultures—prejudice based solely on the color of skin.

These Web sites are devoted to providing information on and links to a wide variety of antiracism sources on the World Wide Web. They provide an enormous amount of information about the way racial prejudice has operated in society, here and abroad, now and through history. Sobering material here: this is a very important Web site!

Cardoner Ripples of Justice
http://www.vicnet.net.au/~cardoner/ripples.html

Cardoner is the name given to these pages and the name of a river in Spain that flows into the Mediterranean Sea. It was on the bank of the River Cardoner and in a nearby cave at Manresa where Ignatius of Loyola, who started the Jesuits, underwent some of the most intense mystical experiences of his life. Out of reflecting on these experiences and discerning the interior spirits came his Spiritual Exercises.

The Cardoner Web pages are about religion, with an emphasis in Christian (and specifically Catholic) topics; social issues, ecology, human rights, and justice topics from a Christian perspective; and the Jesuits (Society of Jesus) in Australia and their works. These pages comprise a project of the Australian Jesuits.

This site features action alerts, places, issues, organizations, and other interesting Web sites. It has interesting information on the indigenous of Australia and the Pacific, including migrant and refugee issues. The site also has information from Chiapas, Mexico. It pays special attention to the situation in East Timor, where the Indonesian army continues its occupation of a largely Catholic land. There is much here on the human rights violations occurring in East Timor. Another country these social justice–minded Jesuits are watching is Rwanda, where a genocidal civil war has devastated the country. The site also has an ecology and environment watch that includes an extensive list of resources. This is an excellent site with quality information and analysis.

CatholicMobile:Activism
http://www.mcgill.pvt.k12.al.us/jerryd/cm/act.htm

> "It is utterly intolerable for Catholics to restrict themselves to
> the position of mere observers."
>
> —*Pope John XXIII, 1959 Christmas*

There are no excuses for sitting on the sidelines after reading through this Web site. It features actions to take and organizations to join to get involved in the pressing social issues of our times. This site directs the visitor to a host of movements and campaigns of the antirace, antipoverty, and antiwar stripe. From parish-based actions to organizing in the neighborhood, from coalition building to Internet activities and lobbying in Congress, this site can tell you the road to take. The site also makes the point—implicitly and explicitly—that the World Wide Web has quickly become the tool of choice for networking and communication among activists for justice and peace.

Amnesty International
http://www.amnesty.org/

This Web site needs no introduction; Amnesty International is the best-known human rights organization in the world. It watches for rights violations and reports them regularly to the international community.

This site features the Amnesty International 1996 report, which covers human rights conditions in 146 countries, exposing abuses in every region of the world. This page gives facts, figures, and summaries of human rights violations worldwide.

This site also features special human rights campaigns. The day I looked at the Amnesty International Web site, it related information on the importance of health professionals who expose human rights abuses. "Medical evidence is a powerful aid in the search for justice by victims of human rights violations," the site stated. Doctors and nurses have been killed and jailed because they refused to cover up medical evidence of torture and other human rights violations or because they gave medical care to government opponents. So, in May 1996 Amnesty International launched a campaign in support of health professionals at risk because they had reported human rights violations and treated the victims. The campaign was launched with the publication of a report documenting the experience of health professionals in 12 countries.

Another campaign on the AI Web site dealt with human rights violations in China, where one-fifth of the world's population lives and where human rights violations are a daily occurrence, according to Amnesty International. While China's economy develops rapidly, the old methods of political control remain. Repressive legislation and the widespread abuse of power mean that everyone is at risk. China's economic revolution has brought greater prosperity for many, but economic reforms have not been matched by greater civil and political freedom. So Amnesty International said it was campaigning for the Chinese authorities and the international community to take urgent steps to protect the fundamental rights and freedoms of 1.2 billion Chinese people.

In addition to information on Amnesty International campaigns, the site features monthly updates, highlighting countries where urgent intervention is required. Amnesty International is a great addition to the World Wide Web.

CatholicMobile:Human Rights

http://www.mcgill.pvt.k12.al.us/jerryd/cm/death.htm

> "Let the United Nations Declaration of Human Rights be ratified by all governments who have not yet adhered to it, and let it be fully observed by all."
>
> —*1971 Synod of Bishops, Justice in the World*

One of the landmark Catholic documents on human rights and human dignity leads this list of documents and sites.

The document, an encyclical by Pope John XXIII, Peace on Earth, is his most magnificent pastoral letter to the Church. It so impressed the world community at the time that the United Nations took it up as a study topic. Peace on Earth was grounded in traditional Catholic natural law teaching, developed by the scholastics in the thirteenth century.

According to this teaching, the world is governed by natural law, which is in harmony with divine law. Natural law is universal and applicable to all, not just Catholics. In other words, there is a governing law of nature that is reasonable and understandable to all. People are called to live in harmony with this law. Natural law expresses the intrinsic dignity of all men and women as sons and daughters of God. Thus, all people have rights that stem from dignity and these rights cannot be violated.

This site also features the Universal Declaration of Human Rights by the United Nations. It discusses human rights as abstract principles and in actual settings. It lists documents on human rights and has information on political crimes, disappeared persons, genocide, political prisoners, and acts of torture and terrorism. The site also links with many other sites that pay close attention to human rights and human rights abuses worldwide.

State of World's Children

http://www.unicef.org/sowc96/

> "I see the world gradually being turned into a wilderness, I hear the ever-approaching thunder which will destroy us too. I can feel the suffering of millions, and yet, if I look up into the heavens, I think that it will all come right, that this cruelty, too, will end."

These are the words of a 15-year-old girl. They could have been written yesterday by a child in Bosnia or Liberia, in Afghanistan or the Sudan. In fact, they were written more than 50 years ago in the Netherlands, by Anne Frank, who died shortly afterward in a Nazi concentration camp.

This site deals with the needs of children worldwide. It commemorates the fiftieth anniversary of the United Nations children's organization, UNICEF. The organization was founded in 1946 in the aftermath of World War II, as the United Nations International Children's Emergency Fund.

"Times have changed—and they have not changed," this UNICEF site states. In 1996, the world's children again face the carnage of war. Millions live with shattered innocence, daily terror, and stifled hopes, which Anne Frank would recognize only too well.

The site asks, "If children are loved and valued, why are they still being used as cannon-fodder?" A weary response might lay the blame on innate human cruelty and duplicity. A cynic would also argue that incessant television coverage has done little more than stun our sensibilities and that all conventions and declarations will inevitably crumple before the barrel of a gun. UNICEF, however, states that it takes a different view. It believes that this gap between rhetoric and reality represents a historic challenge. In response to so much destruction and pain, there have also been unprecedented efforts at peacemaking and caring for the victims. "The urgency now is to vastly enhance the means both to prevent future conflicts and to better support victims."

This site introduces and highlights UNICEF's work and responses in meeting the pressing needs of children throughout the world.

Friends of the Earth Home Page

http://www.foe.co.uk/

The Friends of the Earth Home Page paints a dire picture: "For thousands upon thousands of years, the Earth has sustained a wonderfully rich and interconnected web of life. Now, however, one single species—humankind—is putting it all at risk. The world's forests are disappearing ... our air and water are no longer clean and pure ... species are dying out at a terrifying rate ... toxic waste is piling up ... people everywhere suffer from pollution and environmental damage." The site continues: "It needn't be like this."

For 25 years, Friends of the Earth has led the way in putting forward positive solutions to these and many other environmental problems. This site introduces the visitor to the group's mission and goals. It also features the current national campaigns in which the organization is involved.

Center For World Indigenous Studies Home Page
http://www.halcyon.com/FWDP/cwisinfo.html

The Center for World Indigenous Studies (CWIS) states that it is an independent, nonprofit research and education organization dedicated to wider understanding and appreciation of the ideas and knowledge of indigenous peoples and the social, economic, and political realities of indigenous nations. Its stated aim is to foster better understanding between peoples through the publication and distribution of literature written and voiced by leading contributors from Fourth World nations. The center serves as a clearinghouse for ideas between nations. CWIS receives documents, publications, and undocumented information from throughout the world. These materials are carefully archived. The site also promotes direct exchange of information through people exchanges, workshops, symposia, and conferences. This site intends to help fulfill the mission of the center by linking interested parties.

Engaged Buddhism
http://www.maui.com/~lesslie/

This is one of the most colorful and interesting of the peace and justice sites. Engaged Buddhism is a relatively new idea, developed by Buddhist monks such as Thich Nhat Hanh, who currently lives in exile in a community in France. This site speaks to some of the best religious ecumenical efforts, bringing together the major religions in their common struggles for human rights, a more just and peaceful world, and greater harmony with the environment. This site gets the visitor involved in some of the major global human rights campaigns and introduces the visitor to some of the great twentieth-century human rights advocates and organizations. Lots of great photographs and wonderful links are on these pages. This is a first rate site, and I highly recommend it.

Office of Juvenile Justice and Delinquency Prevention

http://www.ncjrs.org/ojjhome.htm

This site states that its mission is to provide national leadership to support methods to prevent juvenile victimization and juvenile delinquency. This is accomplished, the site continues, through prevention programs and a juvenile justice system that protects the public safety, holds juvenile offenders accountable, and provides treatment and rehabilitative services. The site features the National Juvenile Justice Action Plan, a response to a call by the U.S. Attorney General to take action on behalf of children to reduce crime by and against juveniles. Responding to that call, the sites states, the Coordinating Council on Juvenile Justice and Delinquency Prevention has developed the National Juvenile Justice Action Plan. This site introduces the council, providing an overview, and explains the contents of the action plan.

American Red Cross

http://www.crossnet.org/

The American Red Cross is as American as, well, the American Red Cross. The Red Cross stands for generosity. There is something sacred about blood; it represents and sustains life. It is fitting, then, to support the Red Cross and its work and concerns. Recently, in addition to its normal relief work, the Red Cross has become involved in AIDS education. This site tells the story of the Red Cross and suggests ways supporters can assist the organization. It also explains Red Cross career opportunities.

CHAPTER 11

Renewal Groups

After becoming pope, on January 25, 1959, Pope John XXIII announced he planned to hold an ecumenical council. Throughout Catholic history there had been only 20 earlier ecumenical councils. Called to determine new doctrine or protest against heresy, councils are solemn occasions, gatherings of prominent church prelates and theologians during which they give more definitive shape to Catholic belief. John's idea was different; he wanted this council to be "pastoral" not "doctrinal." He felt that it was time to update Catholic belief and practice to make it more understandable to the modern world. He wanted to reformulate church thinking and practice to make it more relevant, more vibrant. Most simply, he wanted to modernize the Catholic church. It is said—although some call it church lore—that John, speaking of the Church, remarked that he wanted to "throw open the doors and windows and let a little light in." His popularity, meanwhile, mushroomed. Within weeks, during the very infancy of his pontificate, Catholics were calling him "the good Pope John."

The Second Vatican Council, or Vatican II, opened on October 11, 1962. A total of 2,860 prelates attended the first session; between 2,000 and 2,500 would participate in each of the last three sessions. Each day for several months, the world's bishops gathered inside St. Peter's Basilica to discuss, debate, and vote. The atmosphere was highly politicized with sharp differences among the prelates. The last session's last day was December 8, 1965. However, before it was all over, the council had promulgated 16 documents, all aimed at forcing change, or church renewal, as it was called. Vatican II was the most stunning facelift in all of Catholic history.

John XXIII was succeeded June 21, 1963, by Giovanni Battista Montini, the archbishop of Milan. Montini took the name Pope Paul VI and immediately said he would carry through with the work of the council. He, too, wanted to update the Church. Speaking in his first radio address the day after his election, Montini said: "The main duty of our pontificate will be the continuation of the Second Vatican Council."

Pope John Paul I became pope on August 26, 1978, following Pope Paul's death, but he lived only one month before dying of heart failure. Pope John Paul II took the names of his three predecessors, but his inclinations generally have not been sympathetic to the renewal of the council. A conservative, he has been suspicious of change and has talked about church "abuses" that resulted from the council. As a result, there are two major currents of thought in modern Roman Catholicism: post-conciliar "renewal" and reactionary "counterrenewal." Since the early 1980s, the Vatican, under Pope John Paul II, has been staunchly conservative—but renewal activities continue throughout the Church. Groups advocating these renewals see themselves as working out of the spirit of Vatican II.

This chapter contains Web sites of these organizations. I encountered a number of European renewal Web sites in German, Italian, Dutch, and other languages. Some of the sites in this chapter link to these European sites, but since these have no English equivalent I did not include them here.

Association for the Rights of Catholics in the Church

http://astro.ocis.temple.edu/~arcc/

The Association for the Rights of Catholics in the Church (ARCC) was founded in 1980 by lay and clerical Catholics in the wake of Vatican condemnations of such European and U.S. Catholic theologians as Edward Schillebeeckx, Jacques Pohier, and Hans Kung. The association affirms that there are fundamental rights rooted in the humanity and baptism of all Catholics and seeks to put into practice the statement of the 1971 Synod of Bishops: "While the Church is bound to give witness to justice, she recognizes that anyone who ventures to speak to people about justice must first be just in their eyes. Hence we must undertake an examination of the modes of acting and of the possessions and life-style found within the Church itself. Within the church, rights must be preserved."

It is the last sentence in this quotation that AARC emphasizes as it moves from mission to goal. As this site states, ARCS's goal is: "to institutionalize a collegial and egalitarian understanding of Church in which decision-making is shared and accountability is realized among Catholics of every kind. We are Church!"

The Church has traditionally defined itself as a group of bishops, priests, and women religious. AARC wants to dispel this notion. It sees the church primarily as laity, which is the way the bishops who gathered in Rome in 1962 saw it. "People of God," AARC and other reform-minded Catholics argue that until human rights are vigorously respected within the Church, its central mission—spreading the faith—is compromised.

This site highlights AARC's Constitution, newsletters, and press releases and provides plenty of information about what the organization stands for. It also lists documents by prominent clergy who call out for greater justice and openness in the Church. It explains how to join an

AARC discussion group on the Internet and offers many links to other progressive sites on the Web.

Call to Action

http://listserv.american.edu/catholic/cta/index.html

Call to Action is an independent Chicago-based church renewal organization, an engine moving Vatican Council renewal into the twenty-first century. Call to Action, or CTA, is best known for its annual convention, or gathering, at which several thousand like-minded laity and clergy gather to meet and encourage each other to carry out Church reforms—reforms begun at the Council in the mid-1960s but that have been largely thwarted by the very conservative pontificate of Pope John Paul II.

Call to Action, a nonprofit organization, boasts a membership of some 12,000 laity, religious, and clergy. What draws these Catholics together, in the words of the CTA, is "the Spirit of God (who) is at work in the whole church, not just in its appointed leaders." CTA believes "the entire Catholic church has the obligation of reading the signs of the times, responding to the needs of the world, and taking initiative in programs of peace and justice."

This site is a good place to come for tuning into the Catholic renewal effort. It provides basic information about the CTA and news about its annual gathering. It also provides news about regional CTA organizations that are springing up around the nation. CTA publications can also be found on this site, as can related CTA activities and a calendar of events.

One related CTA organization featured on this site is Catholic Organizations for Renewal (COR), a forum of a dozen or more Catholic renewal groups that work together on various projects. CTA also features its Arts in the Ministry Project, cataloguing and promoting artistic productions from many sources. Also on this site is information on Catholic social teachings and links to an array of progressive and renewal-minded sites. CTA's vision of church is spirit-based, inclusive, and centered on the Gospel messages of love, justice, and forgiveness. The CTA is a national network of Catholics helping to keep the spirit of the Vatican Council alive in our times.

Call to Action, Wisconsin, Inc.

http://www.execpc.com/~rakirsch/cta/cta.html

Call to Action, Wisconsin, Inc. was started in February 1995 to meet a very basic need—grassroots reform of both the Catholic Church and our society. It is loosely affiliated with the national CTA, but each state or regional organization has its own identity. Its stated mission: "to be in touch with each other on our journey toward renewal." This is the first upper midwest conference.

This site offers information on general meetings and retreat weekends. It reports renewal developments in the Church and offers a video and audio tape library. It links with other progressive and renewal-oriented Catholic sites and uses the site to provide information about itself as well as offering an email address for further contacts. It is an example of a relatively low-maintenance means of keeping a relatively high profile on the Web.

Catholic Referenda Throughout the World

http://www.austria.eu.net:81/wsk

Throughout Europe and North America, tens of thousands of Catholics have been raising their voices, calling for change in the Church. Their concerns vary, but they agree on one idea: Vatican authority has become too centralized under the pontificate of Pope John Paul II—and it has become abusive as a result. The sharing of authority envisioned by the Second Vatican Council has not gone forward, these reform advocates maintain. As a result of these concerns and hoping for greater participation in their Church, Catholic reform advocates have begun to circulate a number of referenda. They have been seeking signatures to make their concerns better known. The message they want to deliver is their dismay over the direction the Church is taking under the leadership of Pope John Paul II. This site provides information about the various Church protest papers and referenda in both Europe and North America.

Small Faith Communities

http://listserv.american.edu/catholic/cta/sfcintro.html

One of the signs of hope in the Catholic church today is the rapid spread of small faith communities. These are groups of 20 to 40 Catholics, who gather regularly to worship, study scripture, and minister to each other and others. The Chicago-based Call to Action renewal organization has been gathering names of these groups for several years and has published these names for the past two years. This Web site highlights the CTA small faith community directory.

This site is a subsite of CTA. The directory is important not only for networking, but also because the stories of these communities are going to be increasingly important in the historical development of U.S. Catholicism. Catholics often feel their parishes are too big and impersonal. One of the models that has developed in the Church in recent years has been to view the parish as a "community of communities." What the CTA directory points out is that the growing small faith community phenomenon is also a force for Church spiritual renewal. Generally, those who have come to these communities are open to and seeking a stronger sense of faith community. They become agents for change.

The 1995–1996 edition of the *CTA National Directory* lists 235 small faith communities and church renewal organizations. The listing is done alphabetically by city within each state. CTA said the second directory represents almost a doubling of its first directory.

Lesbian, Gay, and Bisexual Catholic Handbook
http://www.bway.net/~halsall/lgbh.html

This is a first-rate site, the work of Paul Halsall, who is doing some of the best Catholic Web work. Of the sites I came across on the Web, this one appeared to be the most thorough on Catholic lesbian, gay, and bisexual issues. I also liked the way Halsall designed his clearly laid-out site.

The Lesbian and Gay and Bisexual Catholic Handbook is an attempt to organize and present a great deal of information, discussion, and argumentation that will be helpful to lesbian, gay, and bisexual Catholics. Halsall says he spent much time organizing, writing, and researching this information, and it shows.

Halsall writes: "To Lesbian, Gay and Bisexual Catholics, other Christians, and friends visiting this site for the first time—Welcome! ... To people who are hostile to gay people, or to those who wonder what is the point or "agenda" of a site like this, please read on." Halsall goes on to state that "Christianity—and its cultural remnants—are among the prime creators of the repression of gay people," adding, "I am concerned to change things. But more: I am also a Catholic who believes very deeply in the revelation of God in Jesus of Nazareth and God's continued presence in the world."

The Lesbian, Gay and Bisexual Catholic Handbook is structured into 10 chapters. Under each chapter heading are documents, images, and links to others parts of the Internet. The visitor can browse the entire handbook or jump directly to a chapter by selecting it from a list on the Web page.

The chapters are as follows: Chapter 1: Basic Bibliographical Guides, Chapter 2: Documents, Chapter 3: Discussion of the Bible, Chapter 5: Lesbian and Gay Catholics, Chapter 6: Lesbian and Gay Marriage, Chapter 7: Witnesses to Truth: Writing in Support of LGB (lesbian, gay, bisexual) Catholics, Chapter 8: Other Ways of Looking at the Issue: Read for Fun, Chapter 9: Miscellaneous

Issues, and Chapter 10: LGB Catholic Resources. There are nuggets in each chapter, whether or not one is gay. Under Miscellaneous, for example, there is "Advice on how to come out," "Origins of the word `faggot'," and "What percentage of the world is gay?"

Dignity/San Diego

http://www.lanz.com/dignity/

It was the letter heard around the world, especially by gay and lesbian Catholics. On October 31, 1986, Cardinal Joseph Ratzinger, prefect of the Vatican's Congregation for the Doctrine of Faith, charged by the pope with upholding church orthodoxy, released a document entitled "Letter to the Bishops of the Catholic Church on the Pastoral Care of Homosexual Persons." Most of the letter covered no new ground. It cited scripture and church tradition to uphold the church's strict judgment against homosexual acts, which are viewed as gravely wrong in all circumstances.

The language that followed was new, as was its characterization of the homosexual orientation. It stated: "Although the particular inclination of the homosexual person is not a sin, it is a more or less strong tendency ordered toward an intrinsic moral evil; and thus the inclination itself must be seen as an objective disorder." Whatever else the Vatican had said, what was heard loudest were the words "objective disorder." Reactions to the letter among U.S. Catholics, including bishops, clergy, and laity, ranged from lukewarm to hostile. Among Catholic gays and lesbians there was only anger and tears.

Most gay and lesbian Catholics have a love-hate relationship with the Church. They love their home but feel forced to live with seemingly hostile parents. As a result, thousands of gay and lesbian Catholics, especially those who are openly gay and lesbian, have found shelter in one of about 100 local Dignity chapters, Catholic communities of gay and lesbians. Contrary to official Church teachings,

Dignity professes that "gay, lesbian, and bisexual persons can express their sexuality in a unitive manner that is loving, life-giving, and life-affirming."

The Dignity/San Diego Web site is one of the better Dignity home pages. It provides information to local gays and lesbians regarding the local chapter's activities, explains the mission and purpose of Dignity and its history, and it links with other Dignity groups across the county. For any gay or lesbian Catholic feeling alienated from the Church but looking for a Catholic community, a visit to this Web site would be an affirming step.

Dignity Writings
http://www.qrd.org/qrd/orgs/dignity/

This site is a subsite to the Queer Resources Directory and the location of significant documents related to the activities of Dignity/USA and its local affiliates. Dignity/USA is an organization of gay, lesbian, and bisexual Roman Catholics and friends with approximately 85 chapters in the United States. The following, taken from the site, explains that Dignity affirms that gay, lesbian, and bisexual Catholics are members of Christ's mystical body, numbered among the people of God: "We believe that gays, lesbians, and bisexuals can express their sexuality in a way that is consonant with Christ's teaching." Dignity is organized to unite gay, lesbian, and bisexual Catholics and to be an instrument through which they may be heard by the church and society.

In order to respect the autonomy of local chapters, Dignity/USA has allowed the creation of what seems to be the most complex membership and dues system of any nonprofit organization in the United States. All members join a local chapter, but if there is no chapter nearby, a potential member may choose to be affiliated with any chapter he or she wishes, or Dignity will automatically assign a member to the closest chapter geographically.

Dues vary with chapter and region, with $40 to $50 being typical.

Besides recent news releases and documents by Dignity, this site contains a Dignity email list, hotline telephone numbers, contacts, and defenders of Dignity and Dignity links in Canada and the United States.

Radical Catholic

http://www.bway.net/~halsall/radcath.html

The author and maintainer of this Web site is Paul Halsall, who clearly loves the Catholic Church and just as clearly believes it is in need of radical reform if it is to fully live out its mission as God's visible sign in the world of love and reconciliation. This Catholic Web site is a favorite of thinking Catholics who, for one reason or another, believe their Church today is hurting and in serious need of reform. The vision of Church that comes out of Halsall's active and engaging Web site is that of an inclusive, sacramental body guided more by scripture and far less by official canons.

"Roman Catholicism," the site states, "is a religion which at its very fundamental level is life-affirming, earth-affirming, and love-affirming." Progressive and/or renewal-minded Catholics will feel at home on this Web site. For those who feel their church is too stuffy or failing to live up to its own teachings, the site will be like a child's visit to a candy story. With the abundance of information on renewal groups or church documents supporting a more radical stance toward the peace, justice, and environmental issues or links to similarly oriented Web sites, the only problem for the visitor will be deciding which delight to consume first.

Besides many links to other Catholic sites, this site lists resources under the following headings: Basic Documents, Women Priests, Liberation Theology, Ecclesiology and Church Structure Issues, Lesbian and Gay Issues. The Death Penalty, Radical Catholic Voices on "Official" and "Conservative" Positions, The Radical Religious Right,

Radical Catholic Witness, Radical Inspiration, About Radical Catholic Groups, Just Very Useful to Have Handy, Miscellaneous, Catholic Social Teaching, Historical Documents, Papal Teaching, Conciliar Teaching, Episcopal Teaching, Links to Other Radical Catholic Sources, Links to Other Radical Christian Sources, Links to Other Radical Sources, and Radical Catholic Approaches.

For the "radical" Catholic, this site seems to have it all.

Partenia
http://www.partenia.fr/indexU.html

This may well be the most publicized Catholic Web site in the Roman Catholic world, the virtual diocese of Bishop Jacques Gaillot, bishop of Partenia. Many Catholics know the story: The progressive French Bishop Gaillot, when called to appear before Cardinal Bernardin Gantin of the Congregation of Bishops at the Vatican on January 12, 1995, had no idea what was about to happen. No bishop in modern history had been summarily dismissed from his See. The then 59-year-old Gaillot recalls the hard-line Vatican conservative, Gantin, ticking off his case against him. It included a list of references to earlier warnings and subsequent "inappropriate" behavior, at least from Rome's vantage, on the part of the bishop from Evreux.

What followed was a litany of Vatican complaints, including matters such as failing to notify other bishops when visiting their dioceses, not adequately depicting official Catholic teachings while appearing on French television, and advocating the use of condoms to prevent the spread of the HIV virus. Gantin ended the session abruptly with a stark demand. He wanted Gaillot's immediate resignation. When the bishop refused, Gantin announced bluntly: "It has been decided that tomorrow you should retire as bishop of Evreux. At noon. And the diocese of Evreux will be declared vacant."

Gaillot marked the first anniversary of his ouster by turning his newly assigned but nonexisting titular See of Partenia, a long-defunct See in the middle of the Sahara Desert, into the world's first cyber-diocese by putting it on the World Wide Web. He said it would be a "place of liberty," open to all. Ironically, the preaching of the bishop now reaches more Catholics than before the Vatican made an example of him. This site tells the Gaillot story and contains his thoughts on a variety of subjects. It has form-driven mail to foster communication with Gaillot. This site is a clear example of how modern technology is changing the very idea of community and bringing the like-minded, scattered around the globe, into closer contact.

Community of the Ascension
http://www.vol.it/IT/IT/ASSOC/ASCENS/ukmain.htm

This is a Naples, Italy–based Church renewal site, reminding North American Catholics that renewal is alive and well in Europe. Many of the themes and ideas that fuel Catholic renewal in the United States are alive in Europe. This site is indicative of this life. The Community of the Ascension refers to the priest, Antonio Maione, who remains in touch with Catholic and non-Catholic groups struggling for democratization of the hierarchy. The community also places high value in ecumenical work.

In 1995, the Community of the Ascension offered its active support to French Bishop J. Gaillot, the progressive prelate who was asked to leave his See in France and was subsequently offered a new diocese, the ancient and inactive diocese of Partenia.

This site gives information on renewal efforts throughout Europe, but particularly in Naples, Italy. It gathers and reprints information on Catholic renewal developments. It serves as a Catholic networking site, especially for Italian Catholics. It has also begun an Internet newspaper. This site is still under construction, but it contains lists of addresses and telephone numbers for progressive links. Reading the information contained on the site is instructive, as it brings another pair of eyes—non North American eyes—to the broader discussion of Church renewal. So not only is the site functional, it is also an education unto itself.

Matthew Fox

http://boris.qub.ac.uk/tony/Fox/

Matthew Fox, since the publication of his book, *On becoming a Musical, Mystical Bear* (1972), has become one of the best-known proponents of creation-centered spirituality in Catholic circles. He was the founder of the Institute for Creation-Centered Spirituality, located at Holy Names College in Oakland, California. In 1992, he left the Dominican Order after a dispute with his superiors regarding his relationship to his province, and in 1994, he left the Roman Catholic Church to become an episcopalian.

The question that led to Fox's expulsion from the Dominicans was not his theology, spirituality, or ministry as much as it was accountability to the Order. A process of negotiation and consultation between Fox and his Order had gone on for years. In the words of the master of the Order, Father Timothy Radcliffe, "every possible avenue of reconciliation was explored without success," and the sole reason for Fox's dismissal "was his failure to accept anything that could be plausibly counted as minimal accountability to his province."

This site acts as a front for the Matthew Fox mailing list. In this sense it is promotional, but it also has useful information about books and other items that deal with creation-centered spirituality, which argues that Christianity has traditionally paid more attention to the Fall than to the Original Blessing of creation itself. In other words, Christianity professes a belief in a Trinitarian God, but Christians, especially in the West, have often built theologies around the Second Person of the Trinity, the

Redeemer, while paying far less attention to the First Person of the Trinity, the Creator. An effect of this has been that Christianity had paid more attention to human sinfulness than to human goodness, Fox contends.

This site also contains a brief bibliography of Thomas Berry, a Passionist priest who has called himself a "geologian." While Fox has been the popularizer of creation-centered spirituality, Berry has been its chief intellectual guru. Berry's thinking has had enormous influence on Catholics and environmentalists. On the list of Berry books is *Dream of the Earth*, which contains his most important essay, "The New Story." This essay is the germ of Berry's writing and should be read by all who prize spirituality and love of planet Earth.

Women's Ordination

http://www.microweb.com/burnside/sfbwomen.htm

The women's ordination issue is arguably the most explosive issue facing the Catholic Church at the end of the twentieth century. Educated Catholic women, especially in the West, have argued that a church that does not ordain women, and therefore does not allow them into key decision-making roles, discriminates and acts unjustly. Advocates of women's ordination argue that only by opening all ministries to women, including the priestly ministry, can the Catholic church maintain credibility in the modern world or grow meaningfully in the twenty-first century.

On October 28, 1995, the Vatican, speaking on behalf of Pope John Paul II, said that it is to be held by all Catholics as "infallible" church teaching that the Church can never ordain women as priests. The stage for conflict could not be more clear. This is especially so because in the October 1995 statement, Rome said the issue is settled and cannot be further discussed. But this has not happened; for example, during 1996 both the U.S. bishops body and the U.S. theologians formally took up the discussion of a woman priesthood. What they found was that like other Catholics, the U.S. bishops and theologians are bitterly divided on the issue of ordination.

This site, run by San Francisco Bay Catholic, offers arguments on behalf of women's ordination. "The New Testament and the whole history of the Church," it states, "give ample evidence of the presence in the Church of women, true disciples, witnesses to Christ in the family and in society." This site contains the latest articles, letters, and documents to come forward on this issue. Along the way it examines the question of papal infallibility.

San Francisco Bay Catholic
http://www.microweb.com/burnside/sfbay.htm

"Don't mistake us for your average 'Bible Board'! San Francisco Bay Catholic is a serious site for adults." So the San Francisco Bay Catholic Web site visitor is warned. To understand why this site is different from other Catholic Web sites, the visitor is invited to read the Bay Catholic mission statement, which reads:

> Most Catholic sites start off by proclaiming their allegiance to the magisterium of the Church. They then provide a list of links, FTP sites and certain restricted lists of "safe" mailing lists or Internet newsgroups which reflect that magisterial position. The SFBAY CATHOLIC web site takes a different approach. We focus on Catholicism, ethics, and Catholic moral issues; however our focus is on presenting both sides of those issues. This site will present links and articles which support the magisterium as we strongly feel that it is important for Catholics to understand what the Catholic Church really teaches. We will also present articles and commentary by knowledgeable Catholics and responsible theologians who disagree with the magisterium on a variety of policy and moral issues. Our goal and mission is to implement and reinvigorate the original spirit of the Second Vatican Council. We are the "progressive" Roman Catholic Web site on a worldwide Internet.

This site delivers. On a wide variety of issues, it offers official Church teaching and what are frequently referred to as "dissenting views." For example, after the former San Francisco Archbishop John R. Quinn made a major speech at Oxford University in June 1996, the site quickly added it to its Documents file. This made the text available to Catholics worldwide. This site is updated frequently and is a major contribution to Catholic Church dialogue.

San Francisco Bay Catholic Special Report
http://www.microweb.com/burnside/sfbbrusk.htm#TOP

> Any Catholics in and of the Diocese of Lincoln who attain or retain membership in any of the above listed organizations or groups after April 15, 1996, are by that very fact (ipso-facto-latae sententiae) under interdict and are absolutely forbidden to receive Holy Communion. Contumacious persistence in such membership for one month following the interdict on part of any such Catholics will by that very fact (ipso-facto-latae sententiae) cause them to be excommunicated. Absolution from these ecclesial censures is "reserved to the Bishop." This notice, when published in the Southern Nebraska Register, is a formal canonical warning. By mandate of the Most Reverend Bishop of Lincoln. (signed) Reverend Monsignor Timothy Thorburn Chancellor March 19, 1996

Such was the unprecedented threat out of Lincoln, Nebraska. No Catholic had seen that kind of use—some called it abuse—of ecclesial authority in recent memory. The organizations listed by the bishop ranged from Planned Parenthood and the Hemlock Society to Call to Action and the Rainbow Girls. It sent reporters scurrying to figure out a rationale for the move. It sent most members of the U.S. Catholic hierarchy running for cover. None wanted to defend the action; few wanted to repudiate it publicly.

The edict also got many Catholics talking about whether their Church's leaders were in touch with the real world; it got other cheering that finally a bishop was standing against modern secular forces undermining the Church. There was, however, one other reaction. The San Francisco Bay Catholic Web page created a page just to dissect and discuss the unusual move. What new surfers found on their Catholic Web sites was one of the first sites devoted entirely to a breaking news story. I expect Catholics will see similar pages in the months ahead as Web sites multiply and Web site creators grow in number. Many Catholics and others interested in trying to make heads or tails of the Lincoln affair will find this site very useful.

SNAP

http://www.ece.orst.edu/~barreta/snap/

The horrifying issue of the sexual molestation of children by clergy first surfaced as a public issue in the mid-1980s. Some 500 cases have since been recorded. The Catholic faithful's criticisms of their clergy may not be new, but the intensity of that criticism, in the wake of these revelations, has been. Given roughly 50,000 priests and roughly 500 abusers, the figure amounts to only 1 percent of the population of the priesthood. Some put the figure of abusers higher; others say it is no higher than the mean in the wider population. Whatever the figure, it represents an enormous violation of trust. It did not take long before victims and victims' families began to organize to support each other and bring their plight to the public.

Survivors Network of those Abused by Priests (SNAP) is a USA/Canadian self-help organization of men and women who were sexually abused by church officials (Catholic priests, brothers, nuns, deacons, teachers, etc). Members find healing and empowerment by joining with other survivors. SNAP is a volunteer group founded by Barbara Blaine of Chicago in 1991. SNAP's stated mission is straightforward: "to reach out to as many survivors of sexual abuse by priests as possible."

This page has been set up to provide detailed information about SNAP, advertise the SNAP email list server, provide links to useful information, and communicate on the World Wide Web.

One of the features on this site is called Tips to Reporters Investigating Sexual Abuse by Priests. Intended to help journalists overcome the barriers that limit effective coverage of sexual abuse, the information is part of the collective lesson that has grown out of this tragedy. Other information on the site includes SNAP national events, memberships, and newsletter updates. The site also offers a database of perpetrators and information on regional offices.

Rosary Crusade for Women's Ordination

http://www.ecnet.net/users/gbattag/rc_ann.htm

This site is a treat! It is based on the premise that "traditionalists" have attempted to appropriate all the Catholic traditions, making it difficult for renewal-minded Catholics to empower themselves with the sacramental powers of 20 centuries of Catholicism. There's some truth to this.

It reminds me of the events of some years back when Vietnam war protesters were making little headway in persuading the American public to be sympathetic to their antiwar views. One of the problems in the early years of those protests was that the war protesters were often carrying the Viet Cong flag! They might have felt good, but they were not acting wisely if their goal was to win public support. In the late 1960s, war protest organizers got smart and began to march in large numbers under the United States flag. That immediately made the antiwar protests more respectable, and it was not long before mainstream Americans were questioning the war.

Who is to say what is going through the minds of those calling for women's ordination while advocating the recitation of the rosary? Maybe some advocates have rediscovered the power of the rosary and its meditative and healing abilities, or maybe this is strategy. Regardless, this site is an oddity worth pondering. It caught my attention.

Are the women ordination advocates ready and willing to join the Rosary Crusade for Women's Ordination? If so, this is where to get information. This is where the networking is beginning. "Join now! Pray the rosary each Saturday in petition to Our Lady to intercede on behalf of the progressive movement in the Church ... that we may feel the direction of the Holy Spirit ... and be strengthened in our efforts." That's the prayer. After all, Mary was a liberator, a radical for all time.

Radical and Progressive Catholic Mail lists
http://www.bway.net/~halsall/radcath/rad-maillist.html

This site begins by saying that "for a long time the internet has been the preserve of conservative Catholics." Since 1994 this has changed somewhat. Now there are places—Web sites, mail lists, and newsgroups—that are more progressive.

It does appear true that conservative Catholics were first out of the blocs on the Internet. It may be that conservatives were quicker to understand the potential power of electronic communication. It may be that they had a stronger "institutional" presence and used technologies at their disposal to populate the Internet. Slowly, however, progressive voices are gaining hold in cyberspace.

This site is an example. It is intended to spawn a greater progressive Catholic presence on the Internet. This document is concerned with mail lists, one of the most enjoyable ways to use the Internet. As explained on the site, the basic idea is that a central program (usually LISTSERV) serves as a "mail exploder." One sends mail to the listserv, and it distributes it to all members of the list. Because this happens within a few minutes—or even seconds—the effect is of a wide-ranging multithreaded conference. The advantage of mail lists is that they develop a community spirit. It seems that the minimal commitment of actually having to "subscribe" leads to more committed group members.

This site lists progressive mail lists; it offers information on these lists, including how to subscribe to them. For some time, one of my favorites has been SISTER-L@LIST-SERV.SYR.EDU. An electronic discussion group, SISTER-L focuses on the history and contemporary concerns of Catholic women religious (sisters and nuns). Its threads are thoughtful, its manner is inclusive and polite. One need not be Catholic or a woman to be part of these conversations. SISTER-L states the only persons not welcome are those whose purpose is to bash or ridicule sisters or religious life.

California Catholics for Free Choice

http://www.stasek.com/ccffc/brochure.html

Catholics for Free Choice is a national nonprofit organization that provides a voice for Catholics who uphold reproductive freedom. California Catholics for Free Choice is a community of faithful women and men who believe in the primacy of conscience and work for social justice in the reproductive arena. California Catholics are multicultural and multilingual, "and a wide diversity of ethnic and racial backgrounds enriches our community," according to the site. Its materials are translated into Spanish and other languages. Its liturgies are multilingual, and information is available in the native language of the individual seeking it.

This site states that Catholics for Free Choice believes that all women have the right to make their own moral decisions about abortion. That's why it is Pro-Choice, it says. The organization states that it is not "pro-abortion," but it believes that abortion must be legal for women even to begin to make moral choices with real freedom.

The site offers information about itself and abortion as an issue both nationally and locally. It provides the following statistics relating to Catholics and the abortion issue:

- 79% of Catholics believe a person could be a "good" Catholic even if they disagree with the Church on abortion. (CBS/*New York Times,* 1985)
- 85% of Catholics agree with the statement: "Women can have an abortion and still be a good Catholic." (Gallop, May 5–17, 1992)
- Abortion should generally be available: Catholics 44%; All Respondents 43% (*CBS News/New York Times,* October 1992)

Old Catholic Discussion List
http://www.cris.com/~jgilhous/oldcath.html

The Old Catholic Discussion List home page is not the work of your ordinary Catholic renewal group. This one has been around for more than a century. These Old Catholics formed after the First Vatican Council in 1870. Their primary complaint was the abuse of papal authority following the declaration of papal infallibility at that council. There are three groups of Old Catholics in the West. This one is centered in Utrecht. Another large group has Polish roots. They all see themselves as a historic part of the One, Holy, Catholic, and Apostolic Church, this one with origins in the Ancient Catholic Church of the Netherlands.

Many of today's renewal groups share the Old Catholics' concern that the Vatican has centralized authority to the point where it is unhealthy for the Church. On the other hand, Old Catholics would be viewed as conservative measured against today's renewal groups.

This Web site is divided into sections: a brief introduction and historical sketch of the Old Catholic Churches in general and the Old Roman Catholic Church in North America in particular; an index of files about Old Catholic liturgies, faith, and practice, and classic spirituality. The site contains the Old Catholics' mission, a series of historical articles by their presiding bishop, and their final and definitive statement of common belief. The site also contains information on Old Catholics' liturgies and links to other sites of interest to these Christians.

This site is meant to be the "electronic library and resource center" for the Old Catholic mailing list. The page was originally set up by Thomas Bridge, but most of the information is from Fr. John-Mark Gilhousen, who serves as parish priest to St. Camillus' Mission in Portland, Maine.

Pro-Life

Catholic teaching on abortion is clear, but what the church demands in the political arena is not so clear. Catholic doctrine does not require Catholics to insist that all their moral values be incorporated into secular law. The Catholic church has opposed the practice of abortion over the centuries, although prominent theologians have debated when "ensoulment" occurs. In modern times, the Church, taking the most conservative position, has taught that life must be protected from the moment of conception. While Catholics have traditionally opposed abortion, they, like others, have often been divided in how they want to work to limit or eliminate the practice. They have also been divided on who should make the decision of whether a woman should have an abortion—the state or the woman herself.

While the sites in this chapter deal primarily with abortion from the official Church perspective, some provide a variety of views. Some are primarily interested in assisting women in a time of difficulty as she faces an unexpected pregnancy. Other sites deal with support for life in a broader context, including work against euthanasia and infanticide. Within the Catholic context, *pro-life* has been an umbrella term also covering the activities of those who work to uphold official church teaching that bans the use of artificial contraception. Some of these links also appear in this chapter.

Abortion Views
http://pwa.acusd.edu/~hinman/abortion.html

There are many resources available on the Web that relate to abortion, including home pages of pro-choice and pro-life groups. This site contains both, making it especially useful for open and honest dialogue. The site is divided into five parts. The first offers useful Internet links related to abortion. The second provides a short survey of some of the more important philosophical work on abortion. It is based on the bibliographical essay in Lawrence M. Hinman's *Contemporary Moral Issues: Diversity and Consensus*, (© 1996, Prentice-Hall). The third part contains references to recent philosophical articles on abortion, and the fourth contains short summaries and links to recent popular articles on abortion. The fifth part is devoted to discussion topics and term paper topics on the issue.

National Right to Life
http://www.nrlc.org/

National Right to Life, the focal point for anti-abortion activities on the Web, examines the issues of abortion, infanticide, and euthanasia. It states its goals as follows:

- **Abortion**: NRL works to educate Americans on the facts of human life development and the reality of abortion and to enact legislation protecting the unborn and providing abortion alternatives in Congress and state legislatures and it supports activities that help women choose life-affirming alternatives to abortion.

- **Infanticide**: NRL works to protect newborn and young children who are discriminated against simply because they have a disability.

- **Euthanasia**: NRL opposes euthanasia and the pro-death ethic that says that certain people do not have a right to life because of age, health, or disability.

This site is, perhaps, the most comprehensive and active site on the Web, helping anti-abortion activists to change attitudes and public policy regarding abortion, infanticide, and euthanasia. Checking the National Right to Life organization's Web site is certainly a quick way to stay abreast with news on the subjects of abortion, infanticide, and euthanasia as it affects government policy in the United States. The site is updated at least weekly, with action alerts for political activists. It reacts to abortion-related developments and attempts to shape the abortion discussion. For example, on June 10, 1996, when the CBS News program *60 Minutes* aired a report on the subject of partial-birth abortions, the NRL quickly issued a reaction and placed it on its Web site, describing what it said were "distortions and errors" in the *60 Minutes* broadcast. This is an example of the Web being used to disseminate information to a wide network of activists who populate the Web.

America's Crisis Pregnancy Helpline

http://www.easy.com:80/crisis/

The America's Crisis Pregnancy Helpline Web site is a Dallas-based nonprofit organization designed to provide facts about the many services and resources available across the United States for women experiencing unplanned pregnancies. It is the stated goal of the Crisis Pregnancy Helpline to provide each woman with a sense of empowerment and hope and to connect her with services in her geographic area. It wants women to know there are positive options as well as people and organizations willing to assist her as she makes informed decisions about her future.

The guiding principles of America's Crisis Pregnancy Helpline are:

1. To provide a confidential service, free of charge to the caller.

2. To remain dedicated to supporting, encouraging, informing, and empowering all women, regardless of their circumstances.

3. To never discriminate on the basis of race, creed, color, national origin, age, marital status, education level, economic status, or political beliefs.

4. To provide a caring, attentive listener to learn each woman's individual story as completely as possible and without judgment.

5. To immediately reduce the caller's sense of urgency, crisis, and despair.

6. To keep current all files and information so as to provide accurate and updated information specific to her needs and to continuously look for new resources and to foster development in areas lacking in appropriate resources.

7. To refer women to organizations that will make efforts to save the life of the baby and preserve the dignity of the mother through honest education and compassion.

8. To never provide information about prospective birth mothers to prospective adoptive parents or adoption agencies.

9. To make follow-up contacts to all women who will allow us to do so, without judgment to what decisions she has made regarding her pregnancy, to ensure her needs have been adequately met.

10. To maintain a positive, encouraging attitude at all times and to take care of ourselves so that we may take care of others.

11. To do all this in the service of God and in accordance with His guidance.

Adoption Network
http://www.infi.net/adopt/

Consider this the one-stop adoption Web site. Not only does this site provide abundant information concerning adoption, it links with other Web sites that are similarly involved in helping with the adoption process. In a society frightfully divided on the morality of abortion, both pro-life and pro-choice advocates agree that assisting child-seeking parents is a good thing.

The Adoption Network is an organization founded by adoptive parents with a personal belief in the value of adoption. Through databases of references to printed articles and testimonials of real adoption situations, it hopes to show the joys and challenges that face these special families. Adoption Network was established in the fall of 1994 to use the Internet as a means to improve the dissemination of information about adoption. The stated founding principles of the network include increasing the number of adoptions; increasing access to government information about adoption; expanding public awareness about government programs that provide assistance for adoptions; providing information concerning state adoption laws; providing a comprehensive library of resources for adoptive parents, adoptees, and adoption professionals; and helping other adoption organizations develop home pages.

According to this site, the number of adoptions of unrelated persons has actually declined in the United States over the last 20 years from 89,000 to 60,000, despite an increase in the number of families pursuing adoption. One possible reason for this decline, the site speculates, is the difficulty of identifying points of contact for information about adoption. The Adoption Network identifies more than 2,500 public and private adoption contact points, and it claims to be the only free electronic service providing this breadth of information.

With the advent of Internet connections in high schools and colleges, the Adoption Network hopes to provide many young birth parents with basic information about the process of adoption. This sort of information is difficult to locate from government listings, and many adoption agencies do not advertise in the yellow pages.

Catholics United for Life
http://www.mich.com/~buffalo/

Catholics United for Life is a nationwide organization with branches in a number of cities. Members gather to pray and give witness for the protection of all preborn humans. This is a politically active organization. It offered an endorsement to Pat Buchanan during the 1996 presidential campaign. Later it endorsed Bob Dole, but only after he chose Jack Kemp as his running mate. The site is punctuated with photographs of organization members demonstrating their opposition to abortion and praying at abortion clinics. The site also has a dozen or more links to other anti-abortion sites as well as documents opposing abortion.

Common Ground
http://www.serve.com/jennj/

This is the site for an organization that has been receiving much publicity in recent months. The group, Common Ground, sees the abortion debate as going nowhere and doing little or nothing to help the women it is fighting for. Common Ground wants to foster dialogue between the two sides. The Common Ground Network for Life and Choice was created to serve that need. The Common Ground movement, an alliance of pro-choice and pro-life, wants to give women the things they need, not just a quick fix.

"If we redirect the energy spent on fighting for choice or life, we can accomplish together the one goal we really do have in common: we want to help women," the Web page declares. The site introduces the visitor to the organization and provides information, including email address, mailing address, and telephone numbers for more contact.

Feminists for Life

http://www.serve.com/fem4life/

This site opens by asking, "Is Feminists for Life a feminist group or a pro-life group? What should our emphasis be? Eliminating abortion or enhancing the status of women?" Feminists for Life declares the answer is not either/or but rather both /and. Feminists for Life seeks to eliminate abortion but believes that the best way to do so is by enhancing the status of women.

The Web site boldly makes the point that "the necessity of abortion arises from the inferior status of women." Feminists for Life wants to raise the conditions surrounding women. "This linkage," the site claims, "was the basic tenet of the philosophy of the first American feminists." These feminists frequently cited the rather widespread incidence of abortion in their times as proof that women were an oppressed class. "The foundresses of feminism saw abortion as a symptom of the many problems imposed upon women; it is excruciatingly ironic," the site states, "that modern pro-abortion feminists see abortion as a solution to those problems." For this reason, Feminists for Life says it must speak to all issues that impact the well-being of women and children.

Project Rachel

http://ivory.lm.com:80/~lou/rachel.html

Project Rachel exists to help women who have had an abortion to reconcile with themselves. The site asks:

> What do we know about you? Others who have walked this path toward healing tell us about you. Before your abortion you were sure that this was the right thing for you: Your problems were insurmountable. You had to make an immediate decision.

You were under extreme pressure. You didn't know your options. You feared rejection. You had a right to your own choice. After your abortion, your emotional reactions to the abortion may have been suppressed for a long time. Now your initial sense of relief, of not being pregnant gives way to: A sense of loss. A feeling Anxiety Depression. Sleep disturbances, nightmares. Separation from God. Whatever the reason for the abortion, if you are now seeking a closer union with God, and spiritual healing, a compassionate, loving Church is waiting.

Project Rachel, then, sees itself as a means of receiving the healing grace of God, helping the individual to move from brokenness toward reconciliation—with self, with the unborn child, the family, the Church, and with God.

Medical Students Supporting Life

http://www.prolife.org/mssl/

Medical Students Supporting Life (MSSL) is a nonpartisan, nonprofit foundation established to promote respect for human life at all stages of development, from conception to death. Early on in one's medical studies, a student has to come to terms with how he or she regards abortion. Often, answering this question will mean deciding if the student, as an intern, will participate in an abortion. This anti-abortion organization aims to help the medical student sort out the theological and philosophical issues involved. It states its goal as follows:

- To provide a forum for nonviolent, collegiate discussion of abortion issues in an effort to establish common ground.

- To inform all individuals about medical and social facts regarding termination of pregnancy.

- To educate the medical community and society as a whole about the impact of abortion on the individual, family, and community structures.

- To reframe the abortion discussion in a moral context.

Nature's Method
http://upbeat.com/family/om.html

While polls have repeatedly shown that more than 80 percent of U.S. Catholic couples practice some form of artificial birth control, it is official church teaching that such practices are sinful. It was in 1968 that Pope Paul VI reaffirmed church teaching on the matter, issuing the controversial encyclical, *Humanae Vitae*. It restated traditional teaching banning all forms of artificial contraception. Over the years, this teaching has helped spawn organizations aimed at upholding Church teaching and supporting various techniques of natural family planning, which use nature's fertility cycles to avoid pregnancies. This site is one example.

It begins by asking, "Did you know that a woman is only fertile about 100 hours during her menstrual cycle? You can now confidently identify these hours using the 100% natural Ovulation Method. This scientifically proven method of avoiding or achieving pregnancy eliminates all health risks associated with contraceptives, and it is 99% effective."

The site then explains the basic premises of the ovulation method of family planning and refers the visitor to various educational products, including books, videos, and correspondence courses aimed at teaching the ovulation method of family planning.

The site is supported by Family of the Americas, which was founded in 1977 for the purpose of promoting programs for the family. Free information, "charting coach" software, support, materials, and articles are available through the sites.

Priests for Life
http://www.priestsforlife.org/index.html

Priests for Life is an officially approved association of Catholic clergy who give special emphasis to the pro-life teachings of the Church. "We offer ongoing assistance to the clergy in addressing the topics of abortion and euthanasia," the site states. This is one of the more active Catholic organizations in the pro-life movement.

Priests for Life claims a mail list of some 40,000 Catholic priests nationwide. The founder was Fr. Lee Kaylor, a priest of the Archdiocese of San Francisco who, in 1994, saying he wanted to encourage his brother priests to preach and teach on the sanctity of life, established a newsletter and began to organize an association to network priests who are active in pro-life work. This association obtained the endorsement of Roger Cardinal Mahony of Los Angeles in 1994, when he was chairman of the Pro-Life Committee of the U.S. Bishops.

The site lists the organization's goals as fourfold:

1. Unite, encourage, and provide ongoing training to priests and deacons who give a special emphasis to the "life issues," especially abortion and euthanasia, in their ministries.

2. Instill a sense of urgency in all clergy to teach about these issues and to mobilize their people to help stop abortion and euthanasia.

3. Help clergy and laity work together productively for the cause of life.

4. Provide ongoing training and motivation to the entire pro-life movement.

The site states that Priests for Life achieves its goals by offering pro-life seminars and retreats, by meeting with pro-life organizations, by offering audio and video tapes and brochures, and by working with the media to spread the pro-life message.

Ultimate Pro Life Resource List

http://www.prolife.org/ultimate/

This site has been acclaimed as one of the most comprehensive listings of right-to-life, or anti-abortion, resources on the Internet. In February 1996, it was proclaimed "Conservative Site of the Day." Its list of anti-abortion links is impressive. This site may be the best place to begin on a cyberspace journey into the pro-life Internet, an active area of the Web. Here the visitor will find mailing lists, organizations, adoption resources, news, political links, publications, opinion pieces, educational facts sheets, health information, and abortion alternatives. The site also has a special What's New section. The day I looked, it had a list of Life Sites of the Week. The information is fresh, and the links listed are current. Simple and clean, this site's home page takes you where you want to go.

AAA Women's Services

http://bertha.chattanooga.net/aaawomen/

This is a Chattanooga, Tennessee–based organization and Web site for women facing unexpected pregnancy. AAA Women's Services is a nonmedical, nonprofit, Christian organization "committed to saving lives by serving women." As the site explains, "The right to choose includes the right to know. As a woman today, you face tough choices. Sexual and pregnancy-related problems can be major personal crises. We understand because we are women who have faced the same choices. Our goal is to be a safe place to talk about your feelings and options." This page is among the many that bring useful information to women who face difficulties and need to reach out for assistance. This site offers a telephone number and says a call can put a woman in touch with other women who can answer questions such as "What if I am pregnant?" "Whom should I tell?" "What are my options?" and "What if I've already had an abortion?"

This site offers connections under the following page headings: Choices, Free, Confidential Services, Appointments, Abortion Information, Post-Abortion Support, Guest Book, and Other Resources. It also offers free pregnancy tests, a 24-hour hotline (423 892-0803), confidential peer counseling, maternity and baby clothing and equipment, an emergency food closet, a "my baby and me" support program, childbirth classes, and educational ultrasound.

There are many local and national resources to help women facing unexpected pregnancy. While this site is based in Tennessee, it matters little because it provides links with similar sites in other parts of the United States. It offers links under nine categories: America's Crisis Pregnancy Helpline, Bethany Christian Services, Care Net, Family Research Council, Internet Adoption Photolisting, Internet Pro-Life Journal, LifeLinks (Feminists for Life), National Women's Coalition for Life, and Ultimate Pro-Life Resource List.

Human Life International
http://www.hli.org/

Human Life International is one of the largest Catholic pro-life organizations. Founded by Benedictine Father Paul Marx, HLI states its mission is to bring "the pro-life/family message to countries throughout the world." This non-profit organization says it is devoted "to educating people about the evils of abortion, sterilization, infanticide, euthanasia, contraception and other modern threats to life and family."

Human Life International boasts that it operates in 56 countries on five continents. It has a dozen chapters in the United States. HLI conducts worldwide seminars and symposia on pro-life issues, the family, and natural birth regulation in several languages. It publishes numerous periodicals. The HLI site lists HLI position statements, has information on its founder, and provides testimonial statements regarding HLI's works by various Catholic bishops and others. The site can be accessed in English, French, Spanish, and Polish.

Partial Birth Abortion

http://www.tidalweb.com/life/

This site has grown out of the political debate over partial birth abortions. It views partial birth abortions as nothing less than barbaric. The site contains a graphic depiction of a partial birth abortion and is an example of how the Web is being used to rally public opinion and influence political discussions. "Partial birth abortion," the site states, is "4/5 infanticide, 1/5 abortion" and is "100 percent wrong." The site makes it clear that it disagrees with President Clinton's decision to veto a congressional bill that would have outlawed the practice. During a partial birth abortion, the doctor places the fetus into the "breech" position (feet first) and pulls it from the mother until all but the head is out. He or she then forces scissors into the base of the skull and inserts a catheter to suction out the child's brain. The information on this site is from the National Conference of Catholic Bishops brochure on partial birth abortions.

CatholicMobile Abortion List

http://www.mcgill.pvt.k12.al.us/jerryd/cm/abortion.htm

This Catholic site contains a first-rate list of anti-abortion links. It may well be the most complete anti-abortion list on the Internet. These links include anti-abortion organizations, information, Catholic church abortion documents, and other statements by anti-abortion activists. It provides a brief history of the abortion issue and its development in the Catholic Church. The site contains homilies on abortion, links to many other abortion sites, including a survey of philosophical work on abortion, discussion topics, and term papers on abortion. This site is a subsite of the Catholic Resource list of CatholicMobile.

Ministry

The word *ministry* comes from the Latin word *ministerium,* service, the public service rendered by members of the Church. Christian ministry, then, is the work of those who have special callings and gifts and respond to serve in the name of Christ. Within the Church there are special ecclesial ministries to which members of the faithful are appointed by church officials, such as the ministry of the priesthood. In this chapter, however, I use the term in a broader sense, in the sense of general service.

The idea of ministry within the Church has changed over the centuries. It has generally moved from a narrow to a broader interpretation. That is, the Church now teaches that all the faithful, by baptism and confirmation, are called to take an active responsibility for the community and mission of the church. All are called to ministry.

This chapter could fill the book. Catholics are ministering, serving the Church, the People of God, in a seemingly infinite number of ways. In this chapter I highlight a few Web sites that exist for the specific purpose of spreading the Word to enhance a given ministry. One could correctly argue that almost any Catholic site would fit this bill. Nevertheless, I wanted to show how the Web is being used to assist Christians. Here are some examples; many more could be listed. I chose these not only because of their intrinsic importance but because they show the rich variety of ministry that exists and how the Web is helping out.

Focolare Movement
http://www.global1.net/users/unity/

This site is the home page of a Catholic who tells of his love for the Focolare movement. What is Focolare? A movement dedicated to unity and peace among all people. "Its message is not complicated; its spirituality is drawn straight from the Gospel," the site explains. From its beginnings in the Italian city of Trent, Focolare has become a worldwide movement that claims some 87,000 members and about 2 million friends and adherents in more than 180 nations. The movement is made up of persons of all ages; it is ecumenical.

It was in the midst of the destruction and hopelessness of the Second World War that a group of young women gathered around a 23-year-old named Chiara Lubich. What bound the group together was their faith and experience that God is love. That experience radically changed their lives. They resolved to live as persons whose actions and thoughts would be based on the Gospel. Some words of Scripture particularly drew their attention: "Love one another as I have loved you" (Jn 13:34).

They discovered that evangelical mutual love united them and they experienced the presence of Jesus. The spirituality that developed was to be a spirituality of unity, a way to go to God together. At first the spirituality of unity spread within the Catholic Church. Since 1958, Christians of other traditions began to come in contact with the Focolare and to feel that its spirituality was also for them.

This site offers information about the movement and addresses and telephone numbers for contacting Focolare. It also offers links to other Catholic sites on the Web.

Collegeville Pastoral Institute
http://www.osb.org/litpress/cpi/cpi.html

This is the home page for the Collegeville Pastoral Institute (CPI), a cooperative service of Saint John's University's

School of Theology and the Liturgical Press. Its purpose is to build pastoral leaders by spreading the word about the Pastoral Institute, which serves people from a variety of ministerial backgrounds. It does this by offering a series of workshops, conferences, and seminars on diocesan, regional, and national levels. These address topics on various aspects of pastoral church work, including leadership and education, skills for liturgical ministry, and other contemporary issues.

Collegeville Pastoral Institute uses the campus facilities of St. John's University. A partner with the nearby College of St. Benedict, St. John's is located 80 miles northwest of Minneapolis/St. Paul on a 2,400-acre tract of woodlands and lakes. Participants at CPI also have the opportunity to pray with the monastic community, visit the showroom and facilities of the Liturgical Press, hike the many miles of nearby trails, and enjoy the lush beauty of the campus.

This site lists a toll-free number, a fax number, and an email address. It lists dates and costs of programs. For furthering church ministries in adult spirituality and faith development, adult catechesis, formation programs, or motivating adult learners, the Pastoral Institute is worth considering.

Process of Annulment of a Marriage

http://www.ring.com/stdan/annulmnt.htm

It is estimated that there are between 6 million and 8 million divorced and remarried U.S. Catholics. The Church does not allow divorce, but it grants "annulments," a practice that is sometimes very slow and often misunderstood. A Catholic can receive an annulment if it can be found that for some reason the marriage was not valid from the start. Between 45,000 and 50,000 Catholic annulments are granted in the United States annually, representing a small fraction of the number of Catholics who get divorced each year.

This site aims to explain the often-misunderstood annulment process. "The Catholic Church," it states, "understands marriage as a sacrament that images God's covenant with His people, a covenant of love for a lifetime. Once a valid marriage covenant is made, it is a commitment for life to faithfulness and the good of the spouse and children." But for a marriage to be truly valid (with the Catholic understanding of covenant), both parties must be capable of such a commitment, fully aware and freely giving consent. Sometimes, one of these conditions is not present and therefore something is wrong from the beginning, something is lacking. In such a case there was never a valid marriage bond. One or both parties may not have been capable of full consent for personal reasons, or there may have been undue external pressure.

The site, through questions and answers, offers helpful information about annulments and the process Catholics must go through to receive them. It is the work of a pastoral minister at a local Catholic faith community. The information, however, is universally applicable.

Real Eucharist Presence

http://www.pitt.edu/~aagst8/a/a

Some in the church feel that modern Catholics have lost sense of mystery and awe. These Catholics feel they want to develop a greater sense of that awe, especially in the Eucharist and specifically in the belief of the Real Presence of Christ in this sacrament. The site states that the Eucharist, above all the sacraments is "the perfection of the spiritual life and the end to which all sacraments, tend." In the sacrament of the Eucharist, "the body and blood, together with the soul and divinity, of our Lord Jesus Christ and, therefore, the whole Christ is truly, really, and substantially contained." These words come from the Catholic Catechism.

"Unfortunately many of us disbelieve or have grown indifferent toward Jesus in the Blessed Sacrament," the site states; its purpose is to counter this trend. To do it, the site introduces a listserv called ADORE-L that "is specifically for people who desire to grow in their own devotion to the Eucharist and to help others to believe and/or increase their devotion as well."

The site also links to other sites that preach the importance of the Eucharist and other aspects of Catholic belief.

Seven Sacraments

http://www.fatima.org/sacramen.html

Do you remember the Baltimore Catechism? Most Catholics over the age of 45 were raised on this book; it was their theology. They read it first in Catholic grade school. It was their Bible, too. Back then Catholics were not encouraged to read the Bible—at least not without a priest's help. Back then, reading Scripture was seen as potentially dangerous. (It's what Protestants did.).

Before the Vatican Council in the mid-1960s, the Catholic faith was taught through simple questions and answers that the young learned. Unfortunately, many Catholics never went beyond this. Adult religious education was not encouraged. All this, of course, changed a generation back. Some hard-line conservatives feel that was when the bottom dropped out of the church. They blame the priest shortage and a host of other current church ills on the weakening of faith that began at the Vatican Council. Other Catholics, however, see the council as the beginning of growth for the church, the start of a journey to theological adulthood.

Whatever one's disposition toward the council and the life of the Church today, many older Catholics have a sense of nostalgia for the Baltimore Catechism and the simpler life it represented. This site recalls the flavor of those days.

Some may see it as an effort by conservative Catholics to return to old teachings. That may have been the original intent. Others, however, may look at it as part of Catholic tradition, a tradition likely to bring back memories to older Catholics. This site excerpts from the Baltimore Catechism some questions and answers that deal with sacraments, beginning with this famous one:

Q: What is a Sacrament?

A: A Sacrament is an outward sign instituted by Christ to give grace.

The questions and answers continue from here. I imagine many will enjoy looking at this site and recalling old times. Others may find this site a real oddity, especially when told that Catholics had to know all these questions and answers by heart.

Steps for Life
http://inet.uni-c.dk/~grant/steps1.htm

This page, a work of the Curia of the Cistercian Order, is straightforward. It begins: "Please Help!"

Steps for Life is an example of the Web being used to solicit money for a needy cause. It is an inexpensive way for nonprofits to ask for money without using direct mail, which is getting more expensive as the United States Post Office raises the cost of second-class mail. Steps for Life is a charitable organization associated with the Cistercian Order. Its mission is to provide help for the estimated 15,000 young amputees in former Yugoslavia. Steps for Life provides not only artificial limbs, but also "financial, emotional and spiritual support for those who have been injured," the site states. "Officially registered since 1991 under Austrian law, any contribution is guaranteed to go directly to those in need," the site goes on to say. It then gives mail and email addresses—and is written in several languages.

Fire4JC
http://members.aol.com/fire4jc/homepage/FIRE.HTM

The main purpose of this page is to announce upcoming Catholic Charismatic events in the Dallas area or around the state. This site is an example of how the World Wide Web is being used to network communities of Catholics within the Church, especially those spread over wide areas but sharing similar interests. The Catholic Charismatic movement has grown in the United States in the past 20 years—but in pockets. The Web, then, is a fast means of connecting. In some ways, it is beginning to replace the ubiquitous monthly or quarterly newsletter.

This site seems to be doing well by doing a lot of different things to help people network. It is sprinkled with quotations from Scripture aimed at enlightening the spirit, such as:

> The word I spoke, the gospel I proclaimed, did not sway you with clever arguments, but with a demonstration of the Spirit's power, so that your faith might be built not on human wisdom but on the power of God.

> —*(I Cor. 2:4-5)*

Among other things, this site lists upcoming Charismatic events in the Dallas area, introduces the Catholic Charismatic Center in Houston and offers its weekly schedule, has a place for prayer requests and a Marion prayer line, offers recommended reading, and lists sites that might be of interest to Charismatics in Texas.

Benedictine Volunteer Program
http://www.benedictine.edu/volunteer.html

How better to reach the young and intelligent than through the World Wide Web? That, at least, appears to be the reasoning the Benedictine Sisters at Atchison, Kansas, hold to when they advertise for volunteers for the

Benedictine Volunteer Program on one of their monastery's pages. This community of women in Atchison is one of the most innovative when it comes to staying abreast with electronic communication. They appear on various pages in the Web. This site aims at stimulating interest in their volunteer program, which they call an "opportunity for women and men to join with the Benedictine Sisters in Atchison, Kansas, in their service to the people of northeast Kansas and northwest Missouri." Volunteers, they say, enter into the communal life, prayer, work, and ministry of the monastic community.

The site explains the program and its term of service: "several months to a year, renewable for a second year." It lists the kind of people the community is looking for: volunteers to help with gardening, domestic, elder care, child care, retreat support services, tutoring, clerical, library, and hospitality for guests. Requirements: a desire to experience monastic life style, at least 21 years old, in good health, and no dependents. Benefits: orientation and formation opportunities, life in community, room and board, with stipend negotiable. "Enjoy educational, cultural, spiritual, and recreational opportunities with our monastic community."

The site offers contact information by mail and email. Finally, the site links with other religious volunteer programs, both religious and secular.

Funeral Ripoffs

http://www.xroads.com/~funerals/

After a home and a car, the most expensive purchase most people make is a funeral. And while it is not unusual for consumers to spend weeks or months shopping for the best deal on a house or automobile, few compare prices when shopping for a funeral. But thanks to Fr. Henry Wasielewski, a semiretired parish priest at St. Margaret Mary Church in Tempe, Arizona, anyone with access to the World Wide Web can get pricing information on common funeral merchandise.

Since last fall, Wasielewski has been publishing a variety of funeral information on the Web. His site is the only one that provides wholesale prices for caskets, usually one of the most expensive elements in a funeral. He also offers advice on shopping for a funeral, the type of casket to buy, and information about prepaid funeral plans. Active in funeral-related issues since 1980, Wasielewski, 66, has become one of America's most outspoken crusaders against an industry that he believes abuses the public. Wasielewski says his interest in the industry was piqued while working at parishes in the Phoenix area.

Wasielewski's Web site contains pictures of caskets, model numbers, and suggested prices. It also contains other information guidelines such as choosing a mortuary and casket, price lists for vaults, phone numbers for companies that sell low-cost caskets directly to the public, and a list of resources for consumers who think they have been mistreated by the industry. This site provides a unique service and represents a creative ministry by a Catholic priest.

Dorothy Day House
http://www.ccseb.com/ddh/index.html

Dorothy Day House is a Catholic Worker community in Berkeley, California. It is nondenominational, embracing volunteers of many beliefs and faiths. Volunteers come from all walks of life. Dorothy Day House originated as a sandwich program at St. Mary Magdalen Church in Berkeley in 1984. This became the breakfast program carried on by the Berkeley Catholic Worker in People's Park and later in the People's Cafe house trailer. After the cafe closed, a number of Berkeley Catholic Workers organized Dorothy Day House.

The site states that the house believes in providing a consistent, caring presence for the poor and homeless. It says that it is a house of hospitality, not an agency, subscribing to the Catholic Worker philosophy as expressed by Dorothy Day: "...we are our brother's (and sister's) keeper and ... we must have a sense of personal responsibility to take care of our own, and our neighbor, at a personal sacrifice. As she believed, so we also believe that the freedom and dignity of each person should be the focus of our service. "

The house site states that it strives to provide sustenance and a loving, nonjudgmental source of community for the poor and homeless. Currently, it serves breakfast seven mornings a week in both the men's' shelter at the Berkeley Veterans Building and in People's Park, Berkeley. It serves an average of 170 people per day. The site explains that the house relies entirely on donations of money and food and on volunteer workers and that it is always looking for volunteers to work in various ways, from feeding the needy to raising funds. It requests money and food, and it gives an address and telephone number to contact the house.

Trappist Preserves

http://www.ultranet.com/~trappist/preserves/

Preserves are made and packed by the monks of Saint Joseph's Abbey, located in Spencer, Massachusetts, as a part of a long tradition of excellence and hospitality.

Preserves are the subject of this site and the ministry of these Trappist monks. In the fall of 1954, a small, chance, stove-top batch of mint jelly was made by the monks who worked in the herb garden. At that time, they had a great excess of mint on their hands. Because monastic austerity at that time precluded the jelly from being served to the monks at meals, it was sent down the hill to be sold at the Porter's Lodge. The response was very encouraging. Other varieties of fruit and wine jellies and preserves were quickly tried, and soon there were hopes that jelly-making would prove to be a successful and compatible monastic industry that would contribute to the monks' self-support.

For nearly 1,500 years, monks following the Rule of St. Benedict have prayed and worked in common and lived by the labor of their hands. Hospitality has always been a special work of monks, who for centuries have preserved food products with conscientious care in order to have a tasty treat to present to their guests. In the spirit of this venerable tradition, Trappist Preserves came into being.

According to this site, what makes Trappist Preserves special can be answered in one word—quality, first in flavor, but also "in the consistency of the gel, and the texture, color and distribution of the fruit in each jar." One factor that contributes to top quality, the site explains, "is the process of vacuum pan cooking, which has many advantages over open kettle. The fruit can be cooked at temperatures of about 80 degrees cooler, resulting in better color and flavor retention. No artificial colorings, flavors, or preservatives are ever used in Trappist Preserves."

This colorful site also gives catalogue information for ordering and information about the abbey.

Young Adults Hanging Out Together
http://userwww.qnet.com/~rbayerl/yacht.html

This is a site placed on the Web by a young adults group at Good Shepherd Catholic Church in Alexandria, Virginia. Young Adults Hanging Out Together is composed of post–high school singles, couples, and young families from the parish community, and they have a three-fold ministry, according to this site:

- To provide spiritual and social fellowship to young adults in the Good Shepherd community.

- To encourage individual and group participation in standing committees and programs at the parish and within the broader community.

- To foster new relationships with other young adult organizations throughout the Arlington Diocese.

The site lists group and individual activities including a biannual retreat/day of reflection with parish deacon or priest, participation in and support of a local International Festival, membership in the parish liturgy committee through music, usher and lay Eucharist ministry programs, membership in religious education committee as catechists, support of social ministry programs and outreach events, and participation in hospitality committee events.

Additionally, the site keeps track of upcoming events and posts them on the Web page. It also links with the home pages and email address of various members of this young adult organization. One click, and you are in touch with another young Catholic. In the case of Raymond Bayerl, one click and you are on his home page, where you can read about his family and farm animals, see photos of his vacation, or learn his Meyer-Briggs personality type. The young seem to be taking to the Web faster than their parents. It seems as if more youth organizations, like this one, are finding their way to the Web to improve communication.

Saint Francis House
http://www.tiac.net/users/sfh/sfh.html

Saint Francis House, located in Boston, Massachusetts, is New England's largest, most comprehensive day program for homeless men and women. Founded in 1984 by the Franciscans, the center evolved from a soup kitchen into a provider of a full range of emergency and rehabilitative services. An ecumenical agency, St. Francis House serves all in need.

"We believe in the dignity of every human being and offer respect to all who enter the house," the site states. "Our mission is to care for those who cannot take care of themselves and to assist those who are capable of becoming self-reliant and fully functioning members of society. We also advocate at the local and state levels for the rights and well being of the poor and homeless."

The site provides information about Saint Francis House, services provided by the house, plans for the future, and offers suggestions about how Web visitors can help the house. I am impressed by the way nonprofit organizations are using the relatively low-cost World Wide Web to spread news of their good works and to solicit assistance to keep these good works going.

International Catholic Child Bureau

http://eric-web.tc.columbia.edu/families/refugees/iccb_mission.html

ICCB is an international nongovernmental organization established under French law in Paris in 1948. ICCB's regional office for North America (ICCB/North America, Inc.) is a not-for-profit 501(c)(3) organization. Its programming is funded through individual gifts, membership fees, foundation donations, and government grants. Headquartered in Switzerland, it has regional offices in the Ivory Coast, Belgium, Philippines, Uruguay, the United States, France, and Austria.

This site explains that ICCB exists to serve the needs of children at risk around the world, regardless of creed. Its commitment to the inherent dignity and beauty of every child stems from a Catholic heritage, the site proclaims, adding that it is the principal international Catholic organization devoted to promoting the well-being of children and their families.

ICCB serves children by assisting those who care for them at the community level. Through the development and implementation of pilot projects, training seminars, educational materials, and action-oriented research, ICCB seeks to attain several goals:

- To further the holistic growth of all children, especially those struggling against poverty, violence, drugs, sexual exploitation, and disabilities.
- To support child development strategies that are family-based and culturally sensitive.
- To build on the capacities of children to participate in their own development.

"ICCB," the site goes on to say, "attends to the emotional and spiritual needs of children—a focus which many organizations, already overburdened in their efforts to meet basic needs, seldom have the resources to address."

ICCB believes in the importance of fostering regional, national, international, and multidisciplinary cooperation to protect the rights and improve the lives of children. It participates in the work of international, civil, and religious organizations that also serve children. It has consultative status with UNICEF, UNESCO, the United Nations Economic and Social Council (ECOSOC), and the Council of Europe. ICCB is recognized by the Holy See.

Opus Dei

http://www.opusdei.org/

This is the official site of *Opus Dei* (Latin for Work of God), a religious movement founded by Monsignor Josemaria Escriva de Balaguer in Spain. It began as a pious association of lay people (and clergy) who decided to dedicate themselves to lives of holiness. The conservative movement has spread throughout the church and has a reputation of trying to draw into it influential Catholics from a variety of professional careers. Opus Dei has evolved over the years, all the while maintaining its conservative and secretive nature. In 1982, Pope John Paul II, who has been fond of the organization, established it as a personal prelature, giving it wider autonomy in the church.

The current structure of Opus Dei has various levels of commitment:

1. Numeraries, who are celibate, live in the organization's centers and work full-time at the apostolate. (Female numeraries do administrative and domestic chores for the houses.)
2. Oblates embrace a celibate life but live outside the centers.

3. Supernumeraries are married members who have professional careers.

4. Cooperators support the work of the organization but do not have formal ties to it.

The organization is often criticized for its secrecy. It protects the identities of its members. Opus Dei claims that in 1995 it had 79,027 members (77,416 lay members; 1,611 priests). There are about an equal number of men and women in Opus Dei.

The site provides more information on these topics: The Founder, Escriva de Balaguer's Beatification, History of Opus Dei, Books and Documents, List of Dates in Opus Dei History, and the Founding of Opus Dei. The site provides contact information and invites the visitor to write.

Camp Ekon

http://www.io.org/~ekon

Looking for an exotic summer camp for the children? This site might be the answer. Camp Ekon is a recreational and leadership program for young people sponsored by Canadian Jesuits. The camp program, the site states, is guided by the 500-year-old Jesuit tradition of educating the whole person for well-rounded living and service to others. Camp Ekon provides healthy recreation and reflection at the same time. It is located at Stanley House, 250 kilometers north of Toronto, on the scenic waters and rocky shores of Lake Joseph in central Canada's historic Muskoka Lakes Region. Founded and operated by the Canadian Jesuits, the camp states that it offers fun, value-based recreational and leadership programming for young people ages 8 and up. This Web site offers information about the philosophy, program, staff, and facilities of Camp Ekon.

MinistryConnect

http://ministryconnect.org

The purpose of this site, sponsored by the Ministry Resource Center in Scotch Plains, New Jersey, is to help people in ministry find jobs. The site offers listings of both "positions available" and "positions sought." It is also a bulletin board for other related announcements. This ministry-sharing site is sponsored by the Ministry Resource Center for Women Religious in collaboration with similar centers and projects. Funding for the site's initial development was provided by the Conrad N. Hilton Fund for Sisters. The stated goal is to assist all interested in supporting, finding, and encouraging meaningful work in the service of others.

God Squad

http://www.midwest.net/scribers/pwpatter/

This site states it has two purposes. First, it is a source of locating sites of a religious nature on the Net. While the thrust of this site is primarily Roman Catholic, it also attempts to locate sites that relate to all the world's major religions. And second, it attempts to furnish links to items of interest to those in prison ministry. Assistance with the furthering of either of these goals would be greatly appreciated, the site's author states. This is a young site and it appears to need assistance, but its intentions are solid. Prison ministers, take note!

Theological Study for People in Secular Life

http://soli.inav.net/~tomlaw/crossing/crossing.htm

Back in the early 1970s, two Lutheran seminary teachers in St. Louis, Missouri, heard the plea of some lay Christians. "Can you help us live out our faith in the world of daily work?" they asked. "Can you help us connect our Sunday worship with our jobs, careers, and callings in the secular world?" That is how, this site states, the Crossings Community began. It is a partnership of Christians studying both the Word of God and the workplace in order to bring the two together. Those two teachers, Robert W. Bertram and Edward H. Schroeder, now retired from seminary work, continue in the community's work, although official leadership has passed on to the next generation.

As Bob and Ed gained experience through the early years, two Crossings programs evolved. One continued to pursue the original request, with weekend workshops around the nation and in other countries. The second program, the site explains, was an outgrowth of the first, a Crossings school with semester-long courses. Some of these were offered in seminaries, others wherever interested students were found. This Web site keeps the thousand-plus Crossings members in contact with each other.

Evangelization

E*vangelization*, simply put, is the proclamation of the Gospel. Jesus understood this to be essential to his own ministry: "I must proclaim the good news of the kingdom of God to the other cities also; for I was sent for this purpose" (Luke 4:43). Jesus, however, evangelized in more than word. He cured the sick, fed the hungry, comforted the afflicted, raised the dead, and gave hope to the poor. For the Church, evangelizing means bringing the Good News to all people, and through it transforming humanity and the world in which the human family lives.

This chapter contains some of the evangelization sites on the Web. The ones I have chosen deal with spreading the faith of Catholicism and the Good News of the Gospel.

RCIA

http://members.gnn.com/tscharbach/ts_rcia.htm

This Web site originates with St. Thomas the Apostle Parish in Chicago and features its RCIA program, a liturgical formation process of adult Christian initiation. This parish-based program is one of the most successful developments in Catholic church life in the past quarter century. The rite, which dates back to at least the third century, when it took three years or more to complete the process of becoming a Christian, was revised and restored in 1972 in the wake of the Second Vatican Council.

Now it takes about nine months to complete the RCIA process. It attempts to involve many in the parish, becoming a catalyst for parish faith renewal. Thus, the program, when it is successful, not only provides a doorway through which the convert enters the Catholic church, but it also becomes a means of renewing the faith of members of the parish. Officially, RCIA, which stands for the Rite of Christian Initiation, involves adult men and women who act as sponsors and guide the prospective Catholic through an educational and liturgical process.

This Web site describes a parish RCIA program, inviting people to join. While the site is maintained by a parish, the RCIA program is universal. Explanations here are applicable, not only throughout the nation, but throughout the Catholic world.

Notes the St. Thomas Webmaster: "The RCIA process is the first step on a lifelong journey of intellectual, emotional and spiritual conversion." This emphasis on faith as a life-long learning process is slowly taking hold in the Catholic church today, where adult religious education continues to develop. Words like "faith journey" and "discernment process" have entered the Catholic vocabulary. The RCIA program builds on this imagery, speaking of the communal nature of conversion, a process involving mind, heart, and soul. The RCIA program culminates at Easter when baptisms occur. For information on the RCIA program, this site is a rich resource.

Youth Apostles Institute

http://csugrad.cs.vt.edu/~membree/ya/

The Youth Apostles Institute, the site states, "is committed to evangelize, teach, advise, challenge, console, and love youth with the ultimate purpose of inspiring them to live a Christ-like life centered on prayer and the Sacraments in the Catholic Church." The institute is a mixed public association of single, married, and consecrated lay men and consecrated clerics. The community is united by a common vision, spirituality and apostolic thrust, although each member retains his or her proper lifestyle as lay person or cleric. The members of this institute state their desire to be "of one heart and one mind" (Acts 4:32) in response to the Lord's call and in imitation of Christ's first followers. They say they are united through a particular promise to a deep spiritual life and a common apostolic service to youth. It is the institute's hope that young people realize through the modeling of committed lay people that everyone is called to holiness, "not just priests and religious brothers and sisters; that everyone is called to live a life of prayer and moral virtue; and that the Church desperately needs the service of all its children to expand God's kingdom." Members dedicate themselves to live out the Lord's commandment of love.

This site features the Youth Apostles Institute, its mission and work and provides information on these Catholic life communities, their retreats and workshops, religious education, human sexuality seminars, counseling, college support programs, and pro-life activities.

That All May Again Be One

http://www.itnet.net/~jbfbrew/convert.html

Converting to the Catholic faith? Cradle Catholic who needs to hear new inspiration? Can you offer assistance? Need prayer? Are you just curious? Need answers? If you answer "yes" to any of these questions, this site proclaims, this is the page for you.

The author of this page, J. Francis Brewer, writes the following:

> I am a convert from the baptist faith, whom the Holy Spirit led to the Catholic Church. Coming into the faith has been one of the most joyous events of my lifetime, and I thank God daily for the Church. However, a conversion experience is not without its trials and troubles. I have found the Internet to be a wonderful place to meet people going through similar experiences.

With this in mind, Brewer decided to use the Web to allow Catholic converts to introduce themselves to each other. "This page," Brewer writes, "is aimed at those Catholics who follow the one, holy, catholic and apostolic Church and its authority through the Bishop of Rome." Going on, Brewer explains that the site's guest book is a place where the visitor may write something about him- or herself. "If you are a convert, you might mention a little about from where you came, when you converted, and other things. It is really up to you what you choose to write, but keep in mind that the page is aimed toward converts to the faith. You will be given an Internet form to fill out in order to sign the guest book. Thanks."

The site lists entrees by month. Visitors can go through these to contact people who have signed the guest book. This site also lists various Catholic links, including sites where Catholics can bump into each other to get better acquainted.

Worldwide Lay Apostolate

http://www.catholicity.com/Cathedral/CSE.html

The California-based Catholic Society of Evangelists was founded by lay Catholics responding to Pope John Paul II's call to the laity to become evangelists of Jesus Christ and His magnificent Bride, the Catholic Church. It is a nonprofit organization that relies mainly on donations. All members are volunteers and receive no financial benefits.

According to the site, the Apostolate's mission is to provide members of the Catholic Society of Evangelists with the basic tools and support necessary to spread the truths of the Catholic faith, help Catholics become better Catholics, and bring former Catholics back "home." Under the patronage and protection of the Blessed Mother Mary, the Apostolate pledges "uncompromising loyalty and fidelity to the teaching authority (*magisterium*) of the Catholic Church and the successor of St. Peter, the Roman Pontiff." Anyone taking the same pledge of loyalty can become a member and receive the society's support.

This site intends to spread the faith, but I must come clean and say I have become a bit cautious about any Catholic group that appears preoccupied with "loyalty and fidelity" to the teaching authority of the Church. Not that loyalty is a bad thing, but it is a matter of emphasis. What's wrong, for example, with "uncompromising loyalty to the Gospels and the teachings of Jesus?" The emphasis on fidelity and authority indicates a conservative theology. For some this is a plus; for others, a minus.

"A new member of the Catholic Society of Evangelists," the site states, "will receive audio tapes and booklets order forms, a signed oath suitable for framing, 25 printed cards with a logo on them, handouts for duplication, a rosary, and a brown scapular."

CatholicMobile Evangelization
http://www.mcgill.pvt.k12.al.us/jerryd/cm/evangel.htm

> The good news of the kingdom is meant for all people of all times.
>
> *—Pope Paul VI: Evangelization in the Modern World*

This site provides links to various documents on the Web that are interesting to Catholic evangelists. Among the sites listed are: Vatican II: Decree on the Church's Missionary Activity, Paul VI: Evangelii Nuntiandi (1975) Evangelization in the Modern World, General Catechetical Directory, Pius XII: Evangelii Praecones (1951) On Promotion of Catholic Missions, and Pius XII: Fidei Donum (1957) On the Condition of Catholic Missions.

PART IV

Catholic Transcendence

Part IV of this book describes Web sites related to transcendence—that component of existence beyond the ordinary boundaries of day-to-day human life and experience. Chapter 15 includes Web sites that feature the traditional and perhaps most accessible routes to transcendence—through the study of Scripture and theology. Chapter 16 describes Web sites devoted to spirituality; it reveals the amazing variety of ways in which Catholics are reaching outward and inward to fulfill their spiritual needs. Chapter 17 focuses on liturgy—the prayers and rites practiced by Catholics when they praise, give thanks, commemorate, adore, or petition. And Chapter 18, mostly through the medium of art, shows how web sites featuring paintings, icons, and architecture can inspire meditation.

CHAPTER 15

Scripture and Theology

Catholics believe that Jesus Christ is the fullest revelation of God. They believe that this revelation is learned through the study of Scripture and Church tradition. Catholics also believe in a reasoned faith, approachable through use of the human mind. In the broadest sense, this is the work of theology, the "science of God." Christian theology has been developing throughout Church history. It has been around as long as Christians have attempted to understand and interpret divine revelation.

This chapter looks at some of the Catholic Scripture and theology sites on the World Wide Web. Scripture, it seems, got to the Web faster than theology, but the latter is growing in number. These sites indicate that the Web is now an accepted medium for study and the communication of Christian thoughts and beliefs. Catholic faith and academic life are being served in a variety of ways on the sites in this chapter. I have chosen these sites both because they seem representative of the wider network and because they serve as gateways to that wider network.

Biblia Sacra
http://davinci.marc.gatech.edu/catholic/scriptures/
vulgata-clementina.html

The Holy Bible
http://www.cybercomm.net/~dcon/drbible.html

Online Catholic Bible Summary
http://catholic.net/RCC/Indices/subs/online-bible.html

Until the sixteenth century, all translations of the Bible into English were made on the basis of the Latin Vulgate version produced by Jerome at the bidding of Pope Damasus (383–384). *Biblia Sacra* offers the complete text of the Latin Vulgate. The authority of the Vulgate as authentic was affirmed by the Council of Trent in its fourth session (1546). It was this version, and its translation into other languages, that remained authoritative for Roman Catholics until Pope Pius XII's encyclical *Divino Afflante Spiritu* (1943) , which allowed and encouraged modern translations of the Bible from the original languages.

The Holy Bible site features the entire Bible translated into English from the Latin Vulgate. The Old Testament was first published by the English College at Douay in 1609. The New Testament was first published in English by the English College at Rheims in 1582. The whole Bible was revised and compared with the Latin Vulgate by Bishop Richard Challoner (1749–1752) and approved by the American Cardinal Archbishop James Gibbons.

So what Catholic Bibles in English are on the 'Net? The Online Catholic Bible Summary discusses the various translations currently on the Internet. It also addresses proposals for further Scriptural efforts.

Bible Gateway
http://www.gospelcom.net/bible

This site, the work of Gospel Communications Network, is one of the most useful on the World Wide Web. It is helpful for anyone who wants to search or research Holy Scripture. Through word searches, the site allows the Web visitor to find out what the Bible says about any one of 22,000 topics. A half dozen translations of the Bible are included here, including the Revised Standard Version. Searches can be done in six languages, including Latin. Two types of searches are available: One search is a "starts with" (example: "love" finds Love, Lovefeasts, Lovers.) and the other is "exact" (example: "love" finds Love.) This site is excellent for sermon writing; it provides Scripture at a glance to be copied and incorporated into a text or homily.

World Wide Study Bible
http://ccel.wheaton.edu/wwsb/

The World Wide Study Bible, the site explains, was conceived as a means of organizing all the Bible-related resources on the World Wide Web according to Scripture reference. Because of the nature of the World Wide Web and the large number of potential contributors, it is possible to index an enormous number and wide variety of resources—commentaries, meditations, sermons, pictures, word studies, musical settings, historical or archeological notes—anything that is relevant. Currently there are some 1,500 HTML files and about 12,000 references on the site.

The author writes: "This is a world wide effort; it will flourish only with user contribution. Please consider finding a public domain commentary and typing in the notes for a section of scripture. Scan an image. Type in a sermon. Enter a midi file for one of the numbers in Handel's Messiah. ..."

The project underwent major revision in January 1996. The original vision of links added by thousands of users had a weak link—the author. It was necessary for one person to verify and add all submissions, and he couldn't keep up. So he changed the operation. The site is currently built on top of an Informix database. Links are added by importing a file of links into the database.

Daily Gospel and Commentary

http://www.netside.com/~jtmood/

This inspirational site offers the Gospel with commentary for the day and every day for the week ahead. It's great for personal reflection and for anyone wanting to write a homily based on Scripture readings. The source of the readings is "The Navarre Bible: Text and Commentaries." Biblical text is taken from the Revised Standard Version and New Vulgate. Commentary is made by members of the Faculty of Theology of the University of Navarre, Spain.

As an added feature, this site invites the visitor to subscribe directly to the "(Daily) Gospel For Your Reflection" and have it sent by email. Private mailings will follow. It's a free service and a nondiscussion list.

The Lectionary Page

http://www.io.com/~kellywp/index.html

This site was created to support all those engaged in an ongoing study of the lesson texts from the Revised Common Lectionary. The Revised Common Lectionary is used, with variations, by the Episcopalian, Lutheran, Methodist, Presbyterian, and Roman Catholic churches. The texts presented here follow the Episcopalian (USA) variation. Most of the time, if you are a member of one of the other denominations, these will also be your lessons, but the visitor is advised to double-check before basing a sermon on them.

The Common Lectionary is a three-year cyclical lectionary. The year starts with Advent The Bible translation used is The New Revised Standard Version, (© 1989, the Division of Christian Education of the National Council of the Church of Christ in the USA) and is used with permission. This site features a liturgical calendar for upcoming weeks, with links to the lessons from the revised common lectionary. Planning liturgies and integrating Scripture into liturgical services is being made easier for liturgists through the Web.

Catholic Biblical Association of America

http://www.cua.edu/www/org/cbib/

The purpose of the Catholic Biblical Association is to promote, within a context of faith, scholarly study in Scripture and related fields by meetings of the association, publications, and support to those engaged in such studies.

The formation of the association was the outcome of the desire of Bishop Edwin O'Hara, chair of the Episcopal Committee on the Confraternity of Christian Doctrine, to improve quality of the New Testament. In 1936, O'Hara called a meeting of American Catholic Scripture scholars to help plan and carry out the project. At this meeting, a proposal was aired and agreed to for the formation of an association of American Catholic biblical scholars. At a subsequent meeting on October 3, 1936, the CBA was voted into existence.

While the CBA began with 50 charter members in 1936, its active and associate members now number 1,280 throughout the world. The faith dimension of the CBA continues to be important, but there is no confessional test for membership, and many non-Catholics and Jews are active members in the association.

The *Catholic Biblical Quarterly*, the official organ of the CBA, first appeared in 1939. It carries scholarly articles and notes on Scripture and related fields, an extensive book review section, news of the association's annual meeting, and other pertinent notices; its circulation in 1996 is roughly 4,100.

This site features a brief history of the Association, its constitution and by-laws, news of the annual meeting, officers and committees, and information on becoming a member. It also features the association's publications, grants, stipends, and fellowships. Finally, information is also provided for contacting the association by mail and email.

What is a Theologian?

http://ballingerr.xray.ufl.edu/sac/sac5_23.htm

What is a theologian? This site provides an explanation. It republishes a personal essay by Lawrence S. Cunningham of the University of Notre Dame Department of Theology. Cunningham is the author of 16 books, including *Thomas Merton: Spiritual Master* (Paulist, 1992).

The site traces Cunningham's life as a theologian from the first time he entered a lecture hall at the Gregorian University in Rome in 1957 to his post at Notre Dame. Cunningham shows how dramatically Catholic theology and the makeup of Catholic theologians have changed in just over a generation. Today, he states, the Catholic Theological Society of America is made up of men and women, lay and clergy, religious and nonreligious. Several of its presidents have been women. "For centuries Catholic theology was the sole domain of celibate male clerics. No longer. As much as anything else fueling change in the Catholic church today, the radical shift in the ranks of its theologians assures new ways of looking at old truths."

Cunningham also traces the development of the ranks of Catholic theologians, not only in his lifetime, but in the lifetime of the Church in this readable and informative site. He speaks about the work of the theologian in the modern world and how modern communication is influencing the work of the church as theologians and others discuss and debate Catholic teachings.

Catholic Perspective on Women in Society and Church

http://www.cco.caltech.edu/~newman/women.html

One of the most heated controversies in theological and episcopal ranks within the Catholic Church today surrounds the roles women should play in church and society. This site offers much information from official Church sources on the roles of women. The official Church position is that women and men are to be treated equally as they are equal in God's eyes. Yet Catholic tradition, only allows men to be ordained as priests, and the Church claims it lacks the authority to ordain women to the priesthood. Critics dispute this lack of authority, arguing that Catholic tradition and practice are culture-bound and that the times call for an inclusive priesthood.

This is what Pope John Paul II had to say about the role of women when he addressed a group of U.S. bishops who were visiting Rome in July 1993:

> In respect to not ordaining women to the ministerial priesthood, this "is a practice that the church has always found expressed in the will of Christ, totally free and sovereign" (Christifideles Laici, n.51). The Church teaches and acts with reliance on the presence of the Holy Spirit and on the Lord's promise to be with her always (Mt 28:20). "When she judges that she cannot accept changes, it is because she knows that she is bound by Christ's manner of acting. Her attitude ... is one of fidelity" (Inter Insigniores, n.4). The equality of the baptized, which is one of the great affirmations of Christianity, exists in a differentiated body, in which men and women have roles which are not merely functional but are deeply rooted in Christian anthropology and sacramentology. The distinction of roles in no way favors the superiority of some over others; the only better gift, which can and must be desired, is love (cf. 1 Cor 12–13). In the kingdom of heaven the greatest are not the ministers but the saints (cf. ibid., n.6).

Whatever one's thoughts on the matter of ordination, this site provides much useful information concerning the thinking and theology that supports Church views on women.

Feminist Theology Page

http://www2.gsu.edu/~reoldc/feminist.html

Laura Cook says she developed this page in response to the lack of information she found on the Web about Feminist theology and subjects related to it. So she put together bibliographies of works by well-known feminist theologians (by name and by tradition), as well as short biographies. She also included on her site links to Web sites dealing with issues related to the theologian's work or areas of concentration. Finally, she invited responses and requests for further additions, offering her email address.

This is an example of how good sites can grow. Interested people, meeting one another, ask each other to comment and respond. Many of the Catholic sites I find myself most attracted to are the work of one or two people who informally assemble information on a given church topic. In this case, it is Laura Cook and the subject is feminist theology.

Cook's bibliographies will be helpful to the amateur and professional theologian. They may help the former enter a new world of theological pursuit; to the latter, they could be helpful for quick references while at the computer.

And who is on her feminist list? One listed on her Web site: Mary Daly who received her Ph.D. and Th.D. from the University of Fribourg, Switzerland, and currently teaches at Boston College. Daly, a pioneer in Catholic feminist theology, early on shaped the discussion for many who followed her in the last generation.

The books cited on the Daly Web page include:

- *Pure Lust: Elemental Feminist Philosophy* (HarperSanFrancisco, 1992)

- *Gyn/Ecology: The Metaethics of Radical Feminism* (Beacon Press, 1990)

- *Beyond God the Father: Toward a Philosophy of Women's Liberation* (Beacon Press, 1973; Woman's Press, 1973, 1986)

- *The Church and the Second Sex* (Harper & Row, 1968; G. Chapman, 1968; Beacon Press, 1985)
- *Radical Feminism: The Spiritual Revolution: Mary Daly's Sophia Lyon Fahs Lectures—June 28, 1974* (Liberal Religious Education Directors Association, 1974)
- *The Problem of Speculative Theology* (The Thomist Press, 1965)

Woodstock Theologial Center
http://guweb.georgetown.edu/woodstock/

Aquinas Institute of Theology
http://www.op.org/aquinas/

The Woodstock Theological Center, one of the most respected Catholic theological centers, is a nonprofit independent research institute at Georgetown University that addresses topics of social, economic, and political importance from a theological and ethical perspective. Interdisciplinary and ecumenical by design, the center engages in research, conducts seminars and symposia, and publishes books and articles on such issues as church and society, business ethics, international relations, technology and culture, public philosophy, and religion and politics. The center is financed by individual donations, foundation grants, and contributions from the Society of Jesus.

The Woodstock site provides a great way to enter the theological discussion taking place in the Church. Not only is this site rich in theological resources, it also lists some of the more interesting Catholic theological links on the Web. Listed are sites that provide useful places on the Web for beginning research on religious and theological questions. Each of these in turn has numerous links to other sites. Many of these are academic sites maintained by individuals.

The Aquinas Institute of Theology is a Roman Catholic graduate school of theology and ministry sponsored collaboratively by the men and women of the Order of Preachers (Dominicans). It is located on the campus of St. Louis University. "Aquinas students and faculty," the site states, "undertake the tasks of education in the Dominican spirit, which is rooted in strong academics and the pursuit of truth, a dedication to liturgy, community, contemplation, and most importantly, a commitment to the preaching mission of the Church." The site features information about the school, programs, degrees, and how to contact it.

Christian Theology Page

http://apu.edu:80/~bstone/theology/theology.html

Internet Theology Resources: Systematic Theology

http://www.csbsju.edu/library/internet/theosyst.html

The Christian Theology site has Christian theology written all over it. It is a site that looks at Christian theology from every which way, linking the visitor with ideas, schools, libraries, fellowships, journals, associations, and news-groups—all having to do with Christian theology.

Consider some of these sites categories: Christian Theological Societies, Fellowships, and Associations; Christian Theology Pages by Tradition; College and University Christian Theology Departments; Christian Theological Seminaries and Graduate Schools; Christian Theology News Groups/Subscriptions; Christian Theology Projects; and Christian Theological Publishers. The site also has a place to post Christian theology jobs. The links here are worldwide, an impressive array of useful sites leading to every nook of the Christian theological landscape.

The Internet Theology Resources: Systematic Theology site is another very thorough Christian theology site. It is not only systematic in presentation, it lists documents chronologically by topic. This helps the visitor to better grasp the development of theological thought over time. This also makes any search easier.

Preaching the Just Word

http://guweb.georgetown.edu/woodstock/pjw.html

Preaching the Just Word is a national program sponsored by the Woodstock Theological Center to help priests and other ministers of the Gospel to be more effective in preaching social justice. Conceived by Walter J. Burghardt, S.J., the project is coordinated by both Father Burghardt and Father Raymond B. Kemp. "Presenting the Gospel and its implications to others with fidelity and felicity is not simply a matter of putting together the correct words or phrases. It requires a deeply felt and personal understanding of the just Word," this site maintains.

The aim is to bring preachers to a lively understanding of social reality or culture: what it is, how it originates, how it operates, how it shapes and forms human consciousness and communities for good and ill, how it improves, and how it deteriorates. The aim is to understand the U.S. culture of the 90s, so as to rejoice in the gifts and opportunities provided and be horrified at the suffering it causes or occasions—with a view to promoting the former and preventing the latter.

"The program," the sites states, "is an attempt to make use of the single situation where the majority of the faithful regularly gather to hear the preaching of the Word, the Sunday liturgy." However, Catholic preaching is not limited to the Eucharist liturgy in the parish; it takes place in a variety of other contexts: retreat houses, prisons, hospitals, college campuses, parish missions, seminars and workshops, conventions, and conferences. To take full advantage of all these situations, it is vital to prepare the messenger as well as the message.

The format is a five-day retreat/workshop, based on themes from the Spiritual Exercises of St. Ignatius Loyola, integrating personal prayer with reflection. The week also offers participants an opportunity to reflect alone and in groups on the nature of their own ministry and how it relates to the just Word.

This site shares the fundamentals and purpose of the program, as well as opportunities. It provides information on contacting the center for further information or for signing up to join the Preaching the Just Word program.

Gaudium et Spes

http://www.knight.org/advent/docs/ec21gs.htm

This is arguably the most important document proclaimed by the Second Vatican Council and, perhaps, of the twentieth-century Catholic Church. The document, the *Pastoral Constitution on the Church in the Modern World*, was proclaimed on December 7, 1965, by Pope Paul VI. It was the last and the longest document of the Council.

The theology of the pastoral constitution is rooted in two sources: the papal social teaching of the twentieth century and the theology developed in Western Europe from the 1930s through the 1950s. It is impossible to understand the highly active social engagement of the Catholic Church in the postconciliar era apart from this document.

The opening words of the document, remembered fondly by many who lived through the council and found new life in the Church in its wake, speak of a renewed Catholic commitment to the work of building the kingdom of God on earth.

> The joys and the hopes, the griefs and the anxieties of the men of this age, especially those who are poor or in any way afflicted, these are the joys and hopes, the griefs and anxieties of the followers of Christ.
>
> —*Pastoral Constitution*

The document has two parts. The theological contribution is contained in Part One, where the conciliar text synthetically presents a Christian anthropology, a theology of human work, and a reflection on the Church's role in the world. Part Two is essentially a development of the themes found in the Church's social encyclicals. Because of the historic role this document has played in the development of Catholic social thought and its underlying theology, this document deserves its own site and citation.

Humanae Vitae

http://listserv.american.edu/catholic/church/papal/paul.vi/humanae-vitae.html

In the wake of reports of an exploding world population and the discovery of "the pill" as a new birth control technique, pressure grew within the Catholic Church for a new statement, updating and possibly or changing church traditional teachings on birth control. During the summer of 1968, rumors spread throughout the Church that the Vatican was about to release a long-awaited birth control statement. The Vatican press office called these reports absolutely false. Then on July 29, word finally came. It was *Humanae Vitae*, literally "Of Human Life."

The encyclical was a sensitively written expression about the sanctity of marital love and the need to nurture life in marriage. Some said the encyclical was almost poetic and came as a much needed statement concerning human dignity. Maybe so, but whatever else it stated, it has been remembered for only one thing: upholding the Catholic Church's ban on artificial birth control. Pope Paul VI rejected the findings of the majority report of a papal commission that had been meeting for several years and reaffirmed the position of Pope Pius XI and Pope Pius XII, who supported the rhythm method (now called natural family planning).

This site offers the complete text of this highly controversial encyclical, which begins with these words:

> The most serious duty of transmitting human life, for which married persons are the free and responsible collaborators of God the Creator, has always been a source of great joys to them, even if sometimes accompanied by not a few difficulties and distress. At all times the fulfillment of this duty has posed grave problems to the conscience of married persons, but, with

the recent evolution of society, changes have taken place that give rise to new questions which the Church could not ignore, having to do with a matter which so closely touches upon the life and happiness of men.

—Humanae Vitae

Reactions within and outside the Church were almost universally negative. Later, polls showed that most married Catholics simply decided to disregard the encyclical. Some years later, Pope Paul shared with confidants his disappointment in the way his encyclical was received. He said he had expected some opposition from the secular media but was not prepared for widespread opposition from priests and theologians. Many bishops were lukewarm to the encyclical. Although the Vatican asked all national episcopal conferences for statements in support of *Humanae Vitae*, many attempted to nuance that support without denying or directly challenging it.

The Lonergan Web Site

http://www.uottawa.ca/~s352983/lonergan.html

This site is dedicated to the thought of Bernard J.F. Lonergan and aims to facilitate Internet-based collaboration among Lonergan scholars and others interested in Lonergan studies. Lonergan was a Jesuit philosopher and theologian. A Canadian born in Buckingham, Quebec, in 1904, he died November 26, 1984. Lonergan was considered by many intellectuals to be the finest philosophic thinker of the twentieth century.

This site states that not much is available on the Internet regarding Lonergan, and it is trying to change this. The site states that the best source for the latest in Lonergan studies is currently the *Lonergan Studies Newsletter*. It provides up-to-date information on recent publications, reviews of publications, and news of interest to Lonergan scholars. Information about this newsletter is provided.

Scripture and Theology

The site also lists Lonergan books still in print and information on where to study Lonergan and research his thought. Listed, for example, are the Lonergan Institute of Boston College; the Lonergan Communications Center in Cebu City, the Philippines; the Lonergan Center in Manila, the Philippines; the Lonergan Center at Loyola Marymount University; and the Lonergan University College of Concordia University.

This site appeared to still be in development when I visited it. Lonergan is not widely known outside academic circles. Yet his influence on Catholic thought continues to grow. It is encouraging to see more attention to his work on the Web.

Theology 100 On-Line Glossary Project

http://www.nd.edu/~jvanderw/theo100/glossary.htm

The Theology 100 On-Line Glossary Project is a glossary of more than 400 terms for beginning study of the Christian and Hebrew Scriptures and other ancient texts. The project was prepared for the Web by 84 students of the University of Notre Dame in the spring semester in 1995. The Theology 100 On-Line Glossary Project, the site states, "is extended to users of the World Wide Web for educational purposes only in accordance with U.S. Copyright laws."

The site lists glossary items under the following categories: The Complete List of Glossary Entries, Biblical Names and Nations, Place Names, The Biblical Books and Their Authors, Technical Terms for Biblical Studies, The Hebrew Bible, and The Christian New Testament.

Examples of Hebrew entries include: Aaron, Abba, Abel, Abraham, Achan, Acts of the Apostles, Adam, Adonai, Adultery, Agag, Ahab, Ahasuerus, and Ahaz. Examples of Christian entries include: Apocalypse; Apostle; Aramaic; Ascension of Jesus; Augustus Caesar; Baptism; Basileia; Beatitudes; Beloved Disciple; Caiaphas; Christology; Christos (Anointed); Circumcision, in Acts; and Corinthians, Paul's Letters to.

Feminist Theology Resources on the Web

http://www.mailbase.ac.uk/lists-f-j/feminist-theology/

Feminist Theology Bibliography

http://www.dur.ac.uk/~dth3nk/fembib.html

The San Francisco Bay Catholic Site: Ordination of Women

http://www.microweb.com/burnside/sfbwomen.htm

The first site is a discussion group that is certain to be helpful to feminist scholars interested in Christian and Jewish feminist theology. Topics discussed on this list vary daily, but they often involve feminist critiques of traditional ways of doing theology. The authors state that the site is meant for the exchange of information, including research and publications. The second site is an online feminist bibliography, a good list of scholarly publications in the field of Jewish and Christian feminist theology and religious studies. The third site deals with the explosive (for Catholics) topic of women's ordination. It begins with a statement of the problem, offering historical analysis, then it outlines recent Catholic statements on the subject. By the way, the site clearly comes down in favor of ordaining women.

Future of Liberation Theology

http://www.umich.edu/~iinet/ii/journal/
v2n2_The_Future_of_Liberation_Theology.html

Changing Face of Liberation Theology

http://www.iclnet.org/pub/resources/text/cri/cri-jrnl/crj0080a.txt

What is the history of Liberation theology? Where is it going? Is it theology or sociology? These sites help sort out these questions and provide helpful background information. For more than 20 years, the central goal of liberation theology has been to empower the poor and make churches active agents of liberation, especially in Latin America. By empowering ordinary people and promoting new social movements, liberation theology has tried to change the assumptions that maintain power. It also hopes to change the structures of power to improve life. Has this worked, or is liberation theology spent? And what is it about liberation theology that upsets Catholic conservatives? These sites feature discussions and analysis of the subject.

Dietrich Bonhoeffer Homepage
http://204.245.208.1/bonhoef/index.htm

For Catholics, this site has an ecumenical flavor. It features the life story and theology of one of the twentieth century's most celebrated pastors and theologians, Dietrich Bonhoeffer. Born in Breslau, Germany, he studied at Tübingen and Berlin, and he left Germany in 1933 in protest against the Nazi enforcement of anti-Jewish legislation. He worked in London until 1935, then returned to Germany to combat anti-Semitism, becoming head of a pastoral seminary of the German Confessing Church until its closure by the Nazis in 1937. He became deeply involved in the German resistance movement and was imprisoned from 1943 until 1945, when he was hanged at Flossenbürg. The site lists his major works, features translation projects and discussion groups, and generally draws together scholars and others interested in learning more about this remarkable man.

Karl Barth
http://www.nauticom.net/www/loathian/barth.html

This site features a fascinating introduction to the life and theology of Karl Barth, one of the most notable Christian theologians of the twentieth century. The visitor learns that Barth was born in Basel, Switzerland, and at 18 he began his theological studies at Berne under the direction of his father. He attended several universities and studied under many of the great liberal theologians of the turn of the century. In 1911, he was appointed pastor of a Reformed Church, where he remained for 10 years. It was during this period that Barth broke with the liberal theology he had learned from his professors. It did not provide the resources that his people needed, he felt, especially with the outbreak of World War I. Thus began an intense period of theological study, particularly of the Scripture, and it was out of this that Barth discovered what he was to call "the strange new world within the Bible." The story of Barth's journey and the work it provided along the way has many contemporary lessons. This site is an important addition to the Web, and I look forward to other home pages devoted to theologians so that scholars and other interested people can gain access to their work.

Draft of the June 1995 U.S. Bishops' Statement Calling the Vatican to Collegiality

http://astro.temple.edu/~arcc/bishops.htm

For years, several dozen U.S. bishops had become increasingly disgruntled with the direction of the U.S. Bishops' Conference. These bishops had also been upset with the way the Vatican centralized authority during the pontificate of Pope John Paul II. In June 1995, after some months of consultation, a dozen of these concerned bishops put together a document expressing their concerns. They delivered it to a committee headed by Chicago Cardinal Joseph Bernardin. The statement showed publicly the intensity of their dissatisfaction.

This site features the full text of the original document. Obviously, Catholics are divided about where their Church should be headed, and this document reveals that bishops are among those whose feelings are at odds with the prevailing trends in Rome.

CHAPTER 16

Spirituality

Christians believe that to be a follower of Jesus is to live in the life of the Spirit. As the Christian experiences a relationship with God, the life, death, and resurrection of Jesus Christ take shape within. Many religious traditions speak of spirituality or experience of the divine. People sometimes claim that all such experiences are really the same, but at least two distinctions can be identified in Christian spirituality: the goal of union with God and the second, which grows out of the first, the goal of perfect service and love of neighbor.

The spirituality sites on the World Wide Web reveal the rich diversity of spiritual journeys among Catholics. It also reveals the important place Mary, the Mother of Jesus, and the saints of the Church have played in the development of Catholic spiritualities. In recent times, especially since the Second Vatican Council, Catholics have experienced yet again an explosion in spiritual writings and experiences. Various forms of meditations, including the Centering Prayer, based on Eastern prayer forms, have gained more acceptance in the Church. The mystics and contemplatives, meanwhile, have taken on new roles as Catholics continue to explore their spiritual journeys.

Contemplative Life by Thomas Merton

http://140.190.128.190/merton/Conners.html

Thomas Merton is one of Catholicism's best known twentieth-century contemplatives. He was a Trappist monk, a convert to the faith, an extensive writer, and novice master at the Abbey of Gethsemani near Louisville, Kentucky, until his death in 1968 in a freak accident in Thailand where he was involved in a conference on Eastern religions.

Merton was also known for his pacifism, his letter writing, and his many writings about topics ranging from the social issues of the day to what it means to pray and be a contemplative. Merton lives beyond his death. His writings continue to be read by millions in and outside the Church. It is fitting that his views of the contemplative life be included in this chapter. Here, spirit and intellect blend and mysticism begins. This Web site features a paper written about Merton and the contemplative life. It is worth reading, helping the visitor to understand the mind and soul of a man who decided to leave the modern world (as most people experience it) to find meaning and fulfillment in a monastery in Kentucky.

Catholic Marian Centers

http://www.missionnet.com/~mission/cathlc/marian.html

The Blessed Virgin Mary is the first-century Jewish woman who was the mother of Jesus. The Church teaches four major doctrines about Mary, two ancient and two modern. Stemming from the patristic period are beliefs in her virginity (before, during, and after the birth of Christ) and divine maternity, the latter summed up in the title Mother of God. The Immaculate Conception (Mary was conceived without original sin) and Assumption (she was taken into heaven body and soul at the end of her life) were officially declared dogmas in the nineteenth and twentieth centuries, respectively.

The veneration of the Blessed Virgin Mary is widespread among Roman Catholics. Virtually every nation has shrines dedicated to the Mother of God. The central Marian prayer is the Rosary, but many other pieties are associated with Mary. This site lists the various Marian centers throughout the United States. The list is by state and is especially helpful to those Catholics who look to Marian centers and Marian shrines as aids to their prayer lives.

The Mary Page
http://www.udayton.edu/mary/

Blessed Virgin Mary Library
http://www.ici.net/cust_pages/ffi/lml.html

Papal Documents on Mary
http://www.mcgill.pvt.k12.al.us/jerryd/cm/mary/papal.htm

Marian Hour
http://netpage.bc.ca/marianhr/

The stated purpose of the Mary page is to present information about the Mother of Jesus and to lead people to a loving knowledge of she who is the first and most holy of the faithful. "Learning more about Mary," the site states, "one develops a fuller knowledge of Christ who is the fulfillment of human existence." The site offers weekly news updates and shares various kinds of Marian resources. It answers questions about Mary and offers Marian meditations and prayers. The site is maintained by the Marian Library/International Marian Research Institute at the University of Dayton.

On the Blessed Virgin Mary Library site, the visitor will find a collection of HTML documents about the Blessed Virgin Mary. This is another example of the many sites on the Web aimed at supporting a Mary-centered Catholic spirituality. According to this site, "the Blessed Virgin Mary is not only the forever first and most perfect disciple of Jesus Christ, the Incarnate Son of God, she was predestined to freely cooperate with Him in the Redemption of Mankind from all eternity."

This site features a short life history of the Blessed Virgin Mary and the papal consecration of the Church and world to Mary, December 8, 1990. It explains why Catholics have a devotion to the Blessed Virgin Mary and offers the history and origin of the Marian title "Queen of Peace" as well as other Mary titles. It also offers many images of Mary.

Papal documents on Mary trace the development of Marian thought within the Church and reveal the special place Mary has in the Church throughout history.

Finally, it was more than 24 years ago, that a radio Rosary first sounded its call to prayer. Throughout these years the Marian Hour has been the inspiration to pray for countless thousands, and now this prayer has been extended to the World Wide Web. The format of this page is similar to that of radio broadcasts. With each prayer there is a link to recorded sound files from the program. To access the multimedia aspects of this page, the visitor will need a browser or helper application that can display JPEG images and sound hardware and software that can play WAV or AU audio files. Other prayers are also available in text and audio format in French. Text-only versions of the prayers are available in Polish, French, Luganda, Tagalog, and Hungarian.

Messages from Heaven:
Information About Marian Apparitions
http://members.aol.com/bjw1106/marian.htm

Nothing in the faith requires Catholics to believe in apparitions, yet many Catholics do and many of these apparitions have to do with purported citings of the Virgin Mary. In most cases, the Church discounts these apparitions; in some, Church officials remain skeptical, and in a very few instances, the apparitions gain wider acceptance. In the last 15 years, interest in apparitions has grown in some parts of the Church. This may be, in part, the result of Pope John Paul II's keen interest in Mary and Marian spirituality. This site provides the visitor with all the Marian apparition information he or she might care to have. In many of these purported apparitions, the message of Mary is the same: "Turn away from sin or catastrophe will follow." Mary then calls for prayer, fasting, conversion, and works of mercy. She is seen entreating all to return to her Son.

First, the site discusses the historical and biblical Mary. It then focuses on whether apparitions are possible, offering various explanations for them. The varied physical phenomena reported at Marian apparition sites are categorized into four basic types: solar phenomena, physical healings, changes in state (including rosaries and statutes said to have changed color or appearance), and a growth in spiritual awareness and prayerfulness. It then goes on to list Mary's well-known appearances through history, giving brief descriptions of each.

Fatima, one of the most famous series of apparitions, is described in detail, and the prophecies at Fatima are examined. Another list tallies the major Mary apparitions in the last 30 years. Also on this site are recent developments and trends (in these apparitions) and "changes you should be aware of!" The site offers conclusions and suggestions and, finally, lists other references, books, pamphlets, and magazines that have to do with Marian apparitions.

Our Lady of Fatima

http://www.cais.com/npacheco/fatima/fatima.html

Our Lady of Fatima is one of the more popular Marian devotions. In question and answer form and with the aid of images and photographs, this site tells the story of Our Lady of Fatima. Fatima is a village in the center of Portugal about 70 miles north of Lisbon. In the backwaters of Europe and Portugal, Fatima in 1915 would have been the last place anyone would have chosen as the location to pronounce prophecies involving the great world powers. But that is what is said to have happened there.

As with Lourdes, the visionaries at Fatima were peasant children: eight-year-old Lucia Santos and her two cousins, Francisco and Jacinta Marto. At the time, the Portuguese government was secular and antagonistic toward religion. Far from accepting the children's reported apparitions, the government treated the children harshly, questioned them extensively, and even placed them in prison with the threat of boiling them in oil unless they confessed to having made up their story. In spite of this, the children never wavered.

Fatima involved a series of six major apparitions of the Virgin Mary, together with several other apparitions of angels and other personages, culminating in the extraordinary "miracle of the sun." It is said the Lady of Fatima revealed three "secrets" to the children. The first secret of Fatima is the vision of hell given to the children, together with the prophesies of World War II, the rise of communism, and the eventual triumph of the Immaculate Heart of Mary. The second secret of Fatima is the devotion to the Immaculate Heart of Mary. The third secret of Fatima was written down, placed in a sealed envelope, and given to the Bishop of Leiria, Portugal, to be opened and read not before 1960, when it was to "become clearer." Rather than assume the responsibility of knowing the "secrets of heaven," the Bishop prudently decided to send it to the Vatican, where it has been reportedly read by at least two popes—John XXIII and John Paul II—but never been officially revealed.

At Fatima today, there exists a large shrine, which has drawn millions of pilgrims to prayer and devotion.

Our Lady of Guadalupe
http://ng.netgate.net/~norberto/materdei.html

This page features a unique apparition of the Blessed Virgin Mary, one in which it is said she left a miraculous life-sized portrait of herself, an image that people can visit and see today in the same condition as 465 years ago.

It is said that in 1531 a Lady from Heaven appeared to a poor Indian at Tepeyac, a hill northwest of Mexico City. She identified herself as the Mother of the True God, instructed him to have the bishop build a temple on the site, and left an image of herself imprinted miraculously on his tilma, a poor-quality cactus-cloth, which should have deteriorated in 20 years but shows no sign of decay 465 years later and still defies all scientific explanations of its origin.

Yearly, an estimated 10 million people visit this shrine, making the Mexico City church the most popular Catholic shrine in the world after the Vatican! His Holiness John Paul II visited her sanctuary twice, knelt before her image, invoked her motherly assistance, and called upon her as Mother of the Americas.

This site tells the story of our Lady of Guadeloupe, complete with images. The site lists the chronology of events related to the Guadalupe image and answers questions about this apparition. It lists the prayer that Pope John Paul II said at the Guadalupe shrine. For those who do not have an image of Our Lady of Guadalupe, it is possible to download one—or various other images related to Our Lady of Guadalupe. This site is available in English or Spanish.

Finally, this site connects with a number of other Catholic sites, many of them associated with the veneration of Mary.

Medjugorje Page

http://www.medjugorje.org

"The Medjugorje Web," this site states, "is dedicated to providing information about one of the most incredible and important supernatural events of our time." Since 1981, in a small village named Medjugorje in Bosnia-Herzegovina , the Blessed Virgin Mary has been appearing and giving messages to the world. She says that God has sent her to our world, and these years are a time of Grace granted by God. In her own words she says, "I have come to tell the world that God exists. He is the fullness of life, and to enjoy this fullness and peace, you must return to God."

Since the apparitions began in 1981, millions of people of all faiths, from all over the world, have visited Medjugorje and, the site indicates, have left spiritually strengthened and renewed. Countless nonbelievers and physically or mentally afflicted, meanwhile, have been converted and healed. This site extends an invitation to explore the information contained on this Web site and decide whether to choose to believe this messenger from Heaven.

The site offers daily Scriptural meditations, Medjugorje statistics, and the latest Medjugorje information. It features Marian groups, associations, and shrines, as well as pictures from Medjugorje and other information regarding Marian spirituality.

Shroud of Turin

http://www.cais.com/npacheco/shroud/turin.html

> And he bought a linen shroud, and taking him down, wrapped him in the linen shroud, and laid him in a tomb which had been hewn out of the rock; and he rolled a stone against the door of the tomb.
>
> —*(Mark 15:46, RSV)*

The Shroud of Turin, believed by many to have wrapped the body of Jesus in the tomb, is a rectangular linen cloth, weaved in a three-to-one twill, 14 feet, 3 inches (4.36 meters) long by 3 feet, 7 inches (1.1 meters) wide. It is wrapped in red silk and kept in a special silver chest in the Chapel of the Holy Shroud in the cathedral of St. John the Baptist in Turin, Italy.

According to the site, the Shroud of Turin's history can be authenticated to the year 1578, when it was known to have been taken to its current resting place in Turin, Italy. However, there is a large circumstantial body of evidence that traces its history back to the early Christian centuries. Some historians, such as author and researcher Ian Wilson, believe that the Shroud may be the same as the "Mandylion," which was a famous Christian relic of the face of Christ on a piece of cloth. The Mandylion was venerated by the early Christians and was exhibited in a wooden case with an oval cutout through which the face of Christ was allegedly seen on a piece of cloth. Wilson and others claim that this was the face of the man on the Shroud, with the remainder of the Shroud image folded within the case. The Mandylion was known to have been in the city of Edessa, in what is now Turkey, and later in Constantinople, which is now Istanbul. It disappeared during the Fourth Crusade in 1203, to be possibly found again and displayed as the Shroud in the city of Lirey, France, in 1353. The Shroud came into the possession of the House of Savoy in 1453.

In 1532, a fire engulfed the Chapel of Sainte Chapelle in Chambrey, France, where the Shroud was kept, and it came dangerously close to being destroyed. The fire was so intense that part of the silver on the reliquary holding the Shroud melted, and a drop of molten silver fell on a corner of the folded linen. This set one of the Shroud's edges on fire, burning through all of the folds before it was doused with water. When the Shroud was opened up, the characteristic geometric set of scorch marks visible today were seen, and yet the part of the Shroud containing the image was scarcely touched by the fire. The burned material was later repaired by sewing linen patches over it. In 1578, it was taken to its current location in Turin.

The site attempts to keep the visitor current with information on the Shroud, attempting to present an overview of the Shroud to a general audience rather than presenting scientific findings.

Catholic Prayers

http://www.webdesk.com/catholic/prayers/index.html

This site lists hundreds, perhaps thousands, of Catholic prayers in English and Latin. Basic Catholic prayers and those for travelers, dog owners, and home owners, morning prayers, the Holy Office, and prayers by saintly people can all be found here. So can prayer requests, the Stations of the Cross, Minute Meditations, and prayers to the Holy Spirit. The Lord's Prayer is examined, and the Act of Contrition is here. Prayers are here for virtually any occasion in life one. This list is seemingly endless. The problem—if there is one—is organization. Looking up a specific prayer is not easy, but if the visitor simply wants to browse Catholic prayers, it is difficult to find a better site.

Centering Prayer

http://www.io.com/~lefty/Centering_Prayer.html

Centering Prayer, as described by Fr. Thomas Keating in his book *Open Mind, Open Heart* and by Fr. M. Basil Pennington in his book *Centering Prayer*, is a simple yet effective Christian contemplative practice based on the method described in the fourteenth-century mystical text *The Cloud of Unknowing*. This site introduces the visitor to the technique of Centering Prayer. The following steps are offered:

1. Choose a sacred word as the symbol of your intention to consent to God's presence and action within.

2. Sitting comfortably and with eyes closed, settle briefly and silently introduce the sacred word as the symbol of your consent to God's presence and action within.

3. When you become aware of thoughts, return gently to the sacred word.

4. At the end of the prayer period, remain in silence with your eyes closed for a couple of minutes.

Some examples of sacred words are: Lord, Jesus, Abba, Father, Mother, Love, Peace, and Shalom. How does one practices this prayer form? "In step 2, "sitting comfortably" means relatively comfortably—not comfortable enough to encourage sleep, but comfortable enough to avoid thinking about the discomfort of your body. Praying in this way after a main meal encourages drowsiness—better to wait at least an hour. Praying in this way just before retiring may disturb one's sleep pattern.

The minimum time for this prayer is 20 minutes. Two periods are recommended each day: one first thing in the morning and one in the afternoon or early evening. The end of the prayer period can be indicated by a timer, provided it does not have an audible tick or loud sound when it goes off. The principal effects of Centering Prayer are experienced in daily life, not in the period of Centering Prayer itself.

Besides offering the outlines of Centering Prayer to the visitor, this site provides a contact address for further information and information for joining a Centering Prayer mailing list.

The CatholicMobile Spirituality
http://www.mcgill.pvt.k12.al.us/jerryd/cm/moral.htm

Eventually, almost every thinking person confronts some basic questions like "Who am I?" and "What am I doing here?" Answers to these questions give meaning to life. Out of these questions, spirituality arises as creature reaches out to Creator. Sometimes religion helps structure these spiritual quests. Roman Catholicism is a worldwide religion embracing a billion people. While these Catholics may share the same basic faith, their spiritual paths are often varied. This site looks at some of these spiritual pathways through documents of the Church. A list like this could be endless. All the more important that a good list help point out healthy spiritual paths. This site serves such a task.

The site opens with the Vatican Council Dogmatic Constitution on the Church, explaining what the landmark council had to say about spirituality (Chapter V) and the call to holiness. Also on this list are the essays *What Is a Psychologically Healthy Spirituality* and *What Is Spirituality*. Many other worthwhile documents dealing with spirituality can be found on this site.

CatholicMobile Popular Devotions

http://www.mcgill.pvt.k12.al.us/jerryd/cm/devotion.htm

Catholic devotions are part and parcel of Catholic tradition. Devotions are rituals used by Catholics to help them pray. Many Catholic devotions, as this site indicates, have to do with Mary, the Virgin Mother. Of these, the Rosary is the most popular. This site connects the visitor with papal documents on the Rosary, information on how to pray the Rosary, and information on something called the Scriptural Rosary. Many other Mary devotions can be reached through this site.

Another popular Catholic devotion is the Stations of the Cross, or the Way of the Cross. This site connects the visitor to a number of sites that explain how the Stations of the Cross are to be prayed. The history of the practice of the Stations of the Cross is also available.

Catholic novenas, a series of prayers, are also explained on this site. The visitor can learn more about the many Catholic novenas by visiting the sites listed on this page. The Catholic Church celebrates scores, if not hundreds, of novenas.

Also on this site are a list of Catholic litanies: to the Saints, the Holy Ghost, the Blessed Virgin Mary, the Name of Jesus, the Sacred Heart of Jesus, and many others. Litanies are repetitious prayers intended to create a meditative mood. Other devotional links are also listed on this page.

Angels

http://www.catholic.org/saints/angels.html

Angels: A Biblical Perspective

http://www.connix.com/~kgeffert/vchome/jk_angel.htm

Maybe Angels has more to do with "spirit" than "spirituality," but the two are connected. The truth is that Angels are often portrayed in Scripture as messengers and communicators. If prayer is anything, it is about communicating.

This site introduces the visitor to angels and all their glory. It describes angels as "pure spirits created by God." The Old Testament theology included the belief in angels as used by God as ministers of His will. Scripture gives no indication of the precise time of the creation of angels; their existence is assumed at the earliest times. God often spoke of angels; in the New Testament various orders are mentioned: Angels, Powers, Principalities, Dominions (ations), Thrones, and Archangels; the Old Testament specifically mentions two others—Seraph (im) and Cherub(im). It is held that God bestowed upon angels great wisdom, freedom, and power, and their many appearances in the New Testament are indications of the leading role assigned to them. Both the New Testament and the Old Testament refer to fallen angels. The Temptation of Adam and Eve presupposes the existence of bad spirits or demons who were cast into hell, from which they have no hope of redemption.

Angels: A Biblical Perspective explains angels in their various biblical roles. It looks to Scripture to understand the phenomenon of angels, offering this definition: "spiritual beings endowed with immortality and attendant upon God." They may be described as heavenly guardians, warriors, ministering spirits or messengers. This site also looks at the division between good and bad angels.

Orientations
http://www.oise.on.ca/~rboys/veltri.html

This site is an electronic version of a work by Jesuit Father J. Veltri, who works at Loyola House in Guelph, Ontario, Canada, where he directs retreats. People from all over the world have taken part in the house's various retreats, institutes, and workshops. The stated purpose of the programs is "the personal growth in prayer and awareness of the individual participant." More specialized programs intend to help participants in their capacity to guide others spiritually.

This site is really a collection of help for prayer growth put together by Veltri for "those who listen to God's word." All methods of prayer, he maintains, are simply human ways of disposing oneself to be open to the mystery of God's unique communication. This collection of methods, prayer exercises, prayer patterns, and suggestions is no different. "Prayer," he states, "of course, is an individual thing." Therefore, many of the items contained here may or may not be a help for one's own prayer life. But there is a lot here from which to choose.

The collection features instructions on prayer, suggestions for prayer and spiritual guidance, spiritual exercises of St. Ignatius, help in decision making, various prayer patterns, various ways of reflecting on experience, 12-step-type help for the inward journey, special readings, special prayers, and special poems. This site also provides information about contacting the house and learning more about the various aids to prayer available through the house and its programs.

Sophia Spirituality Center
http://www.benedictine.edu/location.html

Located in Atchison, Kansas, on 40 acres of rolling hills in a Benedictine environment of a praying community, the Sophia Spirituality Center provides an ideal setting for prayer and reflection. Open to persons of all faiths, the programs include courses on the psalms, monastic theology, spirituality, and history; reflection days for the elderly and for parish ministers; directed and group retreats; Advent and Lenten days of prayer; days of recollection; and much more.

This site is an example of the many centers of spirituality that exist around the nation to help Catholics and others. It is also an example of the Web being put to good use to spread the news about spiritual enrichment programs. The many faces of Catholic spirituality quickly become apparent in the programs available through the Atchison Center. Consider some of these titles: Clay and Fire Retreat, All the Way Home Is Home, Seeking Hildegard of Bingen, Enneagram Workshop, Come to the Water, and the Fourth Annual Thomas Merton Conference. Other programs available through the Center include: How to Give Your Spiritual Life a Lift, Centering Prayer Retreat, and How to Cope with Holiday Frenzy.

The site also tells the visitor about the availability of special direction retreats and provides information on the Center for Benedictine Studies at Mount St. Scholastica, in Atchison, Kansas.

Carmelite Spirituality

http://middletown.ny.frontiercomm.net/~ocarmvoc/spiritua.html

This site portrays Carmelite spirituality through the writings of various Carmelite religious figures. Perhaps the most well known among these was St. John of the Cross, considered by most authorities on the spiritual life, one of the greatest mystics in the history of the Church. Addressed to Christians who aspire to grow in union with God, this site, through St. John's writings, examines various categories of spiritual experience from the spurious to the authentic.

In his Apostolic Letter proclaiming St. John of the Cross a Doctor of the Church, Pope Pius XI wrote that he

... points out to souls the way of perfection as though illumined by light from on high, in his limpidly clear analysis of mystical experience. And although [his works] deal with difficult and hidden matters, they are nevertheless replete with such lofty spiritual doctrine and are so well adapted to the understanding of those who study them that they can rightly be called a guide and handbook for the man of faith who proposes to embrace a life of perfection.

This site explores the mysticism of St. John and Carmelite Sister Teresa of Avila. It also looks at other Carmelite writings, including twentieth-century works.

Prayer Requests

http://www.nb.net/~snoopy/index.html#Inner Healing

This site has a personal nature. It allows visitors to state why they are in need of prayer. Other visitors to the site can add these prayer requests to their daily prayer lists. The kinds of prayers listed on this site are categorized, beginning with Repentance and Inner Healing. Want to pray for someone? Need a prayer? This is one way to make the step. Prayer requests stay online for three months unless an update is added.

Merton Society of Great Britain and Ireland

http://www.ucl.ac.uk/~ucylpmp/home.htm

This site indicates that the influence of Trappist Monk Thomas Merton continues to make itself felt beyond North American shores. The site, sponsored by the Merton Society of Great Britain and Ireland, is one more indicator of the strength of the spiritual legacy of Merton, who died in a freak accident in Thailand almost three decades ago. To this day, men and women meet worldwide to discuss his thought.

The Merton Society of Britain and Ireland came into existence December 12, 1993, in Winchester, England, at a celebration held to commemorate the twenty-fifth anniversary of Merton's death. The society is affiliated with the International Thomas Merton Society, based at the Thomas Merton Studies Center in Louisville, Kentucky. The stated aims of the society are:

- To promote interest in and study of Thomas Merton and his concerns.
- To encourage the formation of local groups or chapters of the society.
- To organize national meetings of the society.
- To encourage the publication of works by or about Thomas Merton in the United Kingdom and Ireland.
- To issue twice yearly *The Merton Journal,* containing articles, book reviews and other information of interest to the members of the society.

Blessings Around the U.S.
http://www2.americancatholic.org/americancatholic/us.html

Catholics proclaim a respect for all life—and this site is an example of how that respect has been part of Catholic thought for centuries.

October 4 is the Feast of St. Francis of Assisi. In many parts of the nation, Catholics gather on this feast day to receive blessings—not for themselves but for the animals they love and for all God's creatures. St. Francis, it is said, spoke to animals, understanding they too were loved creatures of God. This site contains a partial list of events involving animal blessing so Catholics can find nearby locations where they can take their animals on the feast of St. Francis.

Prayers for Meditation
http://esoptron.umd.edu/UGC/Prayers.html

This site is straightforward enough; it contains Catholic meditation prayers. Many are traditional, others less well known. These prayers are generally intended to be read quietly and privately. They include prayers of gratitude and recommitment and other simple prayers—some would say this constitutes their basic strength.

Celtic Christianity
http://www.shsu.edu/~lib_maa/celt_christ.html

Celtic Christianity, this site claims, quoting Ian Bradely from *The Celtic Way*, speaks with almost uncanny relevance to many of the concerns of our age. Celtic Christianity was environment-friendly, embracing positive attitudes toward nature and constantly celebrating the goodness of God's creation. It was nonhierarchical and nonsexist, eschewing the rule of diocesan communities and a rigid parish structure in favor of a loose federation of monastic communities, which included married as well as celibate clergy, and which were often presided over by women.

This site provides much information about Celtic Christianity, its spiritual base, and its soul. It also connects with a host of other sites that deal with Celtic Christianity. I learned a lot spending time here, and I suspect others will too.

Spiritual Gifts
http://www.cforc.com/sgifts.cgi?help

This site features the spiritual gifts of the Bible. If the visitor is not familiar with the spiritual gifts, he or she would be wise to take a minute or two to brush up on them. They are all listed with references to where they can be found in Scripture.

Perpetual Eucharistic Adoration

http://www.concentric.net/~uliv/

This site supports and celebrates a growing movement in U.S. Catholic parishes—the spread of perpetual Eucharistic adoration. The purpose of this site is to be a resource for parishioners who wish to start the devotion in their own parish and included are copies of actual letters, committee agendas, bulletin announcements, invitations, schedules, and guidelines generated by one Illinois parish as it worked to get Perpetual Adoration started. This site, then, amounts to a step-by-step case study, providing its unique lessons and experiences. The author cautions that other experiences might be quite different.

CHAPTER 1 7

Liturgy and Worship

Liturgy, which comes from the Greek word *leitourgia*, "work of the public," refers to the public and official prayers and rites of the Church. The term signifies that worship is an activity of the entire Church—laity and clergy alike. Liturgical worship is an act of the entire church body, an act of praise, thanksgiving, adoration, or petition. Liturgy finds its source and goal in the common glorification of God. In liturgy, all the faithful are brought together. Good liturgy involves recognizable symbols and all worshippers. Good liturgy stirs the soul and unites the worshipping community.

This chapter features some of the many liturgically oriented Catholic sites on the World Wide Web. Some of the sites were chosen for their education value, others simply because they appear to enhance good liturgies. Through all of these sites, one recognizes the attempt by the faithful to reach out to the mystical and connect to the Creator of all.

Liturgy of the Hours
http://www.universalis.com/

This site allows everyone—even those with modest liturgical knowledge—to participate in the Liturgy of the Hours (also known as the Divine Office). These are among the richest prayer resources in the Christian Church. They have existed from the earliest times to fulfill the Lord's command to pray without ceasing. Never monotonous, always new, the Office provides the means for the whole world, united, to pray together and sanctify every hour of every day of every year. All over the world, hundreds of thousands of priests and religious have vowed to pray the liturgy daily, and all over the world they do, in public and private, in tin shacks and cathedrals, in palaces and prison camps.

Everything has its price, and the price of the richness of the Liturgy of the Hours is a corresponding complexity. The liturgical calendar, the four-week cycle of psalms, and the celebrations of saints all interact in an intricate dance of prayer that takes some 6,000 pages of small print to describe. No one with a busy life can afford to undertake the project of praying even part of the liturgy, and so it remains scandalously unused.

As the third millennium approaches, it becomes more important than ever, according to this site, that people should obey the Lord's command and pray without ceasing to sanctify the coming millennium, the world, and themselves. And so this Web site has been created, to give all, wherever they are and whatever the time, the chance to participate in the Church's universal prayer. One click—one bookmark—and people can pause for a moment in their busy lives and contemplate what really matters.

The Liturgy of the Hours used here is the one codified by the Catholic Church. The Protestants and the Orthodox have their own liturgies and their own calendars, all of which derive from the same common source. It is the intention of this site to provide spiritual rather than doctrinal resources, and so all are welcome to use it and to pray, among other things, for reconciliation among Christians.

Readings for Upcoming Sundays
http://www.cs.cmu.edu/web/people/spok/catholic/readings.html

Worship that Works
http://www.dfms.org/worship-that-works/

Sunday liturgical planners, this site is for you. Readings for Upcoming Sundays points to Scripture covering the standard readings for upcoming Sundays and feast days. The text is from the Revised Standard Version. The citations are taken from the listing in the back of the (1977) New American Bible. One's local church might have different readings on a given Sunday, for various reasons.

Worship that Works is a series of weekly sermons based on the texts of the liturgical year and written by a variety of preachers. It is a lively contribution to the mission of the Church. This site is the work of the Evangelism Office at the Episcopal Church Center. The sermons, as well as a related series of sermon notes, will be available online two weeks in advance of use dates. They are published as a resource for preachers and congregations, offering yet another way to experience the rainbow of diversity that is the Episcopal church and the Anglican Communion. Since 1979, this resource has been published in book form with the traditionally long advance print preparation deadlines. With this new format, contributing preachers will be able to think, pray, and write in the context of more current events that shape our world.

Byzantine Rite
http://www.the-hermes.net/~hrycak/Welcome.html

Byzantine Catholic Home Page
http://www.epix.net/~byzantin/byzan.html

As a result of historical divisions, the Catholic Church is divided between Western and Eastern rites. The Byzantine Rite site briefly explains the history of the divisions and provides background information on the Eastern Byzantine rite.

The following is a narrative taken from the site. It explains the development of the Eastern and Western churches:

> The Catholic Church was founded by Jesus Christ nearly two thousand years ago through His apostles and disciples. The Church consists of the faithful united though the Holy Spirit by faith, the seven sacraments, and leadership. The visible head of the Catholic Church is the Pope of Rome who is the successor to St. Peter, the vicar of Christ, and universal teacher of religious truth. The early Church originated in the Middle East and spread throughout the world. As the Church spread, it encountered a variety of cultures. The coupling of Christianity with these cultures resulted in different forms of worship and expressions of faith. While the forms of worship, or rites varied from region to region, the fundamental truths of Catholicism remained the same.
>
> The early Church established local churches in the major centers of the Roman Empire: Jerusalem, Antioch, Alexandria, Rome, and Constantinople. When the Roman Empire was divided into East and West in 395 AD, the local churches became closely related to the structure of the state. Political divisions became models for ecclesiastical division, and the tendency was for each political division to have its own local church. This can be seen in how the Catholic Church is structured today. It consists of Western Rites and Eastern Rites. The Western Rites consist of those ancient traditions whose center was Rome. The Eastern Rites consist of the Christian communities whose centers were Constantinople, Jerusalem, Antioch, and Alexandra.

The Byzantine Catholic home page is the unofficial home page of the Byzantine Catholic church in America. It includes all the parishes, monasteries, and institutions of the Byzantine Catholic Metropolitan Province of Pittsburgh Pennsylvania. These include the Archeparchy (Archdiocese) of Pittsburgh, the Eparchy (Diocese) of Passaic New Jersey, the Eparchy (Diocese) of Parma Ohio, and the Eparchy (Diocese) of Van Nuys California. This page also includes various topics about the Byzantine Catholic church and its spiritual life.

Catholic Prayers
http://webdesk.clever.net/catholic/prayers/prayers.html

This site represents one of the most complete lists of Catholic prayers I found on the Web. All the old Latin prayers are here, as are prayers in English and French. And the visitor can leave a prayer intention on the site for others to see. This is a great site for newcomers to the faith, for old-timers, and for the general Catholic audience. Approach this site prayerfully because the rewards could be great.

Consider some of the prayers on this site: *Oratio Dominica* (The Lord's Prayer), *Ave Maria* (Hail Mary), *Signum Crucis* (Sign of the Cross), *Doxologia Minor* (Glory Be), *Confiteor* (I Confess), To Our Mother of Perpetual Help, To Saint Joseph, Guardian of Jesus, For the Canonization of Blessed Kateri Tekakwitha, For Motherhood, Litany of the Sacred Heart of Jesus, Litany of the Most Precious Blood of Our Lord Jesus Christ, St. Barnabas, Eucharistic Prayers of the Roman Missal, Internet Prayer, Booklet Prayers of the Roman Missal Roman, Liturgy Web Page of Prayers, French Prayers, Hungarian Prayers, On-line Prayers, Polish Prayers, Tagalog (Filipino) Prayers, Prayer to the Holy Spirit, and others. There are also many prayers to Mary here as well as prayers to the saints. There are prayers for those who suffer, for human dignity, for life, for the sick, for the dying, for vocations, and for faith, hope, and charity. The Divine Praises are here, as are prayers for children. Litanies are also on this site.

Catholic Liturgy on the Net
http://www.cs.cmu.edu/Web/People/spok/catholic.html

St. Benedict Liturgy
http://www.osb.org/osb/gen/topics/liturgy/

The Catholic Liturgy on the Net site lists some of the more important Catholic liturgical sites on the Web and provides

links to them. There are several liturgical rites of the
Catholic Church that can be found here. Most English-
speaking Catholics follow the Roman Rite. The Mass of the
Roman Rite is here. The last major revision of the Order of
Mass was made in the late 1960s, after Vatican II. The
Divine Office (of the Roman Rite) can also be found here,
as can the Liturgy of the Hours. Eastern Rites, including
the Byzantine Rite and Coptic Rite, will have links here as
well. Music, Hymns, and Chants can also be found here.

The Benedict Liturgy site features Catholic liturgical
texts, commentaries, and other sites, as seen through
Benedictine eyes. The Benedictines have been known for
centuries as a liturgical-centered monastic order.
Benedictine monasteries were often founded by the nobili-
ty as centers of prayer, communities that would pray for the
people, especially the nobles themselves. The most famous
was that of Cluny; named for the abbey in Burgundy; this
monastery was founded in 909 or 910. Cluny reformed
congregations of black monks, as they were called, in practically all parts of Europe. The abbot of Cluny was in effect
the superior of all the dependent monasteries even though
he administered the multitude of abbeys through appointed priors. Cluny excelled in the splendor and length of its
liturgy—so much so that its monks had little time for manual labor or reading.

Gregorian Chant Home Page

http://www.music.princeton.edu:80/chant_html/index.html

This site is the work of the New York Latin Liturgy
Association. It offers a history of Gregorian chant and asks
visitors to send information to be posted about conferences, workshops, concerts, or other events that deal with
Gregorian Chant. The stated purpose of the Gregorian
Chant Home Page, according to the association, is to support advanced research on Gregorian chant.

The following brief history of the origins of the chant is provided on the page. It explains that with the conversion of the Roman empire to Christianity during the fourth century, Christian worship changed from a persecuted secret cult, practiced surreptitiously by small groups in the house churches and cemeteries, into a formal public liturgy, celebrated in the great basilicas. This inevitably affected the music, as can be told from Christian writings of the period. Sermons by prominent bishops of the time, most notably St. Augustine of Hippo, often cited the Biblical passages that had just been read in the service, and these frequently included psalms in which the congregation responded with an unvarying refrain to the verses sung by a soloist.

By the fifth century, this practice had been formalized in a type of liturgical book known as a *lectionary*, containing the complete cycle of readings and responsorial psalms for each day of the year. The most important lectionary to survive from this period, and very likely the first to be written down, was the lectionary of Jerusalem, the influence of which can be detected in most of the other early lectionaries that survive. To study this period in the history of liturgical chant, therefore, the scholar must be willing to read widely in the literature of the early church and be especially familiar with the Bible and the history of its interpretation, for this is the source of most chant texts. Knowledge of contemporary liturgical studies is equally essential.

Online Devotions
http://members.harborcom.net/~landmark/devotion.htm

I am calling you to pray with your whole heart
and day by day to change your life…
I am calling that by your prayers and sacrifices
you begin to live in holiness…
daily change your life to become holy.

—*Our Lady of Medjugorje*

This site is typical of some of the Catholic devotional piety found on the World Wide Web. This page comes to the Web via the *Militia Immaculata* (MI) (Latin for Knights of the Immaculata). It features Roman Catholic Prayers, Novenas, and Devotions. The prayers on this site are broken down into Basic Catholic Prayers, Daily Meditations, Roman Catholic Prayers and Novenas, a Daily Thought Drawn from the Scriptures, Stations of the Cross, Prayers to the Sacred Heart of Jesus, and Prayers to the Holy Spirit and the Rosary of Our Lady. Traditional-minded Catholics will find this site especially to their liking.

According to the site, Marian consecration is sweeping the Church as a primary means of personal and national renewal. The Militia Immaculatae invites the visitor to come on board by entrusting him- or herself "totally to Jesus's Mother, the Immaculate Woman Full of Grace." The site states that "When you give yourself to her totally, she gives herself to you totally. She puts you under the mantle of her protective care and helps you find your place in God's Kingdom of Love."

This site provides information on the militia and on how to join in its work.

Easter Page

http://www.execpc.com/~tmuth/easter/

Easter is the most important Christian holiday. This is the day that Catholics believe Jesus conquered death.

The Easter Page is a cyberspace journey through scripture, art, music, and other materials that reflect on the mystery and miracle of the death and resurrection of Jesus Christ. This page offers images and text that set the scene for Lenten and Easter meditation and prayer. Some of the masters of art can be found on this page, including the *Last Supper* by Leonardo Da Vinci and the *Last Supper* by Cossimo Roselli (a panel in the Sistine Chapel). On this site, the narrative flows while the visitor gets to meditate on the images provided.

The site also links to other sites that concentrate on the Lenten/Easter experience, including the Virtual Museum of the Cross and other Christian art sites. On this site are sermons and essays on the meaning of the cross and Easter.

National Shrine of the Immaculate Conception
http://www.ewtn.com/Nat_Shrine/index.shtml

This is the official site of the Shrine of the Immaculate Conception in Washington, D.C., "America's Catholic Church." When John Carroll, the first Catholic bishop of the United States invoked the young nation to be under Mary's protection, he foreshadowed the faith and devotion of Catholics, who have made the Shrine what it is today. According to the site, its every stone and artistic nuance proclaim the nation's relationship with Mary begun centuries ago. This spiritual bond between our nation and Mary was formalized in 1847 when Pope Pius IX entrusted America to her protection, proclaiming Mary "Patroness of the United States" under the title of her Immaculate Conception.

The Basilica of the National Shrine of the Immaculate Conception, located in the heart of our nation's capital city, is but one site in our country where this ancient but ongoing tradition of pilgrimage is alive and well. Established by the American Catholic bishops to honor the Mother of our Lord, the National Shrine is more than a space made beautiful by artisans and craftsmen, more than a museum of ecclesial history and art. Rather, "the National Shrine," the site states, "is a living and vibrant place where everyday life continues to be transformed into a meaningful expression of faith by the thousands who journey to worship beneath its great dome."

In an age when there is ever-increasing competition for our time and focus, it is vital, the site states, that people carve out a place reserved solely for getting back to the basics. A pilgrimage, in this sense, takes one out of everyday routines and, at the same time, brings one home.

This site features a history of the shrine and offers a listing of current and future events at the shrine. It also features a schedule for liturgies and pilgrimages. Each year, tens of thousands of Catholics come to the shrine on pilgrimage. This site explains how one can join a pilgrimage and what to expect during such a trip.

Mass
http://www.uccla.org/uccla/UCC/Mass.html

This site features, in English and Latin, the prayers of the Holy Sacrifice of the Mass, the Eucharistic celebration—the central liturgical worship act among Catholics. The site also offers a special guide to help with the Latin pronunciation of words. The juxtaposition of the Latin and English texts is aimed at helping one learn the Latin translation of the English mass.

The site takes the visitor through the entire mass, beginning with the Introductory Rites, Greeting, Penitential Rite, Kyrie, Gloria, and Opening Prayer to the Liturgy of the Word, Homily, General Intercessions, and Liturgy of the Eucharist. This site is helpful for anyone who wants to better understand the structure of the mass and especially those who want to brush up on its Latin translation.

Notre Dame Center for Pastoral Liturgy
http://www.nd.edu/~ndcpl/

This site features the Notre Dame Center for Pastoral Liturgy. Founded in 1970, its stated purpose is to promote the implementation of the liturgical reform launched by the Second Vatican Council and to foster the renewal of the human spirit through worship. Through its research, publications, educational programs, and liturgy network, the NDCPL places in dialogue those involved in academic liturgical studies and the pastoral practice of worship.

"We know that the liturgy and the church influence one another," the site states. The church makes the liturgy and then the liturgy makes the church. Profound liturgical change has influenced and altered the church. Now a changing church promises to influence and alter the liturgy.

The site features information about the center's educational programs, liturgical network, research and publications, staff, and virtual bookstore. The site provides information about the center's annual pastoral liturgy conference, occasional symposia, workshops, consultations, and speaking engagements.

The Easter Page
http://www.execpc.com/~tmuth/easter/

Easter in Cyberspace
http://members.aol.com/REMinistry/devotionals/easter.html

Images of Easter
http://www.tssphoto.com/easter/easter.html

Catholic Online Lenten Page
http://www.catholic.org/lent/lent.html

One of the fastest-growing categories on the Catholic Web (and not among the earliest to the Web) is the liturgical page, which helps individuals and parishes plan liturgies. Part of the process of planning is getting into the spirit of the liturgical season. Because it can provide both text and images and can easily be updated, the Web is an excellent resource for Catholics to use in familiarizing themselves with the tools available for preparing better liturgies. Also available on these sites are simple prayer aids; one does not have to be a liturgical planner to profit from what can be found on these pages.

The first site listed above features prayers, images, and reflections on Easter. Its authors claim it is a "cyberspace journey through scripture, art, music and other materials which reflect on the mystery and miracle of the death and resurrection of Jesus Christ." The second site provides some terrific links to many useful Lenten and Easter season sites. The third site features Easter images, including the Garden Tomb in Jerusalem. The images on this site certainly set a meditative mood. Finally, the fourth site provides reflections on Holy Week day by day, leading up to the Easter feast day.

Funeral Meditations

http://xis.com/~bhs/00Sampler.html#funeral

You run into all kinds of things on the Web. I never imagined there could be a category entitled Funeral Meditations, but I was disabused of that idea after visiting here. This site states that "if your spirituality doesn't sustain you at funerals, perhaps you should take another look at it." It then goes on to list a dozen or so funeral meditations, reflections on funerals. Some of the titles include An Application of the Law of Attraction, You Will be Repaid at the Resurrection of the Just, and Funeral for a Friend (My Mother). Some Catholics might find this a bit out of the mainstream, but these are at least honest reflections by ordinary people coping with loss, and they have their own integrity.

Art and Meditation

The sites in this chapter express some of the sublime in Catholic life. They reveal a Christian spirituality based in art, architecture, iconography—and even gardening. They indicate the importance that art has played through the centuries as faithful Christians have attempted to experience the Divine. Art has been around as long as prayer, and art has frequently been an instrument of prayer. Examples abound in this chapter.

Here icons, feast days, prayer cycles, monasteries, and museums reveal the deep human longing to reach out to the supernatural. In this effort, meaning is found, fulfillment is experienced. Indeed, the longing for this completion, essential to human experience, in its own way indicates seeds of love implanted in all by their Divine Creator.

The sites in this chapter help fill out the Catholic soul. It is a soul that finds special meaning in art and history; it believes in the cycles of life, death, and rebirth; it lives by a calendar of church life that unites the ordinary and the extraordinary, establishing a livable pace for the spiritual journey. The Catholic faith comes out of centuries of practices and beliefs of untold millions of believers. These Catholic lives have lived not by bread alone but also through the spirit—through symbols and other art forms—as they continue their journeys of love.

The Road of Monasteries in France

http://www.imaginet.fr/apollonia/monasteries/monainfo.html

A more intriguing site cannot be found among Catholic Web sites. I thoroughly enjoyed this site. After visiting it I wanted to jump on a plane and fly to France.

This site is a virtual tour of 40 French monasteries, offering all a visitor needs to set a date for visiting one or more of them. Everything is here from maps, beautiful pictures, and history texts to hostel information and order forms for religious art, chants, and ceramics. This site sweeps the visitor into another time and place and state of mind. The photographs are numbing. Consider, for example, the monastery among monasteries, Mont Saint-Michel. Stop for a visit, and reflect on this gem's history. Then move on to any of the other monasteries whose monks and nuns live under the rule of Saint Benedict. Some of them range among France's architectural jewels. Here, the visitor learns, offices and masses are chanted in French or in the age-old Gregorian style, leading minds and souls to a thorough rest from modern life. Most of these monasteries provide sleeping accommodations for individuals and groups, and all sell their own specialty products, such as honey, chocolates, cheese, liquors, pottery, lavender essence, and Gregorian chant CDs.

And, as the site beckons, all are havens for the seekers of beauty, peace, and harmony. Don't miss this one!

Sistine Chapel

http://christusrex.org/www1/sistine/0-Tour.html

Admittedly, it is not quite like being there. It may not even be like owning a $125 art book that features the Vatican's Sistine Chapel, or the *Cappella Sistina* as it is known to locals. Nevertheless, one of the more fascinating Catholic sites on the Web is the Sistine Chapel featuring 325 photographs and explanative text.

The site states that the chapel was built between 1475 and 1483, in the time of Pope Sixtus IV della Rovere. The rectangular chapel measures 40.93 meters long by 13.41 meters wide, the exact dimensions of the Temple of Solomon, as given in the Old Testament. It is 20.70 meters high and is roofed by a flattened barrel vault, with little side vaults over the centered windows.

The architectural plans were made by Baccio Pontelli, and the construction work was supervised by Giovannino de' Dolci. The wall paintings were executed by Pietro Perugino, Sandro Botticelli, Domenico Ghirlandaio, Cosimo Rosselli, Luca Signorelli, and their respective workshops, which included Pinturicchio, Piero di Cosimo, and Bartolomeo della Gatta.

Michelangelo Buonarroti was commissioned by Pope Julius II della Rovere in 1508 to repaint the ceiling; the work was completed between 1508 and 1512. He painted the Last Judgment over the altar, between 1535 and 1541, being commissioned by Pope Paul III Farnese.

The Sistine Chapel, the pride of Catholics everywhere and a tourist attraction for almost every visitor to Rome, appears in vibrant colors—but you need to be patient as some of the rich paintings take time to download. The site has been chosen as one of the five best virtual art museums by *PC Magazine*. The site includes a master plan of the chapel, which helps locate each painting by assigning an alphanumeric code. There are 18 images of Michelangelo's ceiling. Michelangelo's Last Judgment can be viewed through 19 other images.

The site is maintained by Christus Rex et Redemptor Mundi, a private, nonprofit organization.

DominICON

http://members.aol.com/DominICON/homepage/index.html

St. Andrei Rublev Icons

http://maple.lemoyne.edu/~bucko/andre.html

Sampling of Russian Icons

http://www.gac.edu/Academics/russian/www-docs/Icons.html

> Since, in fact, we believe that the venerable and ancient tradi-
> tion of the Eastern churches is an integral part of the heritage
> of Christ's church, the first need... is to be familiar with that
> tradition, so as to be nourished by it and to encourage the
> process of unity in the best way possible for each.
>
> —*Pope John Paul II*

The stated purpose of DominICON is to expand and enhance the appreciation of holy icons, Christian sacred images in the Byzantine tradition. This is the home page of DominICON, a ministry of Western Dominican Province, the Dominican Order (Order of Preachers) of the Roman Catholic church, serving the western United States. It is a ministry to Roman Catholic and Protestant parishes, schools, and other Christian institutions. The ministry offers Art & Spirituality of the Icon—a presentation including slide lectures and icon painting classes, to parishes and other organizations. The site offers information about slide and lecture presentations, three- to seven-day Icon Retreats, and Icon Commissions. The site also features other items of interest and upcoming presentations.

The St. Andrei Rublev Icons site presents the icon art of Jesuit Father William Hart McNichols, and it offers them through a variety of products that include holy cards, greeting cards, Mass cards, note cards, posters, and plaques.

There are more than 55 different icons available. This site explains the importance of icons and offers the visitor information about obtaining the various reproductions.

Sampling of Russian Icons is just that: The site offers a half dozen Russian icons and links to other sites. One is the Icon of the Virgin of the Don, an end-of-the-fourteenth-century icon, a depiction of the *Theotokos* (Mother of God) executed by Theophanes the Greek. The site states that the icon brings a "humanizing" touch to Russian icon painting. The depiction of classical conceptions of facial beauty is innovative in this work. The icon became hallowed as a miracle worker, and legend has it that it protected Moscow from invasion on at least three occasions.

Religious Images and Icons, and Art

http://osiris.colorado.edu/~brumbaug/CHURCH/RES/
images.html#clip

Looking for some good Catholic clip art, including religious icons? It can be downloaded from this site. This page is maintained by a Mountain View, Colorado, United Methodist Church member who states that not everything on the page necessarily represents the views of the author of this page or of Mountain View United Methodist Church. There's lots of art here. The Contents menu includes Images and Icons, Clipart, Denomination-Specific Images, Religious Art and Photography, and Commercial Art and Image sites. Under Denomination-Specific Clip Art, the visitor will find a Catholic category that includes RCIA Graphics. Under Religious Art and Photography, the visitor will find many Catholic images from many Catholic sites. Newsletter writers and editors of parish bulletins will find this site useful.

Calculation of the Ecclesiastical Calendar

http://cssa.stanford.edu/~marcos/ec-cal.html

General Roman Calendar of Solemnities, Feasts, Memorials

http://www.cwo.com/~pentrack/catholic/romcal.html

Catholic Calendar Page

http://www.easterbrooks.com/personal/calendar/index.html

The Calculation of the Ecclesiastical Calendar is one of my favorites sites. But then I've been known to set my clock radio precisely to the hour so I can be awakened to the words: "Good morning. This is National Public Radio. ..." This site calculates the ecclesiastical calendar just in case one might want to know the date of Easter in the year 2010. Having fun yet? This site was first published on the World Wide Web in June 1995 and has since been named both a "Magellan 3-Star" and a "Point Top 5% Site."

The program on this site calculates:

- Easter Sunday in both the Western (Catholic, Anglican, and Protestant) Christian and the Eastern (Orthodox) Christian traditions

- The movable feasts associated with Easter in the Western and Eastern traditions

- Many feasts in the Catholic calendar, usually celebrations of events in the lives of Jesus or Mary

According to the site, before the year A.D. 325, churches in different regions celebrated Easter on different dates, not always on Sunday. The Council of Nicaea (325) clarified this a bit by stating that Easter would be celebrated on Sunday. Still, a number of methods were used until a method defined by Dionyisius Exiguus was adopted in about 532. This method was not widely accepted until 725.

It was Aloisius Lilius (d. 1576) who devised the system that would become the basis of the Gregorian calendar, as well as the tables that would be used to determine the date of Easter. As a reference, Easter is supposed to be the first Sunday after the fourteenth day (after the new moon) after March 21 (roughly, this is the first Sunday after the first full moon after March 21) The fourteenth day of the lunar cycle must occur after March 21; the new moon may occur after March 21.

The General Roman calendar is another fun site. It links the calendar day with the feast, memorial, or saint's day and tells the visitor about that saint. There's a lot to learn, and visiting this site develops a greater awareness of the composition of the liturgical calendar year.

Finally, I liked the Catholic Calendar page, too. It not only tells the visitor the day, but the feast, season, vestment color, and saint. Optional feasts are in italic. The site also gives information about the year's major feast days and holy days and explains the meanings for the symbols used in the calendar. The site also links to other Catholic and calendar links. This is another fine religious calendar.

Mary's Gardens

http://www.mgardens.org:8080/BibLit-Symb-QM.html

"Mary's Gardens," the site tells the visitor, "was founded in 1951 in Philadelphia, Pennsylvania to research the hundreds of flowers named in medieval times as symbols of the life, mysteries and privileges of the Blessed Virgin Mary, Mother of Jesus—as recorded by botanists, folklorists and lexicographers; and to assist in the planting of Mary Gardens of Flowers of Our Lady today."

The initial means for spreading the Mary's Garden idea was to make available, through volunteer lay initiative, "Our Lady's Garden" kits, with informative leaflet, packets of seeds for Flowers of Our Lady, together with lists of additional seeds, bulbs, and plants—for the planting and tending of Mary's Gardens as a prayerful, religious work of stewardship for God's flower riches and artistry with devotion, praise, thanksgiving, meditation, and commitment.

By 1965, research had documented more than 800 flowers named for Christ, Our Lady, and the saints. Proposed initially for home gardens, Mary's Gardens soon became established at schools, parishes, burial plots, institutions, and shrines. Some of the better-known Mary's Gardens today are those at Our Lady's national shrines at Knock, Ireland, and Akita, Japan; at the Artane Oratory of the Resurrection in Dublin; and in the cloister planting of Lincoln Cathedral in England.

The work of Mary's Gardens is carried forward today by an informal association of committed persons in Pennsylvania, Massachusetts, Maryland, Ohio, and Dublin, Ireland. This Web site was opened in September 1995 to make literature and photographs about Mary's Gardens available in electronic form, spreading the work worldwide.

Marytown

http://www.crnet.org/marytown/mtown.htm

This site calls Marytown, in Libertyville, Illinois, a place of pilgrimage, prayer, and peace. Marytown is the home of a group of Franciscans whose life mission is carrying on the work of Jesus Christ according to the manner of St. Francis of Assisi and as reflected in the life of St. Maximilian Kolbe. Friars, volunteers, and lay workers encourage a total consecration to the Immaculate Virgin Mary as the surest way to union with Jesus Christ and the reign of his Sacred Heart. Marytown is also the English-speaking home of Maximilian's Militia Immaculatae (MI) evangelization movement. They sponsor study and prayer groups, operate Marytown Press Books and Tapes, publish *Immaculata Magazine* (now online!) of Marian and Eucharistic spirituality, have a radio and TV ministry, and run a religious gift shop.

Liturgical and devotional events include 24-hour perpetual adoration of the Holy Eucharist, which visitors are welcome to join. Inside the chapel is the Chicago Shrine to St. Maximilian Kolbe, with a first-class relicon display and four 11-foot-tall wall mosaics commemorating the saint's life. Other wall mosaics portray various Franciscan saints. "Marytown," the site states, "is an ideal location for parish days of renewal, group pilgrimages, private retreats and meetings."

The Marytown Eucharistic adoration chapel was completed in 1932 near the entrance of the Mundelein Seminary, according to the inspiration of George Cardinal Mundelein, Archbishop of Chicago. The chapel commemorates the 28th International Eucharistic Congress of 1926, the first held in the United States (Chicago). The festivities of the closing day of the congress were held at the seminary, which attracted an estimated 850,000 on June 24, 1926. Perpetual, 24-hour-a-day adoration of the Blessed Sacrament has been going on continually at the site since 1928, first by the Benedictine Sisters of Perpetual Adoration of Clyde, Missouri, and after purchasing the building from the sisters in 1978, by the Conventual Franciscans now in residence.

Mexico Religious Sites

http://www.msstate.edu/Archives/History/Latin_America/Mexico/photos/church.html

For years, Don Mabry says he took photographs for personal pleasure and to use in classes. Unfortunately, most people in the United States have erroneous visual images of Mexico. So, he began to take photos that would help his students better understand the country and its people. Some of the photos are of traditional subjects, of course. The collection certainly does not represent the rich, fascinating variety of sights and images in the country. In fact, they tend to be photos taken in and around Mexico City, where, as a historian, Mabry spent most of his time in archives and libraries. He owns the copyright to the photos and allows them to be used for nonprofit purposes. He only asks to be given credit.

These extraordinarily beautiful photographs include the Rose Window at the San José Mission (now in San Antonio, Texas), Seashell Doorway, Cathedral, Cuernavaca, and several of the Church of Our Lady of Guadeloupe in Mexico City.

Virtual Museum of the Cross
http://www.netline.net/novus/museum/index.html

Experience the breathtaking series, *The Way of the Cross*, paintings by renowned artist, Ben Stahl (1910–1987). This classic collection, stolen from the original Museum of the Cross in Sarasota, Florida, in 1969, has been preserved electronically for presentation today, in The Virtual Museum of the Cross.

As an artist, Ben Stahl won more than 50 national awards, including the Saltus Gold Medal from the National Academy of Design. In 1965, Stahl opened the Museum of the Cross in his hometown of Sarasota. The idea for the museum came from his wife Ella after a successful commission he had completed for the Catholic Press of Chicago in 1954, which was to paint the 14 Stations of the Cross. These paintings were published in a 1954 special edition of the Bible and became very popular. Stahl then decided to paint a much larger, more dramatic set for the museum, which would be for people of all faiths.

These 6- by 9-foot oils would be housed in their own museum with a specially composed soundtrack narrative. Stahl spent more than two-and-a-half years painting the 15 works. Six months were devoted to making studies, drawings, and other oils before he began painting the 15 large canvases. The museum opened and the national press gave the museum and the paintings wonderful reviews. Tourists from all over the world made a point to come to Sarasota to see the museum. At the height of its popularity, however, in the predawn hours of April 16, 1969, the museum was broken into and the 15 masterworks plus 40 smaller works and studies in the inner gallery were stolen.

The theft that brought an end to the Museum of the Cross is still unsolved and without any major leads. It is the hope of the Stahl family that a visitor to the Virtual Museum of the Cross will recognize these valuable works and revitalize efforts to finally solve the mystery of the theft. The site provides contact information.

Vatican Exhibit
http://sunsite.unc.edu/expo/vatican.exhibit/exhibit/
Main_Hall.html

This is the site of Rome Reborn: The Vatican Library & Renaissance Culture, an exhibit at the Library of Congress. It presents some 200 of the Vatican Library's most precious manuscripts, books, and maps, many of which played a key role in the humanist recovery of the classical heritage of Greece and Rome. The exhibition, the site states, presents the untold story of the Vatican Library as the intellectual driving force behind the emergence of Rome as a political and scholarly superpower during the Renaissance. The exhibit was on display in the Jefferson Building of the Library of Congress from January 8, 1993, through April 30, 1993. The online exhibit continues to be available by anonymous FTP and on the Web.

The exhibit is divided into nine sections: The Vatican Library, Archaeology, Humanism, Mathematics, Music, Medicine & Biology, Nature Described, A Wider World I: How the Orient Came to Rome, and A Wider World II: How Rome Went to China. Each section contains exhibit text and separate image files for each object. This online exhibit includes not only objects from the Library of Congress exhibit, but also the alternate objects (brought from Rome to be used if there were a problem with one of the primary objects) and items omitted later in the planning process. The text and images of this exhibit are for the personal use of students, scholars, and the public. Any commercial use or publication of them is strictly prohibited.

The site contains material from *Rome Reborn: The Vatican Library and Renaissance Culture*, a book published by Yale University Press, which serves as the catalogue for the exhibit and presents outside of Rome for the first time a selection of objects from the Vatican Library's remarkable collections. The excerpts on this site provide a good introduction to the exhibit itself, as presented both at the Library of Congress and through computer networks.

The *Biblioteca Apostolica Vaticana*, the Vatican Library, is the prototypical modern research library of Western culture. Surprisingly, its collections are not primarily theological. From its founding by Pope Nicholas V in the 1450s, the Vatican Library consciously pursued an acquisitions policy that focused on the liberal arts and sciences. Consequently, the library has special strengths in unexpected areas, such as the history of the exact sciences, East Asian languages and literatures, and music history.

Tour the Vatican
http://www.christusrex.org/www1/citta/0-Citta.html

Tour the Sistine Chapel
http://www.christusrex.org/www1/sistine/0-Tour.html

Tour the Vatican Museums
http://www.christusrex.org/www1/vaticano/0-Musei.html

Prepare for a spectacular visit to the Vatican and its museums, including the angelic Sistine Chapel. Prepare to experience some of the finest photography on the Web. Perhaps it is the subject matter, perhaps the quality of the photographs, but these three sites provide the visitor with a spectacular inside look at the Vatican and its properties. Outside of purchasing an expensive coffee table book, these photographs are the best way—short of traveling to the Vatican—to capture its unique flavor.

These sites can be found through Christus Rex et Redemptor Mundi, a private, nonprofit organization dedicated to the dissemination of information on works of art preserved in churches, cathedrals and monasteries all over the world. Christus Rex et Redemptor Mundi has won repeated World Wide Web awards for its work, including the spectacular presentation of its photography. The organization has started building the database for a worldwide tour of churches and monasteries, comprising more than 5,000 images. These are early steps in that direction.

The Vatican City tour has 255 images; the Sistine Chapel tour has 325 images; and the Vatican museums have 596 images on these Web pages. The executive director of Christus Rex and Redemptor Mundi, Michael Olteanu, takes responsibility for the design of this server and states that the content here should not be construed as being endorsed by or representative of the official position of the Holy See.

Franciscan Clip Art

http://listserv.american.edu/catholic/franciscan/clipart/clipart.html

Some folks think clip art is beneath them, but surely it can help make a parish bulletin more attractive. And there is clip art, and clip art! The stuff you'll find here is better than average, with more than 160 images in all. And all the artwork contained here can be used freely by any nonprofit publications, the author states: "No previous consent is needed to be able to include these drawings in any noncommercial publication."

"Share freely what you got freely." That is the artist, Franciscan Father Philippus Philippus speaking. He only asks that users send him copies of their publications.

On-Line Directories

The World Wide Web is growing at a phenomenal rate. Search engines certainly help the browser in locating wanted sites. Often, however, a simple search produces hundreds, if not thousands, of Web pages. The result can be as frustrating as it can be overwhelming. How, then, does a Web visitor find topical sites? The answer is locating directories that can lead to the sites of one's interests. Once a list is found, the Web traveler is on his or her way. Some lists, however, are more helpful than others. Some offer sketchy information about the subject matter on a site; others simply tell the name of the site. This chapter contains the most useful directories of Catholic sites I found on the Web. It would take days to get through all the sites listed here. Even glancing at these directories offers a glimpse at the enormous breadth of the Catholic Web—and it is growing by the hour!

CatholicMobile Directory of Directories

http://www.mcgill.pvt.k12.al.us/jerryd/cm/dir.htm

This Web page is actually a directory of directories. The CatholicMobile claims there are more than 1,800 links on this site. I did not count them, but the number is definitely high. The compiler is Gerald Darring, a young student who says the site is aimed at the more serious student of the Catholic faith. "The purpose of this site is not to provide links to everything Catholic," he explains, adding that he alone is responsible for the choices on his site. This page provides another starting point for the Web surfer who does not fear overdose. The problem with seeing directories of directories, however, is that it can become intimidating fast. To avoid this, Darring provides a one- or two-line description of each directory on his list. He has done a lot of homework.

AlaPadre's Catholic Corner

http://wsnet.com/~alapadre/

This is one of the two or three most complete Catholic Web directories, covering nearly 400 sites. It alphabetically covers every imaginable category of church and church life. The work of Father John Stryjewski, AlaPadre's Catholic Corner came to life on the World Wide Web in 1994, when he began to post hyperlinked directories and search devices on his site. His purpose: to help Catholics locate resources and people around the world. A parish priest and self-described "catfish fryer," Stryjewski is a Web pioneer making a major difference in the church. Working out of the Archdiocese of Mobile, Alabama, Stryjewski is connecting Catholics throughout the world.

Not only does this site link to hundreds of Catholic sites, it also links to a dozen or so Catholic directories that similarly link the Web surfer to Catholic information lists. If the visitor is still unable to find what he or she is looking for, then there are always the normal Web search engines. These too are highlighted on AlaPadre.

Catholic Resources on the Net
http://www.cs.cmu.edu/web/people/spok/catholic.html

This recently reorganized index of Catholic resources is edited by John Mark Ockerbloom, a lay Catholic at the School of Computer Science at Carnegie Mellon University. It is not sponsored by any Catholic organization, and it may link to material, the site cautions, that is not endorsed by the Catholic church. It does, however, attempt to identify official Catholic documents and positions as such. I found the layout of this site clear and simple. Like other directories of Catholic sites, hundreds can be found here in directories and subdirectories. This site is especially good in liturgical matters, offering ample connections with the topics of Liturgy, Mass, Prayer, Hymns, and Chants. Official Catholic teaching is also stressed.

Catholic Information Center on Internet (CICI)
http://www.catholic.net

Founded under the Holy See Observer Mission to the United Nations, the CICI provides a focus for Catholic connectivity. CICI plans to develop the site, including an extensive search device that will connect any visitor to Catholic information and personnel around the world. CICI also has a subsidiary called Catholic Internet Access Organization (CIAO) that helps get Catholic organizations online.

The CICI Internet Directory features Catholic online books, commercial Webs, church councils, early church writings, history, culture and exhibits, liturgy and worship, news bits, Catholic organizations, papal writings, the Pope, saints, Scripture, and the Vatican. There is also a directory of Catholic media sources and a thorough listing of pro-life

Web sites. The site says it is working to build "the world's most extensive database of Catholic dioceses, parishes, clergy, schools, resources, and organizations for World Wide Web and email addresses."

Catholic Online
http://www.catholic.org/

This Web site, the work of Michael Galloway, is a growing enterprise, a work of love by Galloway who had dedicated this site to Our Lady of Guadeloupe. Look for new and exciting work to be achieved on these pages in the months ahead. Galloway is an enterprising young man.

This site may not have the breadth of some other Catholic directories, but what it lacks here, it makes up for in thoroughness. New categories are added monthly. Among the categories now listed and linked are Catholic Community, Human Life International, Priests for Life, and Catholic Educations. The theology on these pages is usually conservative.

The Catholic Goldmine
http://www.cris.com/~stambros/catholic.html

The Catholic Goldmine is the work of Christopher J. Miller, a 22-year-old senior at St. Ambrose University in Davenport, Iowa. He clearly enjoys the Web and has done a terrific job of organizing Catholic Web sites by subject. The Catholic Goldmine has been on the Web for just over a year. It is one of a handful of Catholic directory sites that set the visitor in the direction he or she needs to go in order to gather Catholic Web site information.

Among the categories on this site are Really Good Links, Apparitions, Church Documents, Prayers and Devotions, Pro-Life Listings, Priesthood, Women and Men's Religious Orders, Pope Paul II, Mary, Catholic Apologetics, Saints, Retreat Centers, and Catholic Radio and Television.

Tad Book's List

http://davinci.marc.gatech.edu/catholic/web/

This Web site directory is the work of Theodore Book, a student in computer science at Georgia Tech in Atlanta. Among the Catholic sites on this directory are some good ones, linking the visitor to Catholic authors. Also on this list are links to European Catholic sites. It is helpful here if you read Spanish and German. The directory begins with Art and Architecture, and Bibles and Books and moves through to Saints, Spiritual Resources, and Student Organizations.

Catholic Files

http://listserv.american.edu/catholic/

The Web sites on this directory were compiled piecemeal by a group called the Free Catholic mailing list, which has existed as an electronic mailing list (catholic@american.edu) and on Usenet (or Net News) as bit.listserv.catholic. The two are mirror images of each other. This is another of the growing number of directories available to Catholics wanting to find more links and lists. Maintained by Ed Sayre, it has one of the better lists of religious orders. This site appears to be updated regularly.

Catholic Information Network

http://www.electriciti.com/cin/

Catholic Information Network (CIN) is a free service that was founded in 1987 for evangelization through electronic messaging and text retrieval media. One of the largest Catholic networks in the world, it is carried through BBS CIN host nodes to four continents and the world through the Internet. CIN's mission is to offer information on the Catholic faith, including the texts of papal addresses and encyclicals, news, and other articles as well as to facilitate open discussion on all matters of Catholic life. Art and culture are also here.

Ecclesia Web Service
http://www.usbusiness.com/

A parish youth minister from St. Luke's Parish in Stroudsburg, Pennsylvania, Scott Fabian organized this site in early 1995 as a free resource and conferencing area for other parish youth ministers worldwide. Fabian's Web service is devoted to providing quality Web sites to Catholic organizations and promoting Catholic research and networking on the Internet. Many of the directories on the Web are labors of love of individuals or small groups who want to help others make sense out of the Web. Ecclesia appears to fall into this category. It sponsors several Web sites, including the Catholic Internet Directory.

Brother Richard's Favorite URLs
http://bingen.cs.csbsju.edu/~roliver/bro1.html

Brother Richard's Favorite URLs is an index and navigation guide to the Web that reflects his personal and professional interests. This Benedictine from Saint John's Abbey in Collegeville, Minnesota, lays it out online. The advantage of a personal directory is just that: It is more personal and, therefore, more selective, capturing the sense of church of a single religious man. Looking at such a list, the Web site visitor necessarily ends up in a kind of virtual relationship, sensing the inner thoughts and feelings of the list compiler. Brother Richard's modern monastic interests shine through his selections. This slant alone makes this site worth visiting.

Useful Catholic Links
http://sorrel.humboldt.edu/~cps1/catholic.html

Lots of people are getting into Web directory work. One is Chester Paul S'Groi, a Religious Studies major at Humboldt State University in Arcata, California. He has put together a directory of sites he calls Useful Catholic Links. While this directory is not as long as some others, it is open and nonideological. I find that some directories exclude some progressive Catholic Web sites, apparently believing they are not orthodox enough to be on a list. S'Groi's does not fit into this category. He continues to look for new sites and provides an email address so people can provide suggestions for his list.

Christus Rex et Redemptor Mundi

http://christusrex.org/www1/icons/index.html

Christus Rex et Redemptor Mundi, voted "One of the Top 100 Sites on the Web," links to papal statements and documents, the Bible in different languages, news, art, Vatican City, the Sistine Chapel, and churches around the world. *Christus Rex et Redemptor Mundi* is a private, nonprofit organization headed by Michael Olteanu, who takes responsibility for the list, which has an institutional bent.

New Advent

http://www.csn.net/advent/

This directory will appeal to traditional Catholics. The visitor is greeted to this giant site with the words: "Welcome to New Advent, one of the largest Catholic Web sites in the world." Indeed the site is huge, containing all sorts of information. One could enter here and browse until the next millennium and constantly find new information. The visitor can start, for example, with the *Catholic Encyclopedia*, continue on with the *Summa Theologica*, then for a quick change of pace check out Quizzes and Humor.

Want to fill your head with information, switch to Other Religions or Church Fathers? Much information is available about Catholic Web sites, categorized A through Z. An information junkie, I enjoyed browsing New Advent, because it is one of those starting points that deserves being a bookmark on every "Catholic" computer, or at least on conservative Catholic ones.

Avenue of Catholicism

http://www.avenue.com/v/catholic.html

This site provides a lot of general information about Catholic Web sites. The categories on this list are as follows: General Knowledge, Catholic Knowledge, Catholic Net Daily, U.S. Catholic Feast Days and Daily Readings, Bible Search, The Catechism, Catholic Education, The Ten Commandments, The Works of Mercy, The Precepts, Encyclicals, Catholic Documents, College of Cardinals, The Holy See, Catholic Prayers, and Writings by Pope John Paul II.

Catholic Internet Directory

http://catholic.net/RCC/Indices/index.html

The Catholic Internet Directory is a directory of Catholic-related resources on this site and elsewhere. It is divided up as follows: On the Librarians desk the visitor finds Online Books, Commercial Webs, Church Councils, Early Church Writings, History, Culture and Exhibits, Liturgy and Worship, News Bits, Catholic Organizations, Papal Writings, Pope, Saints, Scripture, Vatican, and Other Related Information Sources. This is one more growing Catholic Internet directory. The site makes the claim to having the world's most extensive database of Catholic dioceses, parishes, clergy, schools, resources, and organizations for the World Wide Web—and provides a search engine to make it useful.

Galaxy Religion Resource

http://galaxy.einet.net/galaxy/Community/Religion/
Christianity.html

This is, as they say, a "non-Catholic" site, but it lists some of the best Christian Web sites on the Internet. It's worth checking out. It has the salutary effect of breaking down Catholic chauvinism.

Yahoo on Religion

http://www.yahoo.com/Society_and_Culture/Religion

If you are familiar with the World Wide Web, you must be familiar with Yahoo, a search engine with a people's touch. A staff assesses sites before entering them in the Yahoo domain. This makes topic searches more successful. This site is Yahoo on Religion, falling under Society and Culture. Some Web browsers get hooked on Yahoo and never try another search engine. After the visitor to this site gets a taste of what appears under Religion, he or she may get hooked on Yahoo too.

INDEX

A

AAA Women's Services, 319–320
Abbey of Gethsemani, 57, 72, 72–73, 118, 368
Abbey of Our Lady of the Holy Trinity, 74, 74–75
Abbey of the Genesee, 67–68
The Abbey Quarterly, 36
Abolition Now!!!, 255–256
Aborigines, 248–249
abortion issue, 9, 306–307, 309–321
discussion of, 87–88, 98, 156
Abortion Views, 310
absolutism, discussion of, 129
ACE. *See* Alliance for Catholic Education
Action of the Month update, 236
activists, 230, 251, 270
addicted persons, ministries to, 84–85
Ad Gentes (The Church's Missionary Activity), 141
Adoption Network, 313–314
ADORE-L, 327
adult education, 141, 159–160, 341–342
adultery discussion, 201
affirmative action, 12
Africa
missionaries in, 77
Saint Anthony and, 110
Saint Augustine in, 106

African-American ministries, 21
agriculture, 353
Abbey of Our Lady of the Holy Trinity, 74
AIDS issues, 9, 194, 205, 286
A.J. Muste Memorial Institute, 246
Alabama
bishops on poverty, 258
Web sites in, 24, 194, 203–204, 414
Alan Shawn Feinstein World Hunger Program, 236–237
Alapadre, 166
AlaPadre's Catholic Corner, 414–415
Alberione, Father James, 53–54
alcoholics, ministries to, 84–85
Alexander IV (pope), 39
Allentown College of Saint Frances de Sales (Pennsylvania), 184
Allentown College of Saint Francis de Sales (Pennsylvania), 51
Alliance for Catholic Education, 172–173
Aloisius Lilius, 405
Alverno College (Wisconsin), 184
Amazing Facts, 224
Ambrose, bishop of Milan, 107
American Catholic, 205–206
American Catholic Online, 204
American Indians, 26, 122–123
American Red Cross, 286
American Theological Library Association

423